W9-BBC-744

DOUBLE AGENT

DOUBLE AGENT
The Critic and Society

MORRIS DICKSTEIN

New York   Oxford
OXFORD UNIVERSITY PRESS
1992

Oxford University Press

Oxford   New York   Toronto
Delhi   Bombay   Calcutta   Madras   Karachi
Kuala Lumpur   Singapore   Hong Kong   Tokyo
Nairobi   Dar es Salaam   Cape Town
Melbourne   Auckland

and associated companies in
Berlin   Ibadan

Copyright © 1992 by Morris Dickstein

Published by Oxford University Press, Inc.,
200 Madison Avenue, New York, New York 10016

Oxford is a registered trademark of Oxford University Press

All rights reserved. No part of this publication may be reproduced,
stored in a retrieval system, or transmitted, in any form or by any means,
electronic, mechanical, photocopying, recording, or otherwise,
without the prior permission of Oxford University Press.

Library of Congress Cataloging-in-Publication Data
Dickstein, Morris.
Double agent: the critic and society
Morris Dickstein.
p.   cm.
Includes index.
ISBN 0-19-507399-1
1. Criticism—Social aspects—United States—History—20th
century.   2. Criticism—Social aspects—Great Britain—History—20th
century.   3. American literature—History and criticism—Theory,
etc.   4. English literature—History and criticism—Theory, etc.
5. Arnold, Matthew, 1822–1888—Knowledge—Literature.   6. Literature
and society.   7. Historicism.   I. Title.
PS78.D5   1992
801'.95'09730904—dc20   91-43271

9 8 7 6 5 4 3 2 1

Printed in the United States of America
on acid-free paper

To the memory of
Robert A. Greenberg and Paul Zweig
friends, teachers, critics

"Where I'm Calling From"

Though many of my colleagues who teach English have made the study of criticism their specialty, I never expected to add to the expanding shelf of works on the subject. There have been times, over the last two decades, when it seemed that a fascination with criticism among literary academics would displace the interest in literature itself. Some of this shift toward critical theory was a valiant effort to look beyond individual cases, to examine the general conditions under which poems and stories come into being. But there was a tendency, especially in the heyday of deconstruction in the seventies, to locate these conditions not in authors as individuals and social beings but, more often than not, in the formal operations of language alone. Too much of this theory grew out of an overweening concern with the activity of criticism itself—with interpretation, evaluation, canon formation, academic instruction—usually at the expense of the flesh-and-blood people who wrote the books. In famous essays by Michel Foucault and Roland Barthes, the individual author was reduced to a fictional construct, the product of an outmoded and sinister aesthetic ideology; the writer gave way to the "author function" that was to be understood as a mere convention of literary discussion.

Despite my dislike for this kind of speculative paradox, which goes so much against the grain of how we normally read, I found that over the years I had written about criticism quite often, sometimes lovingly, often polemically. I've been drawn less to abstract critical issues than to the life and work of critics who themselves belonged to literature. Either they were drawn to the essay as an art form—a risky venture in discursive prose—or they were disappointed novelists and poets surrendering themselves to criticism as another way of soliciting the muse and changing the world.

Some, like Matthew Arnold, were writers who were increasingly blocked in their own work and began writing criticism with the left hand, without quite intending to become critics. Others, like Arnold again, were impelled by a sense of social or intellectual crisis. The upheavals in England in the 1860s or in the United States in the 1930s fired up critics and made their work impure, angry, socially engaged, caught up in polemical concerns that violated the classical ideal of disinterestedness. At times a strong critical commitment could be inspired by exciting new directions in the arts: Romanticism, impressionism, naturalism, modernism. Here the critic was often the friend of artists, the tireless campaigner, the semiofficial expositor of the avant-garde. Or the critic could become the embattled opponent of new movements, sorting out daring innovations from clever experiments but still writing with the same sense of passion and commitment.

The more central role of criticism didn't originate with poststructuralism but goes back to the New Criticism, itself a highly theoretical movement, and even further back to Arnold, Pater, Wilde, Yeats, Shaw, and the ferment of late Victorian literary journalism. Arnold was one of the first to articulate what Wordsworth, Coleridge, and Hazlitt had already understood before him—that the complexity of modern literature and modern life cried out for criticism. With literature and society in almost constant flux, the critic became the necessary adjunct to the writer, the apostle of art to a mass audience, as well as the privileged interpreter of the spirit of the age.

Arnold understood this in a special way. With his Victorian sense of crisis, he turned from the private realm of his poetry to a mixture of literary and social criticism, insisting on astringent, cosmopolitan values in an era of intense provincialism yet rapid cultural change. For Arnold, as for Eliot and Leavis after him, criticism was diagnostic, even therapeutic. But Arnold's successors, beginning with Pater, tended to separate the "purely literary" aspects of criticism from the social criticism, and it was this literary side of Eliot and Leavis that most influenced the critics who followed them.

When I first encountered F. R. Leavis's *Great Tradition* and T. S. Eliot's *Selected Essays* in college, I had no notion that these critics also had strong social views. When I read and reread Cleanth Brooks's *The Well Wrought Urn* I knew nothing of the Fugitive group and the agrarianism of their 1930 manifesto *I'll Take My Stand*. These critical models simply struck me as more hard-edged, demanding, even heroic ways of reading than anything I'd encountered before. This was an era of strong technical criticism, though neither Eliot nor Leavis practiced minutely detailed close reading, as Brooks did. But each of them gave the impression that literature was so elusive, so problematic, that it gave the lie to those sweeping correlations between art and society so common in the nineteenth century, when literature was seen as a vehicle of national identity and self-realization. Then the great figures—Taine, Brandes, De Sanctis, Lanson, even Sainte-Beuve—still lived in the shadow of Hegel, of totalizing systems and grand narratives. They were impelled to write enormous works of literary history rather than formal criticism.

Fortunately, I had the good luck to be exposed to other influences besides the New Critics. Columbia, where I spent my undergraduate years, had strong links to an urban intellectual tradition that extended beyond the university. Its faculty included maverick radicals like C. Wright Mills, liberal centrists like Richard Hofstadter, and critics whose background lay in the literary and political battles of the thirties, such as Lionel Trilling, F. W. Dupee, and Meyer Schapiro. These men would have been surprised to hear that politics and the arts could ever be fully separated, or that strong technical criticism had to detach literature and art from life in society. In the opening essay of *The Liberal Imagination* (1950), a book I read with great excitement at the end of my sophomore year, Trilling had talked dramatically about "the dark and bloody crossroads where literature and politics meet." The whole book could be seen as a demonstration of his ambivalence about this shadowy encounter.

Alfred Kazin, a younger member of the New York intellectual group, had put the matter more simply in the preface to his first book, *On Native Grounds,* in 1942. Faced with the vulgar sociologism of Stalinist critics and the formal approach of the early New Criticism, Kazin wrote: "I have never been able to understand why the study of literature in relation to society should be divorced from a full devotion to what literature is in itself, or why those who seek to analyze literary texts should cut off the act of writing from its irreducible sources in the life of men." This could serve as a motto for many of the critics discussed in this book, who were notable for seeing literature not in private, academic, or technical terms but in relation to what Jürgen Habermas called the "public sphere," the sphere of the citizen rather than the specialist. They expressed this in the public style of their criticism—the clarity of language, the address to a wider audience—but also in their concern with social, political, and moral issues, their way of connecting the act of writing to the life of the community.

But even as Kazin wrote these words, the tradition he represented, with its sources in the historicism of the nineteenth century, was being reduced to a countercurrent within the new academic mainstream. The universities were expanding, and the New Criticism, though despised by the older scholars who ran the English departments, made even difficult literature teachable. Starting with *Understanding Poetry* in 1938, Cleanth Brooks and Robert Penn Warren were turning the experimental methods of Eliot's *Sacred Wood,* I. A. Richards's *Practical Criticism,* and William Empson's *Seven Types of Ambiguity* into pedagogy, something every instructor could convey to his or her classes even in high school. And Marxist criticism, meant to put the social approach on the same "scientific" basis, proved no competition at all. Instead, its stale formulas and insensitivity to art helped bring the sociology of literature into near-fatal decline, hastened by McCarthyism soon after the war ended.

The postwar period saw a retreat from historicism in nearly every field, even the study of history. The case against historicism had always been a strong one, for this broad term had embraced the soupy *Geistesgeschichte* of the Hegelians, the sometimes mechanical environmentalism of Taine and the naturalists, and the positivism of the philological scholars, who were more concerned with sources and analogues than with literary works themselves. Though the historical method had been a radical innovation in the study of literature at the turn of the century, it soon evolved into a shallow contextualism that marshaled facts for the historical "background," with only a dim sense of the literary foreground. In the aftermath of the New Criticism, the failure to read closely seemed like a radical failure to read. With the arrival of modernism, even older literary works began to look too complex for the periodized narratives and the facile determinism of the reigning forms of literary history.

Finally, the war itself struck a serious blow to the historical method. In Hegel, in Marx, among the liberal and populist historians in the United States, the historical method had always been a way of telling a story, of organizing the brute facts of history into a progressive pattern. But just as the carnage of the First World War had cast a whole literary generation into disillusionment, so the costly victory in the second war, concluding with the detonation of the bomb and the gruesome exposure of the death camps, had in a sense brought history to an end—a feeling amplified by the long paralysis of the cold war.

Much of Western culture took an inward turn. To explain the numbing obscenities of the camps and the bomb, it seemed more meaningful to appeal to Freud and psychology than to Marx and history. Hollywood expressed the public malaise in its dark, cheaply made *films noirs,* then in a wave of horror and sci-fi films in which the paranoia is almost palpable. The politics of affluence and the cold war helped privatize American life. For the first time since the Crash, Americans went on a spending spree, became consumers, homeowners, automobile owners. Just as ordinary Americans were moving to the suburbs to cultivate their gardens, so novelists, poets, and critics began cultivating *their* gardens, along with philosophers, sociologists, and historians, all devoted to small-scale projects which showed, finally, how much could *not* be known. The New Criticism was a literary version of what sociologists were calling the End of Ideology: it was technical, incremental, meliorist. As F. O. Matthiessen—who had contributed so much to applying the new methods of close reading to American literature—complained in 1949, it was criticism deliberately wearing blinders: "We have come to the unnatural point where textual analysis seems to be an end in itself."

This book is not an elegy for the work of critics like Edmund Wilson, George Orwell, and Lionel Trilling, who held the fort as public critics during the dark days of a reigning formalism. The question it raises is how a strong sense of literature in itself can be reconciled with an equally strong sense of the place of literature in the course of history and the lives of men and women. It asks whether a meaningful criticism is still possible, or whether the professionalization of criticism has turned it simply into an academic "field" where the criticism of criticism now has its own comfortable niche.

Insofar as my concern is with socially oriented criticism and cultural studies, this book could be read as a success story. Surely there's much to celebrate in the widespread and wholly unexpected return to history in recent criticism. An emphasis on the social construction of reality is the latest twist of critical theory. Not since the twenties and thirties has the human environment made such pressing inroads into the academic study of literature. Never before has criticism been so eclectic, so varied, so polarized, so open to influences from other disciplines.

Not since H. L. Mencken and Van Wyck Brooks have literary critics been such superstars, in demand on talk shows and the lecture circuit. Philosophers like Richard Rorty and Stanley Cavell, historians like Hayden White, and anthropologists like Clifford Geertz pay tribute to critics for doing what philosophers and social thinkers *should* be doing: raising the right questions, self-consciously refining their techniques, destroying complacent assumptions, especially the illusion of objective knowledge. Even legal scholars have been influenced by the new work in critical interpretation.

When has literature attracted so many of the brightest students? How long has it been since literary issues like the canon, cultural literacy, and multiculturalism have been at the center of a national debate, from "Nightline" and the op-ed pages to the glossy magazines? Even a subject as arcane as the early collaborationist articles of Paul de Man quickly bridged the formidable gap between *Critical*

Inquiry or university press publishing, on the one hand, and *The Village Voice, Newsweek,* the *New York Times Magazine,* and trade publishing, on the other. Our widely discussed critics are fortunate even in their neoconservative enemies, whose know-nothing assaults, at once strident and complacent, have only trumpeted their renown. If the object of criticism is to gain attention, then our star academics certainly have the nation's ear.

Why, then, do I feel that this splendid uproar, though sometimes good for professors' salaries, has been less than ideal for criticism itself, especially the kind of cultural criticism to which this book is largely devoted? Half a century ago, Kazin found himself caught between a narrow Marxism and an equally limited formalism: "We are all bound up in society, but we can never forget that literature is not produced by 'society,' but by a succession of individuals and out of individual sensibility and knowledge and craft. It has been given to our day in America, however, to see criticism—so basic a communication between men—made into either a scholastic technique or a political weapon."

Even if, in our advanced wisdom, we bridle at the dated reference to "men," his description applies remarkably well to the impasse of academic criticism today. Indeed, it would be hard to improve on this as a thumbnail sketch of the tensions within poststructuralism: between what remains of the kind of deconstruction grounded in language and the newer cultural studies that focus on race, class, and gender. Both kinds of work have contributed greatly to the sophistication and self-awareness of our criticism. Among the respected if controversial figures in critical theory today, who would willingly sacrifice Jacques Derrida's philosophical playfulness, Geoffrey Hartman's range and erudition, the late Paul de Man's dry irony and analytical rigor, Harold Bloom's prophetic eloquence, Stanley Fish's polemical verve, Sandra Gilbert and Susan Gubar's provocative feminist challenge to literary history, Edward Said's synthesis of culture and politics, Henry Louis Gates, Jr.'s mastery of the whole field of black cultural expression, Gerald Graff's precision and clarity of argument, or Jerome McGann's textual and historical learning—to mention just a few names that show the scope and variety of current literary theory.

Yet we also have room for public critics and intellectuals like Kazin, Irving Howe, Frank Kermode, and Denis Donoghue, who are among the best-known exponents of the literary and journalistic traditions explored in this book. Though you wouldn't know it from the current debates or recent histories, some of the best criticism of the postwar years can be found in collections of literary journalism by part-time critics like Randall Jarrell, Mary McCarthy, Wilfrid Sheed, Elizabeth Hardwick, and John Updike, or by idiosyncratic professors like Helen Vendler, John Bayley, and Christopher Ricks, whose best work can be found in reviews and essays rather than full-length books. The same can be said for collections of theater articles by Eric Bentley, Kenneth Tynan, and Robert Brustein or film criticism by Pauline Kael, Andrew Sarris, and Stanley Kauffmann. It would be virtually impossible to find academic work that could match them.

Despite the much-discussed obituaries for "the last intellectuals," as if academic specialization and clumsy jargon were the only mode of writing left to us today, the notion of the critic as generalist—as book reviewer, film critic, higher journalist, cultural commentator, museum curator, social researcher, political pamphleteer, and concerned citizen—is still very much alive today among younger writers in magazines as different as *The Village Voice* and *The New Criterion, The New Yorker* and the *Threepenny Review, Salmagundi* and *Vanity Fair.* I could list two dozen superb young critics still in their thirties and forties who write for such general magazines. They may never achieve the influence of a Wilson on a Trilling, who lived and wrote in a more literary culture, but they have inherited some of that older tradition. Some of them are also novelists or poets who bring to their criticism a feeling for the creative process. Others are cultural critics as much at home with social and political issues as they are with literature and popular culture. They would rightly resent the notion that criticism today has become entirely academic, or that the "last" intellectuals were those of some preceding generation. The traditional subjects have changed, the old mandarin style and dry wit are long forgotten, and the number of outlets for nonprofessional criticism has plummeted. But neither the vocation of the intellectual nor the desire to reach a larger audience shows any sign of disappearing.

Even among academic critics there has been a noticeable retreat from the excesses of the seventies. Sharply etched autobiographical prose has begun to appear from writers who once set out to deconstruct the human subject. Even among theorists, few critics today would call themselves strict deconstructionists. Yet deconstruction, for all its arid emphasis on the cul-de-sac of language, at least reminded us of how slippery and subjective the interpretive process could be. The rise of cultural studies, including women's studies, African American studies, and the New Historicism, was a direct reaction to the dead-end skepticism of deconstruction. It restored the sense of social reference that deconstruction had effectively banished from criticism.

It unwittingly revived the older academic historicism that predated the New Critics. It reclaimed popular culture from the obtuse polemics of mass-culture theorists of the fifties. It rescued forgotten writers, and changed our angle of vision on many familiar works. Zora Neale Hurston and Kate Chopin are well-known examples of "missing" writers whose strengths were illuminated by a criticism focused on race and gender, just as John Donne had been rediscovered—perhaps even overpraised—by a criticism focused on metaphor, paradox, and ambiguity.

Like the New Criticism, cultural studies quickly ran to excess. The old fetishism of the text, centering on the ambiguities of language, was replaced by a fetishism of the context, which showed how everything in the work was culturally determined. Criticism as literary judgment gave way to criticism as cultural history. Minor works were promoted either for their exemplary content, because they fit into some critical argument, or because of their impact in their own time. (This too was typical of an earlier academic scholarship, which subdued literature into a documentation of its age.) Meanwhile far greater works were warily examined for their concealed ideological freight. Little credit was given to the variety and complexity of the Western tradition, including its internal dissonances and subtexts. Yet Western skepticism and pluralism, with their traditions of free expression, had nurtured the dissenting views of these same critics, and had, in fact, produced a strong line of cultural criticism that stretched back to Rousseau, Carlyle, Ruskin, Tocqueville, and Marx.

Matthiessen in 1944 expressed the faith that "aesthetic criticism, if carried far enough, inevitably becomes social criticism, since the act of perception extends through the work of art to its milieu." In the postwar era, when aesthetic criticism thrived, he would find that this simply did not happen. But now we have a politically committed version of cultural studies which is perhaps *too* oriented toward history and not enough toward aesthetics. The crossroads between literature and politics are still dark and bloody, and a middle ground between formal analysis and literary sociology remains difficult to find. But many of the critics examined in this book managed to do so. Like their successors today, they played the double agent, combining a deep feeling for art with a powerful sense of its changing place in human society.

New York   M.D.
November 1991

Acknowledgments

My original debt is to the editors and conference organizers who solicited earlier versions of some of these chapters as essays, lectures, or reviews, often contributing valuable suggestions that helped me in formulating or revising them. These include Walter Kendrick, M. Mark, Robert Langbaum, W. J. T. Mitchell, Robert von Hallberg, William Phillips, Edith Kurzweil, Gerald Graff, Mark Krupnick, George Core, Neal Kozodoy, Marc Chénetier, Rhoda Koenig, Louis Menand, and A. Walton Litz. I am pleased to be able to reprint material that first appeared in the *VLS, Critical Inquiry, Partisan Review,* the *Sewanee Review, Commentary,* the *Revue Française d'Etudes Américaines, New York* magazine, as well as in two collective volumes, *Criticism in the University,* ed. Gerald Graff and Reginald Gibbons (Evanston, Ill.: Northwestern University Press, 1985), and the *Cambridge History of Criticism, 1900–1950,* ed. A. Walton Litz and Louis Menand (New York: Cambridge University Press, forthcoming).

I have learned much about the issues in criticism today in conversation with Eugene Goodheart, Louis Menand, Leo Braudy, Rachel Brownstein, Gerhard Joseph, Geoffrey Hartman, Larry and Suzanne Graver, Richard Locke, Marshall Berman, Charles Molesworth, and my late and oft-lamented friends Robert A. Greenberg and Paul Zweig, to whom this book is dedicated. I have been educated about critical theory by a number of patient graduate students, past and present, including Eric Mendelsohn, Peter Hitchcock, and Bill Mullen. For nearly two decades I've had the benefit of participating in the Columbia Seminar on the Theory of Literature, chaired by Edward Said, which led me to think that some literary theory is best taken orally. Richard McCoy, Lindsay Waters, and Joseph Wittreich gave me some timely bibliographical suggestions as I was completing the book. Finally, I owe a special debt of thanks to Eugene Goodheart and Larry Graver for reading and commenting on the manuscript of this book, indeed, for convincing me there *was* a book here. Needless to say, none of those named should be held accountable in any way for errors, arguments, and prejudices that somehow found their place in this text, since I have not always taken good advice.

My wife, Lore Dickstein, has always been my first and most sympathetic reader, encouraging me to write clearly and forcefully for a general audience. Her own work as a scrupulously honest reviewer exemplifies the conscience and literary judgment of the public critic. My daughter, Rachel Dickstein, offered many bracing challenges as she made her own way through literature, criticism, and theory. My son, Jeremy Dickstein, was a frequent source of encouragement, humor, and support.

I brought this manuscript together in 1989–90 while engaged on another project as a Mellon Fellow at the National Humanities Center in Research Triangle Park, North Carolina. Among the always helpful staff I was especially grateful to Linda Morgan and Karen Carroll for their expert typing and to Librarian Alan Tuttle for his timely computer assistance.

A Note on Sources

Since my approach in this book is broadly essayistic rather than academic, details on sources, along with suggestions for additional reading, will be found primarily at the end of the volume. However, for the sake of additional documentation, I have preserved the reference notes in the two chapters that originally appeared separately with footnotes. These notes too will be found at the end of the book.

Contents

DOUBLE AGENT

1

Introduction:
What Happened to Criticism

When we think of American critics before 1945, we think mainly of the independent man of letters, H. L. Mencken, Van Wyck Brooks, Lewis Mumford, Paul Rosenfeld, Edmund Wilson, Malcolm Cowley, Kenneth Burke, R. P. Blackmur, Otis Ferguson, James Agee. With the boom in higher education after the war, criticism migrated into the university, first as the New Criticism, doing battle against the old belles lettres and scholarly pedantry, then in the last twenty years as critical theory, challenging the humanistic curriculum that the New Critics had recently transformed into a close study of selected literary masterpieces.

The arrival of a more philosophical approach to literature should have been the fulfillment of a dream. I certainly wasn't the only graduate student in the early sixties who was bored with the deadening routine of line-by-line explication. We looked to European critics, less hemmed in by pragmatism and positivism, for more insight into the nature of writing and its social and historical context. In 1961 I first heard of the work of Georg Lukács and the Frankfurt school from a Brazilian friend at Yale, and began occasional visits to Paul de Man's brilliant lectures at Cornell. Within a few years I had graduated from existentialism and was devouring the work of Barthes, Blanchot, Auerbach, Spitzer, and Poulet. I was reading Lukács and Benjamin in French translations, trying to translate Blanchot on Kafka, and (in 1965) helping Jacques Ehrmann organize a colloquium on all these critics at Yale.

As fate would have it, those great European names were not the ones who would most influence the next generation of academic critics in America. Other stars from the Paris firmament were on the critical horizon. The following year at a conference at Johns Hopkins, two saucy Jacks, Jacques Derrida and Jacques Lacan, made their Amer-

3

ican debuts. Back in Paris soon afterward, the almost simultaneous publication of Lacan's *Ecrits,* Michel Foucault's *Les Mots et les choses,* and no less than three books by Derrida, including his *Grammatology,* challenged the authority of the previous generation of European intellectuals, especially Sartre, with his quaint idea of political engagement. In the face of this massive and dauntingly difficult assault on the humanist conception of man—which should have included the work of Marx, Freud, and the great modern writers—I began to part company with European theory just as many others were beginning to sign on.

As everyone knows, it was the failure of the revolutions of 1968 that provided much of the impetus as well as the foot soldiers for the explosion of literary theory in the seventies. This doesn't mean that the student radicals of the sixties became the deconstructionists of the seventies—only that the spirit of unmasking, of rebellion against authority, was transposed in defeat into a far more limited sphere. For at least 150 years Parisian intellectuals had struggled against their middle-class origins, against the rigid patriarchal order in which some of them were raised. Now the strategies of confrontation that had failed in the streets succeeded on the page. Roland Barthes had already deconstructed the bourgeois myths encoded in mass culture, but Foucault and Derrida challenged the discursive categories of writers like themselves, philosophers, critics, humanist intellectuals. In the first heady phase of Derridean deconstruction, every form of critical language was arraigned for its self-deceptions, its internal contradictions, for its residue of dubious metaphysical assumptions.

A pervasive skepticism, sometimes bordering on nihilism, sought to undermine the whole terminology of representation—the relation of writing to anything outside itself—including its connection to the inner world of the individual personality and the outer world of social practice and community. With Derrida's dictum that everything was a text, that "there is no outside-the-text," both self and society became constructs of language, arbitrary verbal categories, dim referents in a ghostly allegory of texts about texts, language about language. Especially in the later work of de Man, the language of literature came to be seen as inherently duplicitous. Since there was no genuine criterion of truth in interpretation, only the assurance of a multiplicity of readings, all meaning was rendered unstable and all reading became a form of misreading.

One might have thought that this skeptical turn would have brought criticism to an end—the rest is silence. Far from it! Since every text could now be read and reread without fear of exhausting—or even approaching—its meaning, the New Criticism was reborn in America in a philosophical guise. Critical make-work thrived. Where the New Critics had searched for organic unity in every work, the new "hermeneutics of suspicion," taking virtually the same trajectory in each "reading," set out to show the work's inner contradictions, which were not so different from the irony, ambiguity, and paradox highlighted by the New Criticism.

In this free-for-all atmosphere, with theory and ingenuity in the saddle, with older interpretations virtually discarded, with literature sealed into an airless space of endless "misreading," many new schools of criticism thrived. The annual convention of the Modern Language Association became a great fair at which young merchant-scholars exhibited their wares while the biggest traders in theory and methodology attracted enormous attention for their new line. Though the universities were contracting and jobs were scarce, though literacy itself was collapsing among the ultimate consumers of these academic products, the business of criticism was booming. As Vincent B. Leitch writes in *American Literary Criticism From the Thirties to the Eighties,* a book entirely devoted to the growth of these competing and overlapping "schools": "In conjunction with reader-response, feminist, and Black Aesthetic criticism, hermeneutics, structuralism, deconstruction, and leftist cultural criticism made the field of literary studies in America during the Space Age seem a carnivalesque site; it appeared less a loosened hierarchy than, say, a series of interlocking sideshows."

Unfortunately this cornucopia, with its happy network of graduate programs, research institutes, conferences, journals, and university press publications, left little ground for the independent critical voice. Leitch fails to see the comedy inherent in these flourishing schools directing their competing theories to fewer and fewer readers. As journalistic outlets for criticism disappeared, the very idea of accessible criticism as a public activity came to seem retrograde. With apologies for his omissions, Leitch excludes from his generous volume any critic who cannot plausibly be attached to some theoretical school, including straight practical critics, critics of the old humanist dispensation, critics who persisted in writing for a wider public, and poets and novelists who write some of our best criticism (and always have). The critical terrorism and guerrilla warfare of 1970 became the critical supermarket of the eighties, but it stocked only name brands. Despite their limited audience (or because of it), competing schools became like Hollywood studios, with their established stars and ingenious marketing devices. As theory prevailed over literary judgment, an overwhelming concern with interpretation itself replaced an interest in the creative process.

This is not to say that the era of poststructuralism, not yet ended, has left us nothing of value. Above all, it made us more aware of the precarious and subjective nature of all interpretation, the degree to which our categories of understanding, grounded in language, condition all our reading. Though deconstruction itself was initially abstract and apolitical, it proved to be but one step from the deconstruction of language to the critique of ideology. Thus deconstruction helped engender its opposite, a resurgence of social and cultural criticism, including Marxism, feminism, and the so-called New Historicism, all flirting dangerously with the idea that there is a world *outside* the text that is nevertheless inscribed *in* the text.

Yet these critics have risked marginalizing themselves by remaining strictly academic, by falling into jargon, unnecessary abstraction, and cliquishness, by exhibiting only "to the trade." Some of their writing was predictable—tied to an obvious political agenda. Some of it was not political enough. Lest they be accused of epistemological backsliding, many of the New Historicists wrote more about "discursive practices" than about social realities. Sometimes they seem to have turned history itself into another self-enclosed text: the *idea* of history as an interpretive conundrum rather than a tissue of lived experience. Meanwhile, academic Marxists like Fredric Jameson proved that they could be as hermetic, as remote from politics and persons, as any aesthetic formalist. Only certain black and feminist critics, though they had no shortage of arcane theories, held strongly to the sixties idea that the personal is political and that the way we live is bound up closely with the way we write and read.

As Alfred Kazin wrote in 1962, "criticism should never be so professional that only professionals can read it." In spite of the revival of cultural criticism in the eighties, the main task for criticism today is to recapture the public space occupied by the independent man or woman of letters not only between the wars but throughout the nineteenth century. The first step would be to treat criticism as a major form of public discourse, as conservatives like Allan Bloom and Hilton Kramer continue to do. For anyone who feels that, despite the blind alley of academic specialization, despite the promotional hype and glitzy trash and celebrity gossip that surround us, the critic can once again become the mediator between art and its audience, a few points of principle should be stressed.

First, a critic is not a plumber, an electrician, or an engineer of human souls. Criticism is not a technical diagram or a user's manual.

For that matter, it's not social science, philosophy, or psychoanalysis; the canons of evidence are different. It is *writing,* and hence its first goal is to interest and hold its readers.

Second, like all good writing, criticism is personal or it is nothing. "Who touches this book touches a man," said Whitman. Roland Barthes's posthumous book about photography, *Camera Lucida,* is less about the medium or its history than about how certain photographs reach him, *puncture* him.

Finally, criticism, like art, is a social activity, however solitary its origin. Vibrating with human meaning, radiating will and desire, good criticism is an intervention in the world that seeks subtly to change the world, starting with the mind of the reader, the auditor, the spectator. Only in defeat can we say that it makes nothing happen.

Cultural Criticism:
Matthew Arnold and Beyond

Matthew Arnold was the prototype of the modern critic, the man who created the role of the critic as we still know it today. His work became uniquely identified with the *cause* of criticism—a controversial issue in his own day—so that T. S. Eliot, in a typical jibe, could label him "rather a propagandist for criticism than a critic." He was also a progenitor of the line of cultural criticism that Raymond Williams studied in *Culture and Society,* the critic situated at the "bloody cross-roads" of art, politics, and social policy. As such, he was the kind of writer the more technical critics associated with Eliot and the modern movement reacted against—partly because of their conservative politics, which recoiled from Arnold's vague and qualified liberalism, partly because of their formal interests, which led them to seek a more rigorous, less intuitive critical methodology.

This leads us to ask: What *is* criticism for a writer who, like most of his English colleagues, has critical habits but can't really be said to have a method? Though Arnold does have much to say about critical practice and malpractice, he might also have agreed with Eliot that "the only method is to be very intelligent." Arnold insisted that his main aim was to direct a free play of thought onto subjects that had become petrified by received opinion. His constant theme is that he lives in a period inhospitable to speculation and criticism, in a nation actively hostile to criticism. His work is like a dictionary of received ideas, a mélange of quotations and satiric portraits made up of attitudes held staunchly but unreflectively. Above all he is a *writer,* like so many cultural critics who followed him—musical, polemical, evocative, aphoristic. He has a born satirist's fascination with absurdity and nonsense and a satirist's instinctive irony and distance. A common feature of his style is an almost musical orchestration of themes, quotations, names, and catchphrases which—despite his urbanity and reserve—finally take on an almost Swiftian or Flaubertian animus toward a world full of bêtise and irrationality.* Arnold is a master ironist, after Jane Austen perhaps the best in English in the nineteenth century. His polemical passages can be crudely reductive: the art of the puppeteer, jerking his creatures, reduced to a few moronic tag lines, through their fantastic paces. At times the effect— the implied contempt—becomes so intense, the world so ludicrous, that it's a wonder he stops short of nihilism. But the reserve and urbanity intervene, an Augustan "good humor" looms up, the limits of convention and good taste reassert themselves, and the possible savagery and freedom of the Swiftian imagination diminish into something more constrained and well mannered. Where Arnold challenges Swift more directly and tries to sustain a longer satire, with consistent characters, as in *Friendship's Garland,* the result today is unreadable, a feeble piece of facetious topicality.

After setting out to describe Arnoldian criticism, I've been drawn to practice it instead. Arnold habitually tried to "place" interesting writers, including those he most loved, by comparing them to the greatest who had written, whose very names were touchstones of high achievement. Surrounded by the literary work of his contemporaries, the critic, he felt, should move nimbly between harshness and appreciation. He should maintain exacting standards yet try to banish his own preconceptions ("he must at all times be ready, like the Christian convert, even to burn what he used to worship, and to worship what he used to burn"). He should be alert to "relative success" without confusing it with something greater: "He is to keep his idea of the best, of perfection, and at the same time to be willingly accessible to every second best which offers itself."[3]

Arnold's sensible, even platitudinous prescriptions, sprinkled throughout his work, helped set a standard for modern criticism, though even for him they were harder to observe than to propagate. Coming to America to lecture on Emerson soon after his death, Arnold was determined to provide Emerson's countrymen with an instructive demonstration of disinterested criticism. He fondly recalls

---

* Arnold's echoes of Swift are not confined to phrases like "sweetness and light." Near the beginning of "Democracy," one of his strongest dissenting essays, he takes on a sonorous Burkean tone: "No sensible man will lightly go counter to an opinion firmly held by a great body of his countrymen."[1] Compare this to the wonderful opening of Swift's essay on abolishing Christianity: "I am very sensible what a weakness and presumption it is to reason against the general humour and disposition of the world."[2] Arnold lacks Swift's grit but sometimes shares his sense of being a lone sane voice in a swirl of irrational babble. Like Burke, he is an heir to Swift's polemical style.

his youthful enthusiasm for the writer yet sets about "resolutely to come at a real estimate of Emerson, and with a leaning even to strictness rather than to indulgence." "Time," he explains, "has no indulgence; any veils of illusion which we may have left around an object because we loved it, Time is sure to strip away."[4] This "real estimate," which Arnold in "The Study of Poetry" calls the ultimate aim of criticism, presumes a perspective outside of time, which the veils of Maia and the *ubi sunt* of the transitory world cannot touch. Though Arnold in many crucial ways is a historicist and a relativist, he insists that the "historical estimate" is caught up in an antiquarian interest in the past, just as the "personal estimate" can be blinded by the judgment of the present. Arnold can only praise Emerson after first showing that he stands neither among the greatest poets, the greatest prose writers, or the great philosophers. "And now I think I have cleared the ground," he says. "I have given up to envious Time as much of Emerson as Time can fairly expect to obtain."[5] In the lecture on Emerson, criticism is a talisman that anticipates and wards off the ravages of time. It reflects our suspicion that we might easily be trapped, that our whole age is trapped, in the transient and second-rate, that the great work has already been done. But criticism compensates for what we fear we have lost as artists and creators by enabling us to live outside of time *as readers,* to live among the indubitably great, and to have a sure hierarchy of values and reputations. In this sense Arnold was a strictly canonical critic—determined to identify a core of exceptional classics, ancient and modern, and to distinguish them from the literature of his own time.

By these same standards of critical discrimination, we must say that the lecture on Emerson was not one of Arnold's great performances. It neither convinces us of Arnold's feeling for Emerson nor identifies Emerson's real importance. One reason Arnold dealt so rarely with recent writers and almost never with living ones was that his mode of discrimination was of little use as a predictive instrument. (As he wrote in 1884, "A hundred years hence . . . George Sand will have established her superiority to Balzac as incontestibly as Rousseau," because her lyricism evoked more timeless values than his realism.[6]) His method worked best on writers less freshly dead than Emerson or George Sand, when envious Time has already taken as much as it could expect to obtain. Such is the case with Arnold himself today. We needn't pause to criticize *Friendship's Garland* because envious Time has already swallowed it without a trace. (I was staggered when Arnold's major biographer described it as "always fresh, never to be put aside."[7])

Arnold loved to appeal to continental models to bring out the provincialism and narrowmindedness of the English—nearly the whole first series of *Essays in Criticism* is a sequence of such vantage points—and we could imitate Arnold's "strictness" by comparing him on the subject of the Greeks to his contemporary Nietzsche. We find in Arnold an idealized image of Greek wholeness and serenity—hardly an unusual stereotype—and in Nietzsche the beginning of the modern perception of the darker, more irrational side of Greek culture. Arnold's viewpoint was the Rugby-Oxford equivalent of what E. M. Butler called "the tyranny of Greece over Germany," while Nietzsche on Socrates or Euripides is idiosyncratic, opinionated, and still inspiriting today.

We needn't draw out this comparison, at least not for the purpose of ranking or "placing" the writer. By his own standards of strict judgment Arnold has already taken up his position among the secondary writers rather than the great original thinkers. But, in his remarkable account of the rise and fall of literary reputations in the last pages of his essay on Joubert, Arnold sketched out another mode of survival from which he himself has since profited. He speaks there of writers who are not permanent parts of the canon, outside of time—the Homers and Shakespeares "whose criticism of life is a source of illumination and joy to the whole human race for ever"—but writers like Joubert who are picked out and kept safe by the advanced spirits of a succeeding generation for their own purposes.[8] This certainly happened to Arnold: he was needed, he was useful.

In his curious inaugural lecture "On the Modern Element in Literature," Arnold talks of the need of the modern age for an "intellectual deliverance."[9] But he believed not simply in the spread of knowledge and the free play of mind but above all in usable knowledge, knowledge that could take on flesh and blood and make a difference, knowledge that was also poetry. (This was a point Wordsworth made when he compared poetry and science—living knowledge and abstract knowledge—in his preface to the *Lyrical Ballads*. This passage must have influenced Arnold as deeply as any piece of criticism he read.) Arnold's whole critical enterprise may be seen as an attempt to make literature "adequate," to give it that vital relation to conduct and feeling that the religious literature once had. For both the individual and his society, literature is thus obliged to become a secular instrument of salvation, a burden few modern writers are still willing to bear.

In such a vision the classics become a crucial part of a new Protestant canon. Arnold's view of the Greeks may be conventional and, for the present age, untenable, but in one sense he is the founder of our modern pedagogic emphasis on the classics in translation. His lectures on translating Homer were daring and effective skirmishes aimed at rescuing the classics from the pedants and philologists, to give them back to the poets who would put them in language that could be read and felt. In that sense he himself belonged to the wave of democratization that he saw as historically inevitable and whose effects he analyzed in *Culture and Anarchy* and in essays like "Democracy" and "Equality." Everyone knows that Arnold was the first Professor of Poetry at Oxford to lecture in English rather than Latin. Affecting the pose of an amateur, he exploited his chair to insist that poetry too had a point of view. Poetry has an *interest* in problems of translation that rivals the claims of pedantry and academic scholarship, just as the true critic sees literature "not as an object of mere literary interest but as a living intellectual instrument."[10]

It's a curious paternity, but Arnold is undoubtedly the first spokesman for the modern demand for "relevance" in literary studies, as he is a source of the curricular turn toward the Great Books—a Protestant encounter with the text itself, free of the haze of commentary and critical dogma. Thus Arnold's "canon" was in many ways anticanonical, existential. In one essay he tried to do for Marcus Aurelius what he had already done for Homer, to make him a living classic. He praises the translator for treating his writings "as he treats all the other remains of Greek and Roman antiquity which he touches, not as a dead and dry matter of learning, but as documents with a side of modern applicability and living interest." In the same man's notes to Plutarch, Arnold tells us, "he deals with the modern epoch of Caesar and Cicero, not as food for schoolboys, but as food for men, and men engaged in the current of contemporary life and action." In a rare gesture Arnold even invokes the spirit of his father to justify "this lively and fruitful way of considering the men and affairs of ancient Greece and Rome." And since Marcus Aurelius is not a master who lives in his own style, "an Englishman who reads to live, and does not live to read, may henceforth let the Greek original repose upon its shelf."[11] Thanks in part to Dr. Arnold and his son, "the classics" soon began to take on a different meaning; the age of mass education was already on the horizon.

To perform a truly Arnoldian critique, then, we must determine to what extent he too is a classic "with a side of modern applicability and living interest." We know that not so long ago Arnold really did have such a currency, that thanks to the work of Leavis in England

and Trilling in America, Arnold was reestablished as a vital influence by the end of the thirties, and that through the forties and fifties he was largely exempt from the ridicule and neglect endured by many Victorian writers, even Dickens. To be genuinely Arnoldian on this subject—in other words, to be a historicist, a Hegelian, as Arnold usually is in explaining cultural change—we must show why Arnold's hegemony not only happened but *had* to happen, because the moment demanded it. Arnold reappeared during the Marxist decade because his defense of Hellenism against Hebraism, the free play of the mind against the practical, activist spirit of English liberalism, paralleled the reaction against ideology that set in by the end of the 1930s. All around him in the England of the 1860s Arnold saw a "preference of doing to thinking." He saw a working class claiming the liberties of middle-class Englishmen, doing as one likes, taking to the streets to demand enfranchisement. He saw a middle class making a fetish of free trade while the poor starved. He saw a Puritan mass pursuing its own form of activism by choosing obedience over intelligence, imagining—like the Marxists later—that they were in possession of the *unum necessarium,* the one thing needful, the single rule of life that gave all conduct meaning.

All these activisms, whether reformist, laissez-faire, or religious, Arnold saw paradoxically not as motors of progress but as dangerous forms of complacency and self-confirmation. The message of culture, as Arnold framed it, was a message of *Bildung* or self-development, as opposed to personal stagnation or merely institutional change. Culture tells us that there are many sides to human nature that must be developed. "There is no *unum necessarium,* or one thing needful, which can free human nature from the obligation of trying to come to its best at all these points."[12] Culture and criticism, according to him, must provide a balance against whatever side of human nature has been overstressed. Arnold's criticism and political writing are always corrective, diagnostic—attuned to his acute sense of the moment and the audience. Arnold's goal was not to create a timeless canon, a perfect society, or an absolute set of values, but to find whatever was needful for a given age. Therefore, in an activist period of robust Victorian self-confidence, in a country that, as he saw it, had always preferred energy and heartiness to thinking and intellectuality, Arnold emphasized the reflection that should precede action; he insisted on the many-sidedness of the traditional humanist ideal.

To say that Arnold's Hellenism was tactical and relative is not to say that it wasn't deeply felt. Arnold's political writings were music to the ears of a generation of modern intellectuals turning inward, away from the rigors of social conflict and ideological polarization; his literary criticism had a similar appeal to those who were reacting against the Marxist politicization of aesthetic issues. Arnold could have been writing an epitaph for the 1930s when he said that "everything was long seen, by the young and ardent among us, in inseparable connection with politics and practical life. . . . Let us try a more disinterested mode of seeing them."[13] Inevitably, despite the scrupulousness of Trilling and Leavis, Arnold was inducted into the vanguard of the End of Ideology, just as in his own day, because of the Hellenist emphasis of his polemical writings in the 1860s, his key phrases were incorporated by Pater and others into the nascent aesthetic movement. Such appropriation, however subtly done, could only distort Arnold's ideal of many-sidedness. His vision of culture was a totality, a dialectic between thinking and doing, an insistence on *both* "spontaneity of consciousness" (Hellenism) *and* "strictness of conscience" (Hebraism).[14] He saw his role as a goad and a gadfly, a party of one, a Liberal of the future rather than the present, and his emphasis of the 1860s as a timely corrective rather than an absolute. Earlier in the 1860s, in fact, before the crisis that gave rise to *Culture and Anarchy,* he himself had put more stress on activism. As Park Honan has argued, his social criticism grew out of the frustrations he experienced in the laissez-faire world of education. His important essay "Democracy" (1861), published as the introduction to one of his school reports, is an appeal for state action to diminish social inequality. It contains, in one brief passage, a full-scale rationale for the welfare state, another theme that would make Arnold exceptionally timely in the 1930s.

Arnold insisted that in France, amid the aesthetes, he would have been much more of a Hebraist. In fact the French subjects of the *Essays in Criticism,* Joubert and the Guérins, were men and women of the most fastidious conscience: Arnold depicts them as exempla, almost secular saints in the probity and moral purity of their spiritual lives. In his last decade Arnold *did* become more of a Hebraist; in essay after essay he inveighed against "the Goddess Lubricity," which he identified with the new French literature and the younger generation in England that ardently admired it—the same generation that had helped itself to some of the catchphrases of his earlier Hellenism and tried to make him an avatar of its own aesthetic ideals. In Pater's essay on Wordsworth, for example, Arnold's tactical emphasis becomes an absolute principle, to whit, that "the end of life is not action but contemplation—*being* as distinct from *doing*—a certain disposition of the mind."[15] Hence the centrality for Pater of poetry and art, which "by their very sterility, are a type of beholding for the mere joy of beholding." His aim therefore is "to treat life in the spirit of art," in the spirit of "impassioned contemplation" which he finds at the heart of Wordsworth's poetry.[16]

Nothing could be more revealing than Pater's deliberate, and honorific, use of the word "sterility" to describe the essence of art—and as a model for life. For Arnold the value of art, the whole thrust of "culture" as he defines it, is that it issues in conduct—not in a crude and immediate way but through an arduous process of *Bildung* and cultivation. Responding to those who reduced his idea of culture to belles lettres and ridiculed it as "a desirable quality in a critic of new books,"[17] Arnold insists that culture is conduct, or at least a firmer, more thoughtful ground on which conduct could be based. To impatient activists Arnold recommends a pause for reflection, but he urges action on those who would imprison art in a separate sphere called Culture, where it would be safely impotent or merely decorative. His culture is "a study of perfection" which "moves by the force, not merely or primarily of the scientific passion for pure knowledge, but also of the moral and social passion for doing good." It's an endeavor not merely "to *see* and *learn*" but to make its ideal "*prevail*" in people's lives.[18]

Pater's inversion of Arnold, his partial and absolute use of him, found its parallel in our own period, in the forties and fifties, when some read Arnold as a prop for their own academic quietism, their retreat inward from social to aesthetic values. Trilling and Leavis gave little support for such a reading—indeed they were at pains in their own work to reproduce his strong moral passion and yet to show how little it conflicted with aesthetic discrimination. But soon after Arnold, such a split occurred nonetheless, and it survived in English literary life long afterward as a timid, conservative version of Arnold, full of naive, defensive assumptions about humanism and tradition, that reared its head in many tired controversies. How ironic that Arnold's attacks on English insularity—his insistence on a broader, more vital, more troublesome Western tradition from Homer to the nineteenth century—became the ground of a new traditionalism, the justification for a new insularity not very different from the insularity he attacked. Arnold himself would not have been surprised. After all, his cast of characters includes a Member of Parliament who told him "that a thing is an anomaly, I consider to be no objection to it whatever."[19]

With his sober sense of the intransigence of cultural habits and prejudices, Arnold could hardly be surprised that the complacency he satirized has persisted so tenaciously.*

The conservative American misreading of Arnold created a similar distortion. In "The Function of Criticism at the Present time" Arnold attacked "the practical spirit of the English liberal movement" and, as I have already noted, its tendency to see everything "in inseparable connection with politics and practical life."[20] He called for a period of hard thinking while new and more broadly humane goals could be articulated. Arnold assailed not simply the crude reformist spirit, caught up in the machinery of merely institutional change, but also the complacency and self-congratulation of middle-class liberals. No one who reads the essay is likely to forget that remarkable pair, Mr. Adderly and Mr. Roebuck, who tell the English that they belong to "the best breed in the whole world" and that their "unrivalled happiness" has no parallel "the world over or in past history."[21] Nor will the reader forget the story of Wragg, the child murderer, whose fate Arnold, in perhaps the most brilliant passage in all his prose, interweaves so effectively with the eulogies of Roebuck and Adderly. Behind their dithyrambs of self-congratulation lurks the hideous reality, "short, bleak, and inhuman: *Wragg is in custody.* The sex lost in the confusion of our unrivalled happiness; or shall I say, the superfluous Christian name lopped off by the straightforward vigour of our old Anglo-Saxon breed."[22] But we in America in the forties and fifties had our own period of self-congratulation, when social thinkers told us that our major economic problems had been solved, when we put ourselves in the thrall of the technocratic spirit, the same utilitarianism that Arnold attacked as Carlyle, Dickens, and Ruskin had done before him. Mistaken for a conservative, Arnold belongs if anything to this great tradition of cultural radicalism which recoiled from the alliance between liberalism and "progress," and hence did much to establish the modern humanist critique of industrial society.

These issues only *seem* to take us far afield from Arnold's literary criticism. Like the poets he admires, the Goethe and Wordsworth whom he describes as healers and physicians to "this iron time / of doubts, disputes, distractions, fears,"[23] Arnold is above all a diagnostic

---

* Interestingly, an American critic sympathetic to deconstruction once cited Arnold's resistance to the viewpoint of the Honourable Member as evidence of his blind pursuit of a chimerical objectivity. Arnold might have relished this as confirmation of his sense of American provincialism—a weakness for crank theories. It's amusing to think of Colonel Blimp as an antifoundationalist.

critic who uses literature instrumentally, to advance social health and human wholeness. Perhaps Leavis was the last critic who believed that literature could in some way save us, but in this belief he was quite faithful to Arnold. Nothing could be more interested, more deeply engaged, than Arnold's ideal of disinterestedness (which today is under renewed attack from poststructuralists, who misconceive it as false and inhuman neutrality, or worse still, as a mask for specific social interests: white, male, and middle-class). Disinterestedness was a social as well as literary goal—really, a utopian ideal. We can't draw a line between Arnold's literary and social criticism because Arnold never does. The first series of *Essays in Criticism,* which first established Arnold's presence on the scene of English opinion, is full of both, and the key essay on the function of criticism—the most important he ever wrote—reverberates in both directions. His very first essay, published as a preface to his *Poems* of 1853, was as much a social diagnosis as a change of literary credo.

Thus the *cause* of criticism, which Arnold espoused so articulately, was not quite the cause which animated that heroic period of modern English and American criticism which lasted roughly from 1920 to 1960. It was an *age* of criticism, as Randall Jarrell labeled it, and it coincided with the heyday of the modernist movement, whose difficult masterpieces helped bring it into being. As far as it was an age of interpretive criticism, even of technical criticism, it could not really be comfortable with Arnold, though it honored him as a forebear and gave him a fresh currency. Even today academic writers on Arnold feel obliged to apologize that he doesn't do "close reading," and one even explains ruefully that he read poetry rapidly rather than carefully. But the great critical books of the modern period, unlike the pedagogic work that followed, were not mainly exegetical; just to name some of them is to renew one's sense of the grandeur and seriousness of their ambition: *The Sacred Wood, Axel's Castle, Maule's Curse, The Wound and the Bow, The Well Wrought Urn, A Grammar of Motives, The Liberal Imagination, Form and Value in Modern Poetry, American Renaissance, Fearful Symmetry, Revaluation, The Great Tradition, The American Novel and Its Tradition, The Lion and the Honeycomb,* and so on. Perhaps this is an arbitrary list of works that meant a great deal to me, but many of us will remember a time when books like these had an almost biblical authority for us. There were moments when not many works of literature had for us the electric impact of certain key books of criticism, perhaps of criticism in general.

The decline of criticism in England and America began during the

1950s, when its sway seemed strongest; this was the time when academic exegetes busily laid claim to the mantle of Eliot, Leavis, Richards, and Blackmur, who sometimes gazed incredulously at their unwanted offspring and shifted dramatically in their own later work. Many of the works just listed drew pioneering attention to the complexities of literary form, in reaction to the woolly generalities of their predecessors. But in the academic busywork that followed, a formal approach seemed all that was necessary.

Finally, the social and political ferment of the 1960s—which in a way resembled the climate of the 1860s that had galvanized Arnold—made a purely technical criticism seem trivial and beside the point. When the dust of 1968 settled in France and the United States, some of the energies of revolutionary turmoil were transferred from the larger world into the sphere of criticism itself. Yet the surge of critical theory that followed, though long overdue in this country, meant something quite different from what it meant to the French. The long-resisted arrival of formalism, Freudianism, and literary modernism in insular France, best symbolized by the sudden discovery of Joyce, was as belated as the attention to critical theory in the United States. In France the rigor of structuralism, as it had first been practiced by the Russian formalists, was a healthy release from a genteel academic humanism, still tied to nineteenth-century critical categories, and from a widespread Marxist dogmatism. But in the United States post-structuralism was a tired reversion to the New Criticism, gussied up with radical slogans yet denying the social energies that had helped bring it into being. The humanism to which the events of 1968 had boldly appealed could now be seen "as based on false Romantic myths of human depth and coherence."[24] In this context Arnold's work was attacked as the mainspring of academic criticism *and no more,* though it was more truly radical and less academic than the work of the deconstructionists themselves.

Arnold might have applied to the new formalists some of the "vivacities of expression" he used on Francis Newman's idiosyncratic and self-indulgent translation of the *Iliad.* In his lectures collected under the title *On Translating Homer,* he took Newman to task for his wildly misplaced erudition, appealing instead to the claims of poetry and the needs of the common reader. Newman's prolix reply led Arnold to one of his first and best statements on the function of criticism. Ironically acknowledging his technical ignorance, Arnold claimed it as a virtue:

> To handle these matters properly there is needed a poise so perfect that the least overweight in any direction tends to destroy the balance. Temper

destroys it, a crotchet destroys it, even erudition may destroy it. To press to the sense of the thing itself with which one is dealing, not to go off on some collateral issue about the thing, is the hardest matter in the world.

If Arnold is the founder of any critical school, it is not academic criticism but a criticism of *sensibility,* which stresses the encounter between the supple, receptive temperament of the alert reader and the literary work, the "thing itself." Far from idealizing the critical act and endowing it with any absolute truth, Arnold is a relativist who anticipates the deconstructionists' sense of the endlessly elusive quality of what we have come to call "the text":

> The "thing itself" with which one is here dealing, the critical perception of poetic truth, is of all things the most volatile, elusive, and evanescent; by even pressing too impetuously after it, one runs the risk of losing it.

In other words, the text is not a fixed object that can be dismantled mechanically, but an infinitely variable palimpsest of suggestions and implications. Meaning is a kind of grace which cannot be forced, nor can it be ferreted out by theory or dogma; the learned Newman, so full of himself, lacks humility as well as poise. He exhibits "erudition out of all proportion to its owner's critical faculty." His pedantry outruns his sensibility and his judgment.

> The critic of poetry should have the finest tact, the nicest moderation, the most free, flexible, and elastic spirit imaginable; he should be indeed the "ondoyant et divers," the *undulating and diverse* being of Montaigne.[25]

When critics like Eliot and Leavis, who rely on sensibility, sound dogmatic, they partly betray the Arnoldian heritage. But they do so as part of the most earnest grappling with the "thing itself." Arnold's stress on sensibility opened the door to Pater and aestheticism, which eventually degenerated into the kind of hazy impressionism he himself loved to castigate, as when he attacks the "rhetoric" of Macaulay as gorgeous language passing for criticism yet failing to keep an eye on the object. Arnold's notion of sensibility, like Pater's, was a tougher growth than the kind of polite verbiage and interior ramblings that Eliot and Leavis came along to explode. In him, as in Ruskin and Morris, sensibility provides part of the grounding for social criticism, a humane standard, adapted from the arts, according to which the social world can and must be judged. For all Arnold's pluralism as a critic, his aim remains "to see the object as in itself it really is,"[26] a goal of illusionless clarity he wistfully urges on readers, translators, and Members of Parliament alike. He approaches but does not accede to the main insight of the deconstructionists: that the viewpoint of the observer creates the thing observed. Park Honan, Arnold's biographer, cites an apt passage from a minor essay in which Arnold expresses tolerance for every kind of subjective viewpoint except the one most fashionable today, the theoretical one. All the others, he feels, can connect us with the text, however partially, and therefore can advance the cause of truth.

> There is the judgment of enthusiasm and admiration . . . the judgment of gratitude and sympathy . . . the judgment of ignorance, the judgment of incompatibility, the judgment of envy and jealousy. Finally, there is the systematic judgment, and this judgment is the most worthless of all. The sharp scrutiny of envy and jealousy may bring real faults to light. The judgments of incompatibility and ignorance are instructive, whether they reveal the necessary clefts of separation between the experiences of different sorts of people, or reveal simply the narrowness and bounding views of those who judge. But the systematic judgment is altogether unprofitable. Its author has not really his eye on the professed object . . . of his criticism at all, but upon something else which he wants to prove. . . . He never fairly looks at it, he is looking at something else.[27]

What Arnold seems least able to tolerate is ideologically motivated criticism, which appropriates literature to prove a point; late theorists, on the other hand, tended to mobilize literature to prove its pointlessness: that was their point. A hostile observer might argue, as David Bromwich did in 1982, that Arnold's residual faith in the objective character of the text—and in the critic's "real estimate" of it—is the kind of positivism that vitiates his flexibility as a critic.[28] Such an observer might well see Pater, with his "impressions," as a more usable ancestor for contemporary criticism.

For all Arnold's effort to introduce continental influences into English criticism and to impress a skeptical English public with the importance of "ideas," he himself was ironic about the excesses of French rationalism and German metaphysics. He was amused when the young Comtean Frederic Harrison criticized him for not developing "a philosophy with coherent, interdependent, subordinate, and derivative principles," just as Leavis (in "Literary Criticism and Philosophy") would resist René Wellek's demand that he articulate the general assumptions underlying his discrete judgments.[29] In this essay, one of Leavis's best, he restates the importance of poise and sensibility— and the centrality of the literary work itself—that was part of Arnold's legacy to modern criticism. Both Arnold and Leavis, English to the bone, feared that theoretical self-consciousness could interfere with the intuitive, visceral nature of the critical encounter. They saw a danger if the critic pursued the will-o'-the-wisp of his own "ideas" or the hobbyhorse of a method.

Arnold could be extremely mischievous about critics who faced literature without the emotional equipment to do justice to it or the disinterested impulse to tell the truth about it. Part of the way he established criticism as a serious enterprise in England was the lovingly destructive attention he paid to negative models, just as he did in his political writings. One of his best essays, a little-known piece called "A French Critic on Milton," is a subtle series of masks which enable Arnold to express his ambivalence by looking at Milton through other critics' eyes. He leads us in an ascending curve from the empty paeans of Macaulay to the conventional but dated analogies of Addison to the bluff and pithy directness of Johnson and finally to the outsider's viewpoint of an intelligent Frenchman unblinkered by English national pride. Through this multiple perspective the piece becomes yet another essay on the nature and function of criticism, with Arnold's own viewpoint focused on Milton's relation to the present moment. He asks of Milton's poems what he had already asked of the classics in translation—to what extent do they remain living works? Just as he had mocked the middle class in *Culture and Anarchy* for its "incomparable self-satisfaction," in his Milton essay he pillories that class's literary equivalent: criticism without judgment, humility, or disciplined attention. He shows how Johnson kept his eye on the object, as Macaulay and Addison did not. Arnold summarizes his argument by saying that "nothing is gained by huddling on 'our great epic poet,' in a promiscuous heap, every sort of praise. Sooner or later the question: How does Milton's masterpiece really stand to us moderns, what are we to think of it, what can we get from it? must inevitably be asked and answered."[30]

To most academic critics the kind of relevance and timeliness Arnold demands is too slippery, too personal, to provide the basis for any critical methodology. Arnold never really asked himself whether this contemporaneity—which he saw as a continuous dialogue with modern life—did not contradict what he elsewhere called "the severe discipline necessary for all real culture."[31] Arnold's influence was like a divided stream, part of which led toward up-to-date literary journalism and subjective impressionism while the other part, the academic current, aimed for rigor by objectifying the text and detaching it from the mind and purpose of both writer and reader. Before the New Criticism the gap between these two tributaries was not yet wide;

Arnold was followed by a succession of minor critics who were comfortable in both worlds—men of letters who spoke loosely about large
issues to a broad cultivated audience.

In Arnold's day this public tacitly allowed critics to occupy center
stage, though Arnold achieved real notoriety only when he turned
from literature to political and religious controversy. The critic was
something of an oracle, a generalist who could claim wide latitude
and authority, even a sort of national entertainer. Reading about
Arnold's lecture tour of America in 1883–84, we're amazed at the
degree of interest his presence aroused across the country—though
this is partly due to America's sense of itself as a cultural backwater.
Arnold had to restrain newspapers from reporting his lectures too
fully, and he was astounded that someone like General Grant should
come to hear him speak in New York. Despite his mild manner,
Arnold was a genius at provoking and exploiting controversy. He
needed no press agent, for he wielded the machinery of publicity in
the rhythm of his sentences and his choice of occasions. He may have
misjudged Americans; even as he died, the anger aroused by his
remarks about them was still breaking over his head. But in tight little
England he knew his audience, knew that his points would be attacked, defended, and ridiculed but certainly noticed and discussed.
His tone comes from this awareness; he called it "urbanity, the tone
of the city, of the centre."[32]

During the great period of modern criticism after 1920, the split
between journalism and pedagogy, between the public at large and
the academic discipline, widens. As the audience becomes more miscellaneous, the Arnolds turn into middlebrow figures like Clifton Fa-
diman, J. B. Priestley, the later Van Wyck Brooks, while the
important work of criticism abandons the public arena and tries to
draw more complex attention to the literary object. Criticism becomes
more technical, more private—a condition immensely exacerbated by
the arrival of structuralism and deconstruction. In "A French Critic
on Milton," Arnold's final example of ersatz criticism is conveyed
with a sarcastic quotation from Addison, even more mischievous today
than it was in 1712 or 1877: "A few general rules extracted out of the
French authors, with a certain cant of words, has sometimes set up
an illiterate heavy writer for a most judicious and formidable critic."[33]
As in his remarks on "the systematic judgment," Arnold suggests that
this kind of criticism lacks discrimination and style, that it is fundamentally unable to respond and communicate, and masks an inability
to read. This is Swiftian exaggeration, to be sure.

With little reference to Arnold, recent critics pursued his argument, developed throughout "The Function of Criticism," for a near parity between the critical and the creative faculty. While seeming to exalt criticism, they undermined it by attacking its truth-telling function—by vaporizing the literary object while endlessly multiplying opportunities for redescribing it. Criticism has promoted itself by sacrificing an essential part of its raison d'être; never has it received so much attention at the *expense* of literature. Arnold, anticipating Derrida, described the object of criticism as "of all things the most volatile, elusive, and evanescent."[34] But he never fell into skepticism or nihilism, despite the darker forces, modern anxieties, and elegiac moods at work in his poetry. As a critic Arnold historicized texts just as his poetry historicized his own predicament. But he never ultimately doubted the object and hence he was able to validate his quest for it, since what he said about it deeply mattered.

Right now the professionalization of criticism, its renunciation of a public language and a wider audience, plays into the hands of the new oracular figures of recent decades: the social scientists, the influential journalists, the popular psychologists, and the media celebrities. Wrapped up in language, seeing even public events as linguistic incidents,* criticism lost its old connection with conduct and bottled itself up with a literature it no longer believed in. Meanwhile a large, excitable, but easily distracted audience, unwilling to follow the abstract critic down this path, has a genuine claim to make: it wants something concrete, it wants to hear about the real world, it yearns for something with dash and liveliness that might have a bearing on the way we live.

This has caused some critics to turn dramatically toward life histories. One of the signal evidences of the decline of the New Criticism in the sixties and seventies was the resurgence of literary biography— books which resituated the text within the texture of the writer's world. While literary theory grew more arcane and often lost touch with particular cases—violating Arnold's dictum that "the great safeguard is never to let oneself become abstract"[36]—literary scholarship has become more fascinated by the connection between text and con-

---

* Writing about *The Empire of Signs*, Roland Barthes's book on Japan, Edmund White says: "If Japan did not exist, Barthes would have had to invent it—not that Japan *does* exist in 'The Empire of Signs,' for Barthes is careful to point out that he is not analyzing the real Japan but rather one of his own devising. In this fictive Japan, there is no terrible *innerness* as in the West, no soul, no God, no fate, no ego, no grandeur, no metaphysics, no 'promotional fever' and finally no meaning. . . . For Barthes Japan is a test, a challenge to think the unthinkable, a place where meaning is finally banished."[35]

text. Literal-minded biographers, hunting for sources, can easily simplify the relations between art and life. They can mire a writer's career in a bog of day-by-day facts or fashion it into an all-too-fluid narrative that expands where the evidence is copious and contracts mysteriously where the known facts are sparse. But good critical biographies can be an ideal way of integrating the social, psychological, and historical influences on a writer's work. Park Honan's biography of Arnold is seriously deficient as criticism but exceptionally valuable, for example, in examining the social context of Arnold's experience as a school inspector and showing its impact on his criticism.

The intelligent general reader chooses biography over straight criticism not simply out of intellectual laziness—because it is less technical, easier to read, and more like a novel—but because he wants to be in touch with something hard and real, something that actually happened. He prefers, I think, not to be sealed up in someone else's mental space, in an airless private world where terms and concepts can be manipulated with impunity. Even as theory and speculation have flourished, many of the key works of literary study in the past three decades have been biographical rather than strictly critical. Books like Ellmann's *Joyce* and *Wilde,* Edel's *James,* Painter's *Proust,* Bate's *Keats* and *Johnson,* Holroyd's *Strachey,* Bell's *Virginia Woolf,* Lewis's *Edith Wharton,* and Holmes's *Shelley*—to say nothing of the revealing biographies of T. S. Eliot himself—were simply of more *use* to the reflective critic than many works of literary criticism. Meanwhile, historically oriented scholars like Samuel Hynes wrote biographies of a whole era.

In my flaming youth the very idea of reading a writer's biography was almost enough to turn my stomach; the work itself, and the very best commentaries on it, were all that mattered. Not many years later it seemed that only a full-scale life (and letters, and memoirs) would satisfy my hunger for more information. For some writers like Eliot, biography let loose a wave of revisionist criticism. Our whole view of the modern movement was strikingly altered by the turn toward a more biographical, more political perspective. (Only gender questions have had a similar impact: a new lens to examine old writers.) Whatever the limits of its critical insight, a biographical work promised something more fresh and solid than yet another dose of exegesis or opinion, or another half-cocked theory that applied to no writers whatsoever. At its best, biography enables us to recover the human context of a writer's work and world. How fitting that Arnold himself should finally have received the same full-scale treatment, against his expressed wish. (What other book on Arnold besides Honan's could plausibly claim that three-quarters of its material had not appeared in any previous study?)

Among the critics of the last generation it was precisely the Arnoldians who held out against the divided stream of his massive influence—against both the professionalization of criticism and its frequent trivialization in evanescent literary journalism. The careers of Wilson, Trilling, and Leavis were successful attempts, each in its own key, to bridge the gap between the professional critic—weaned on modern literature, and using advanced tools—and the remnant of a cultivated literary audience. They were historical critics who wrote during a period of New Critical hegemony. Their sensibility was shaped by difficult writers and advanced modern thinkers, yet they wrote like the old nineteenth-century men of letters. Trilling's best book, *The Liberal Imagination* (1950), had precisely the mix of literary and social criticism we find in Arnold. In his essay on the Kinsey Report, for example, we see the literary critic functioning with his old freedom and authority—earned authority—applying analytic methods to the "social text"—in this case to our changing sexual mores. Like many of Orwell's occasional essays and Leavis's lethal assault on C. P. Snow, the piece belongs directly in the line of Victorian cultural criticism, applying a moral standard of human value to what others discussed in crudely mechanical terms.

In his misguided attack on Leavis in *The Rise and Fall of the Man of Letters,* John Gross accuses Leavis and *Scrutiny* of killing off the man of letters and replacing him with the cold-hearted academic specialist. A fairer account would show that Leavis, following Eliot and I. A. Richards, revived and intensified Arnold's struggle against the vague lucubrations about literature that still passed for criticism. It was Arnold, not Leavis in *Scrutiny*, who wrote that "whoever sets himself to see things as they are will find himself one of a very small circle; but it is only by this small circle resolutely doing its own work that adequate ideas will ever get current at all."[37] Like Wordsworth and Coleridge before him, Arnold was one of the inventors of the idea of a critical avant-garde, a handful of militant spirits whose stringent but humane ideals would save culture from commercial vulgarization and the cheapening of taste in mass society. Unlike the present-day avant-garde in critical theory, Arnold's heirs continued to project for criticism a mediating role between an increasingly difficult art and an increasingly fragmented, distracted audience. Holding to ordinary language and a public style, the Arnoldians resisted this fragmentation. Instead of imitating the gestures and claiming the prerogatives of art, they remained interpreters who saw art within its social framework. Unfortunately, their work also presumed a more unified audience and a more consistent standard of value than anything we have today.

At the risk of special pleading, I would like to draw attention to a few other old-fashioned but still powerful elements in Arnold's criticism, in the hope that they have some bearing on the current hiatus and uncertainty in critical method. They are offered in the spirit of Arnold's own tactical and relative sense of what any age might need ("at the present time") to balance off its own prejudices. My comments on biography were rooted directly in Arnold. During the New Critical period it was often noted, usually with embarrassment, how much biographical detail there is in Arnold's criticism, especially in his final work, the posthumous second series of *Essays in Criticism* (1888). One reason was that Arnold's generation lived in the shadow of a great literary movement, whose creative impetus had exhausted itself by the time he came on the scene. It was left for him and his contemporaries to sort out the remains. Just as we find ourselves in a creative trough following the titanic wave of the modernist movement, so Arnold was a latecomer at the feast of Romanticism, as we were to the heyday of modernism. Great figures had walked the earth: he had known Wordsworth in the poet's old age as we, in a lesser sense, "knew" Eliot as an old man. In "The Function of Criticism," when his career in poetry was almost exhausted, Arnold tells us that major creative work is not possible at some periods; criticism may be essential to prepare the ground for a new creative phase, a promised land he and his contemporaries may be fated not to enter. We can see Arnold turning his own creative crisis into cultural theory: it was not *Arnold* who could no longer write poetry, but *poetry* that was no longer central, or "adequate," to the spirit of the age.

By the time Arnold, in his own old age, came to write his celebrated essays on the Romantic poets, his poetic career was long behind him; the struggle and the passion with which he had wrestled with Keats in his early letters to Clough had long since been spent. What provided fresh impetus for a reevaluation of those figures was the same sort of posthumous material *we* are now getting on the modern writers: letters, biographies, personal revelations, the fugitive hints of an epoch as it passes into history. The severe moralism of Arnold's last decade made him recoil from some of these traces. The revelations of Dowden's *Life of Shelley* and Keat's letters to Fanny Brawne, revelations especially about the poets' sexual lives, made him wish they had never been published. Despite his critical commitment to "see the object as in itself it really is," he preferred his ideal image, the image of his own romantic youth, to what these volumes told him. But once they were published he read them assiduously, hungrily—Arnold was always an eager reader of letters and biographies, despite the caution he hedged about his own. And at least in the case of Dowden's *Shelley* he used the material brilliantly, to come to conclusions about the man that were acute and telling points about the work—did so in a way some modern critics, still hemmed in by constraints left over from the New Criticism, can only envy.

What inspired Arnold to write these essays, after many years away from literary criticism, was first of all a series of occasions—books coming out, reviews to be written, anthologies that demanded introductions—as well as a valedictory impulse to do justice to figures in whom his sensibility was so deeply grounded. But Arnold's immediate model was none other than Dr. Johnson. It's scarcely remembered today, but a year before the first and most brilliant of these essays, the one on Wordsworth, Arnold edited a textbook—for money, his biographer claims—of the six chief lives from Johnson's *Lives of the Poets,* which he had praised many years earlier in "The Function of Criticism" and again more recently in "A French Critic on Milton." Arnold was hardly sympathetic to the eighteenth century, which he repeatedly belittled as an "age of prose," but his feeling for Johnson grew out of his commitment to the cause of criticism and his instinctive affinity for Johnson's biographical method. Arnold's essay on Gray is a direct reply to Johnson's unsympathetic portrait, and his essays on Keats, Byron, Shelley, and Wordsworth show the vigor of judgment and independence of mind as well as the stern moral force he praised in Johnson. Arnold saluted Johnson for giving a complete account of a whole phase of English poetry, and in a haphazard way over a ten-year period he did the same for the Romantic era. The result was a book of essays more truly disinterested than the polemical collection of two decades earlier, with its idiosyncratic cast of all-too-marginal subjects and its oblique, comparative angle on these same Romantic poets.

Besides his attempt to assimilate literary criticism to social criticism and his biographical method, another feature of Arnold's work that came into sharp disfavor in the twentieth century was the emphasis on value judgments. Just as social science in our time made repeated attempts to imitate pure science and become "value free," so literary critics—whether formalist, archetypal, or structuralist—have been pursuing an ultimate "science of literature," like Casaubon in *Middlemarch* seeking a "Key to All Mythologies" (*Mythologiques*?). In the 1960s structural analysis, based on linguistic models, became what explication had been to the New Criticism. Meanwhile Northrop Frye's *Anatomy of Criticism* (1957), which rejected both rhetorical criticism and evaluative criticism, continued to exert its influence. A formalism of the individual work gave way to a formalism of the whole oeuvre, and finally of the whole body of literature. For a time it became more fashionable to diagram the permutations of plot in the *Decameron* than to respond to it with any kind of human fullness or historical awareness. Even today "narratology" threatens to become the next critical pseudoscience, replacing semiology. If translation is verse with the poetry left out, then such analysis is criticism with the literature left out, the mechanical operation of the spirit.

We can never resurrect the sense of social hierarchy on which Arnold's value judgments were partly based, nor can we hold on to the crumbling cultural hierarchy of highbrow, middlebrow, and lowbrow that was dear to our own Age of Criticism. Both the money culture and the media culture have been universal levelers, turning art into a commodity and trash into art—an effect which has exhilarated some artists.

When a representative Philistine in *Culture and Anarchy* appeals to the opinion of a publication called the *British Banner* against that of the *Saturday Review* (a periodical that had vigorously attacked Arnold), he comments: "The speaker had evidently no notion that there was a scale of value for judgments on these topics, and that the judgments of the *Saturday Review* ranked high on this scale, and those of the *British Banner* low."[38] An unquestioning confidence in such a "scale of value" puts a gap between us and Arnold; so does his whole insistence on a firmer center of authority in matters of culture and politics. There's too much emphasis on law and order in *Culture and Anarchy,* an assertion of the sacredness of state power, whoever may be administering it, and however it may fall short of the ideal role Arnold sketches for it. Arnold was enamored of the permanent government he thought he saw embodied in the French and Prussian bureaucracies.

In fairness to Arnold we should add that even this message had a corrective thrust, as he himself tried to make clear in "Democracy," his first major political essay. In France, he insists, he would be the first to criticize state power, just as in England he attacks unbridled individualism. There is hardly a statement in Arnold's prose that cannot be counterpointed with remarks elsewhere which qualify it. This "thinking against oneself" and against the prevailing prejudices of the moment is one of his sovereign values, embodied in the very undulations of his prose, to say nothing of the larger shape of his career. A critic like Trilling faithfully modeled his own "ondoyant et divers" manner on this kind of inner dialectic.

This is why Arnold finally retreats from recommending an English equivalent of the French Academy. Enlightenment cannot be fixed or legislated. For all his admiration for how the French maintain standards, Arnold's literary judgments depend very little on any external authority, be it social or cultural. His "culture," as he always emphasizes, is an "inward" culture, in principle fatal to all mechanical codes and unexamined assumptions. At their worst his judgments betray a touch of snobbery—the same snobbery that makes him so severe on the style of life of the English nonconformists, which he knew so well from visiting their schools. Thus Keats's letters to Fanny Brawne not only offend Arnold morally but reduce him to the ugly vein of the first reviewers of *Endymion:* "One is tempted to say that Keats's love-letter is the love-letter of a surgeon's apprentice. It has in its relaxed self-abandonment something under-bred and ignoble, as of a youth ill brought up, without the training that teaches us that we must put some constraint upon our feelings and upon the expression of them."[39] This sort of constricting reserve is an aberration in Arnold—a Rugby-Oxford recoil from the mess of living and feeling—like the grotesque aberrations of judgment Arnold found in Johnson. What he praised in Johnson, what *we* value in both Arnold and Johnson, is the character of the man in the work, the force of personality that gives power and consistency to all the disparate opinions. No one claims that writers and books cry out to be ranked and placed, one atop the other; that's the feeblest sense of the role of evaluation in criticism. We need value judgments not mainly for the instruction of taste, though criticism does have an educational mission, especially when literacy declines and cultural life becomes chaotic and miscellaneous—the cultural supermarket, as it had already begun to be in Arnold's time. We need them because they're the surest index of something irreplaceable: the full human engagement of the critic in his work, and in literature. This lies at the heart of Arnold's notions of critical poise and suppleness. This is what makes the continuity between literary and social criticism, between literature and conduct, possible and viable.

The modern period, with its fragmented audience, with its scientific aspirations but also its nihilistic skepticism, scarcely favored this sort of criticism based on discrimination and sensibility. Yet it gave us two signal instances of critics who put the evaluative function first. However much we may disagree with particular judgments by F. R. Leavis, which we inevitably do with a critic so opinionated, we must admit that they emerge from the deep core of a unified sensibility. In the welter of his many encounters with specific books, we can trace a depth of feeling and a consistency of vision that only the greatest critics possess. On the other hand, in Yvor Winters a consistency of vision and a distinctness of personality don't prevent the literary judgments from being wildly idiosyncratic. Where Leavis at least *aims* to speak for an objective standard, to engage in a common pursuit, and often does so with astonishing tact and delicacy, Winters can seem madly willful and clumsy. Yet Winters too had a powerfully unified though narrow vision of literature and a set of values we ridicule at our own risk. Even when he gives the wrong answers, Winters seems to ask the right questions. He takes literature so seriously that he always wants to know exactly what it's saying. He demands to know, for example, how Frost's poetry bears upon life, what sort of behavior and values it puts forward. He may be wrong to call Frost a "spiritual drifter" and to insist that this has a crippling effect on his poetry. But he's really asking where Frost lives, and the poet's admirers would do better to refute his argument than to ignore it.

There's another kind of important critic who is not evaluative in the mode of Arnold, Eliot, Leavis, or Winters, but whose work still shows a deep and full engagement with literature. This is the critic who submerges himself in his subject's mental universe, who tries to reconstruct and refine the writer's vision and lay bare his secrets. In this criticism, intimacy and subjectivity replace judicial detachment; when the method fails, the critic becomes a bad philosopher using art as a pulpit or pretext for his subjective musings. Yet when it works, this criticism proceeds by intuitions like those of an artist rather than a critic. Two modern examples of this kind of "criticism of identification" are G. Wilson Knight's *Wheel of Fire* (1930) and Georges Poulet's *Studies in Human Time* (1950), though the names of Bachelard, Sartre, Starobinski, and other French phenomenological critics could be added. The spiritual father of this mode—by precept at least, if not always by example—is Pater rather than Arnold (or Pater and Ruskin, if Ruskin were a more sustained, coherent writer). Since I criticized Pater earlier as a falling off from Arnold, I'd like to conclude by showing one way Pater is superior to Arnold and represents an important advance.

In Pater's chapter on Botticelli in *The Renaissance* he gives obliquely one of the most appealing formulations of his own aestheticism, more appealing, I think, than anything in the famous preface and conclusion.

So just what Dante scorns as unworthy alike of heaven and hell, Botticelli accepts, that middle world in which men take no side in great conflicts, and decide no great causes, and make great refusals.... His interest is neither in the untempered goodness of Angelico's saints, nor the untempered evil of Orcagna's *Inferno;* but with men and women in their mixed and uncertain condition.... His morality is all sympathy; and it is this sympathy, conveying into his work somewhat more than is usual of the true complexion of humanity, which makes him, visionary as he is, so forcible a realist.[40]

He extends the same point from art to criticism in his essay on Charles Lamb in *Appreciations:* "Working ever close to the concrete, to the details, great and small, or actual things, books, persons, and with no part of them blurred to his vision by the intervention of mere abstract theories, he has reached an enduring moral effect also, in a sort of boundless sympathy."[41] This emphasis on sympathy and openness gives a hungry, expansive character to Pater's aestheticism. It enables him to elude the deadening generality of abstract morality and abstract theory. We almost never think of aestheticism in connection with realism; we think of it usually in terms of artifice, even Camp—a refinement and stylization of life rather than a robust novelistic openness to all its littleness and multiplicity. Yet Henry James's advice to the novelist to be "one on whom nothing is lost" is a perfect Paterian formula.

It was Arnold, not Pater, who complained to his friend Arthur Hugh Clough that "Browning is a man with a moderate gift passionately desiring movement and fulness, and obtaining but a confused multitudinousness," and observed that both Keats and Browning failed to understand "that they must begin with an Idea of the world in order not to be prevailed over by the world's multitudinousness."[42] It's no coincidence that Browning was the most novelistic of poets and Keats a writer with great powers of *Einfühlung,* or empathy. Nor is it accidental that Arnold had a lifelong insensitivity to fiction—and a special antipathy to realism—just at a time when the novel was experiencing its greatest flowering. He disliked realistic novels because they were too immersed in the phenomenal world, including the realm of the passions, too much "inspired by a disinterested curiosity,"[43] though he himself had given "disinterestedness" its critical currency. To him Balzac's work was bounded by its subject matter, by the life of the "homme sensuel moyen," just as he had privately attacked Clough's poetry for yielding too much to the spirit of fiction. Clough eventually responded with an essay that attacked Arnold's poetry and exalted the superior creativity he saw at work in the contemporary novel.[44] In both his youth and his old age Arnold feared in realism an excess of curiosity leading to a debauch of feeling, though in the interim he preached openness and spontaneity to his Hebraizing countrymen.

The same impulse toward control and detachment showed itself at many points in his career, from his suppression of his own poetry in the name of an anachronistic classicism in 1853 to his insistence on "constraint upon our feelings and upon the expression of them" which I've already quoted from the late essay on Keats. In his 1853 preface Arnold created a new personality for himself, a prose personality that turned detachment into a principle. This foreshadowed the ironic mask that would shield him in his later work, and as he achieved it his poetry began to dry up. Arnold was one of those rare writers, like Thomas Mann, who consciously remade himself in public, who became something else—a more Apollonian spirit, a version of his father. It was a kind of Faustian compact in reverse—a deal with the angels to quit serving the devil. Except that, as Blake knew, "a true Poet" was "of the Devils party," which doomed frigid experiments like the verse tragedy *Merope*. Like Mann, Arnold purchased longevity with a certain distance and pomposity, a note of falseness in his literary persona. J. Hillis Miller has passed a severe judgment on this strain in him: "Arnold always keeps himself erect and aloof, like a man fording a rapid, muddy river, holding his head high and walking on tiptoe. He never has the courage to try that mode of understanding which seeks to comprehend the rationale of an alien way of life by seeing how it would feel to accept it as one's own."[45]

This is unfair, though it points up a real limitation. We've already seen how the detachment Arnold commends in "The Function of Criticism" is the subtler language of an intense commitment. It's equally true that the sympathy Pater commends is, in his own critical practice, inhibited by a temperamental detachment; it's more a critical credo than a truly novelistic appetite for experience. Pater's essays aim at intimacy and identification with his subject, where Arnold sets himself the more detached goal of keeping his eye on the object. Yet most of Pater's essays turn out to be idealized self-portraits, images of himself in the guise of, say, Wordsworth or Lamb, best at rare moments of ingenious accommodation between the idealized self-image and the recognizable reality of Wordsworth or Lamb. To an extent, this is true of the early polemical Arnold as well. But Arnold's great final essays, which, with the lightest touch, crystallize a lifetime of reflection, can still be read for an illumination of Wordsworth, a perspective on Shelley, not simply another morsel of Arnold.

Yet Pater's cultivation of feeling and personality gives his criticism a dimension that Arnold's lacks. Pater's ambivalence on this issue comes through in a direct piece of self-contradiction in his essay on Lamb. In one passage he says of Lamb's criticism that "he has the true scholar's way of forgetting himself in his subject." Three pages later he says just the opposite: "With him, as with Montaigne, the desire of self-portraiture is, below all more superficial tendencies, the real motive in writing at all—a desire closely connected with that intimacy, that modern subjectivity, which may be called the *Montaignesque* element in literature. What he designs is to give you himself, to acquaint you with his likeness."[46] The discrepancy arises because these comments, like much else in the essay, have only a tenuous connection with Lamb but have everything to do with Pater's ambivalence. He honors Lamb for staying close to the concrete and avoiding the swirl of the great issues. But Pater is every inch the Victorian sage, and poor Lamb is too often reduced to an occasion for his teaching, the material for a credo.

The sort of oblique self-portraiture we find everywhere in Pater is rare in Arnold, though it certainly forms part of his attraction to writers like Sénancour and Joubert. Arnold is most unbuttoned in his poetry, which voices the darker, more anguished feelings that are officially banned from his buoyant prose. Sentiments that other writers confine to their private journals Arnold gives vent to mainly in his poetry, though he often strikes romantic poses, and sometimes begins with little more than the desire to write a poem, as if to ratify his precarious existence as a poet. Still, his poetry is the crucial diary of his emotional life; but as the public persona takes hold, he resorts to this diary less and less frequently. In the Aristotelian preface of 1853 he rejects his own best verse along with much of modern literature. The incipient critic has begun his adversary dialogue with the modern mind, and the terms of this dialogue still interest us because they belong to the mental framework we still inhabit. The poetry itself, sometimes so bare and intellectual, sometimes quite clumsy in style, moves us today mainly as another version of the same predicament, the same dialogue with modernity, which is one of its primary subjects.

Arnold became a much better critic than he usually was a poet, so it's hard to regret the dwindling of the poetry except as a symptom of the diminution of the man. As a critic Arnold put his new detachment to remarkable use. To his discredit, Arnold was almost completely out of touch or out of sympathy with the literary activity of his time, in poetry as much as in prose. (On this point Leavis's career proved all too similar to his.) And his hostility to the modern mode of subjectivity in literature makes him somewhat unsatisfactory even on the Romantic period, as in his insistence that there was "something premature" about the Romantic movement—the poets "did not know enough."[47] This was in 1864. By the time of the late essays his struggle as a poet with his great precursors was a thing of the past. It's certainly true that Pater is an underrated critic; his essay on Wordsworth is not only eloquent but has moments of unique insight, though in the hush of "passionate contemplation" we miss the more masculine figure Coleridge knew and described. But Arnold's splendid essay on this poet, perhaps his best piece of "practical" criticism, is of another order entirely. Founded on a lifetime of affection and a zeal for critical justice, it restored Wordsworth's reputation and (along with the *Golden Treasury*) established his image for the next fifty years. Like Pater he believed that Wordsworth's greatness was buried under a mass of inferior work; in his Wordsworth selection and its introductory essay he cut this dross away and created a canon that would endure, at least until *The Prelude* was rediscovered in our own century.

Arnold's purpose was criticism rather than eulogy. He makes light of the "Wordsworthians" who honor him as a teacher and philosopher rather than as a poet. But in a brilliant twist in his final paragraph, Arnold reveals that he too is a Wordsworthian, that he grew up in "veneration" of the man and still reads with pleasure nearly all the verse his essay has been at pains to criticize. The decline of the critical spirit in our time, the rise of idiosyncrasy, scientism, and academicism, makes Arnold's strategy difficult for us to comprehend. It's one thing to distinguish in the abstract between the "personal estimate" and the "real estimate." It's quite another to write an essay of two completely different minds about a poet's work. His explanation beautifully justifies not only the spirit of detachment but the whole social enterprise of criticism:

> If we are to get Wordsworth recognised by the public and by the world, we must recommend him not in the spirit of a clique, but in the spirit of disinterested lovers of poetry. . . . Wordsworth is something more than the pure and sage master of a small band of devoted followers, and we ought not to rest satisfied until he is seen to be what he is. He is one of the very chief glories of English Poetry; and by nothing is England so glorious as by her poetry.[48]

3

The Rise and Fall
of "Practical" Criticism:
From I. A. Richards to Barthes
and Derrida

In an 1891 essay on criticism, Henry James, who had long suffered from the obtuseness of reviewers, posed a dilemma which looms larger as the territory of criticism expands: "The bewildered spirit may ask itself, without speedy answer, What is the function in the life of man of such a periodicity of platitude and irrelevance? Such a spirit will wonder how the life of man survives it, and above all, what is much more important, how literature resists it." For all his exasperation, James was no enemy of criticism, not the artist determined to keep the mysteries of his trade intuitive, unspoken. The prefaces he later wrote for the New York Edition of his novels aimed to provide a formal ground for the criticism of prose fiction. James could not anticipate the forest of signs and symbols that would grow from his formalist acorn, nor could he imagine that technical sophistication would one day pose as great a threat to literature as the philistine platitudes of reviewers. Once long ago, while I was looking for a thesis topic, a gust of inspiration picked me up and whispered in my ear the word "Conrad." I went to the Cambridge University library to scout the terrain, but soon gave way to an almost physical nausea at the sheer quantity of what had already been done, enough to weigh down and bury all inspiration forever.

Problems of quantity are quickly translated into problems of quality. Our understanding of both James and Conrad has benefited greatly from what Roger Gard describes as "the absolutely unprecedented increase in this century of 'professional' students of literature." But as the amateur "gentleman of letters," who remained anonymous to protect his social status, gave way early in the century to the academic busywork of "practical criticism," the increase of knowledge threatened us with a bureaucratization of the imaginative, while artists, out of an instinct for self-preservation, stopped paying attention. It's easy to see why this quantitative explosion of criticism did not always contribute to the March of Mind. As literary criticism became academicized, scholastic work learned to stay within the parameters of the "field"; the existing literature, with its prevailing categories and methodologies, the whole discipline, with its hierarchical channels of certification and advancement, often became so much dead weight on the shoulders of the living. New views were encouraged to differ, but only minutely, from the academic consensus; when such views gained acceptance, they too became part of the conservatizing inertia of that body of received opinion.

In the secondary world of literary criticism, where everything is commentary, new views were not even required, only new "readings," only texts that could be "read" and re-"read" without going too obviously dead on you. Before exegesis was displaced by the changing fashions of literary theory, the specter that haunted practical criticism for decades was the plague of numbers, the proliferation of mediocrity, the multiplication of redundant readings to which theorists themselves now contribute so abundantly. Of what earthly use, outside the classroom and the certification rituals of the academy, was yet another reading of a poem or play that has been continuously understood and intuitively enjoyed for at least three centuries, or even three decades? Some forms of close reading had no relation to how anyone actually *read*. The New Criticism provided some excellent tools for pedagogy, but it also bound criticism over to the pedagogic spirit, while severing it from the free play of mind that gives the intellectual life its excitement and its value. This is what drew many of us to literature and criticism in college. Where history seemed in thrall to "the facts," the archives, the minutely circumstantial, criticism was the best possible arena of ideas. The philosophers might lose themselves in thickets of abstraction, remote from all immediate human concern, but literature could pose the largest issues of social and personal destiny in a vividly human context. The study of literature demanded a sheer love of language and storytelling for their own sake, yes, but the great writers also had something to say; the cognitive mysteries and affective intensities of the work of art lay before the young would-be critic like a land of dreams.

It didn't take many months of graduate school to disabuse the novice of these prospective ecstasies. The routines of professionalism and apprenticeship, combined with the pseudoscientific methods of positivist scholarship, quickly made an interest in ideas a hindrance, if not an irrelevance, and turned affective intensities into a distracting luxury. A personal stake in books had to give way to a personal stake in one's career, and to a casual facility masquerading as authority. During the seventies the graduate study of English closed down shop, a casualty of the job market, but the best that could be said about it even earlier, when it was thriving, was that a really deep love of literature could survive it, though it couldn't expect much encouragement. When the word "literature" was used in graduate school, it usually referred not to the work of art but—preceded by a definite article—the body of writing that has been secreted around it, like the biblical glosses which, sentence by sentence, made up the edifice of the true church.

Even by the early sixties, however, this traditional scholarship was on the defensive; the spirit of practical criticism, with its emphasis on the text itself, had made serious inroads even into such bastions as the scholarly journals and the major graduate departments. Yale, where I was a graduate student, had long been the redoubt of a softened, academicized version of the New Criticism, which combined a focus on literature itself with a proper respect for what everyone else had said about it. The New Criticism was already a tired movement, a toothless lion, well past old insurgencies. It had made its peace with the old scholarship, whose occasional value it acknowledged. Interpretation and critical thinking had by then acquired some status and respect even in graduate study. But the New Criticism itself was not interested in ideas, which it considered a little extrinsic to the literary work, and it showed relatively little interest in theory, except as an afterthought to justify its procedures of close reading.

There was a body of New Critical theory concerning such matters as organic form, the intentional fallacy, image and metaphor, and so on, but it followed on the heels of the movement's practical work. The New Criticism spread its influence more through textbooks like *Understanding Poetry* (1938) than through much later theoretical polemics like Wimsatt's *Verbal Icon* (1954). In Cleanth Brooks's *Well Wrought Urn* (1947) the theoretical chapters are a postscript to the exegesis of individual poems, and by the time of Wellek and Warren's *Theory of Literature* (1949) the battle was essentially over: the time for handbooks and codification had arrived. And as an academic procedure, churning out new "readings," the New Criticism could be as spiritually deadening as the old scholarship. By successfully turning the New Criticism into theory, Yale professors like Wellek, Wimsatt, and Brooks laid the ground for the insurgent theorists of the next generation, some of whom were their own students.

For all its formal sophistication, for all its attention to the stresses and internal contradictions of the literary work, the New Criticism, by objectifying and hypostatizing the text, never really broke with the positivism of the philologists and the source-and-analogue hunters. For the scholars the text was the sum of its traceable influences. René Wellek recalled taking a seminar on Goethe's *Faust* which began with sources so far back in time that it never reached Goethe. "All we ever established about *Faust*," he said, "was that it existed." For the New Critics, those inheritors and exegetes of modernism, the text's existence was of more complex concern than its background or its relationship to other texts. Sources and analogues—*Quellenforschung*, philology, along with social and biographical contexts—belonged to the old historical scholarship. The New Critics heard the battle cry of modernism, MAKE IT NEW, and behaved as if this rupture had actually been achieved, or desired, by every significant work, past and present. Just as they tried to sever the practice of criticism from theory and ideas, they failed to see that in a way the scholars were right: the text was a living tissue of its manifold contexts. Everything that went into it—the mind that composed it, the language that articulated it, the literature that preceded it, the social moment that conditioned it, the generations that had put their mark on it, the minds that received it—were flickering, prismatic, and unstable. For all their lip service to a Coleridgean idea of organic form, the practice of the New Critics usually betrayed a surprisingly mechanical notion of form. Paradox and ambiguity were there *in the object,* existing not as fragments of internal drama, diversity, and self-contradiction but as elements of a higher unity, a conservative principle of order.

What finally signed the death warrant for the New Criticism was not its conceptual weaknesses but its practical triumphs. Like all successful movements, the New Criticism died when it was universally assimilated. Its techniques of close reading, its vision of formal coherence, its attention to patterns of metaphor and narrative personae, were integrated into the useful equipment of every teacher and critic of literature, and influenced many readers who had studied with them, some of whom became editors, journalists, book reviewers, and even authors. Few have ever suggested returning to the days of genteel impressionism or dry factual scholarship. But by the late fifties and sixties, many began to feel bored and constrained by the anatomical approach to literature. They were eager to see the work reconnected to the wider sphere of history and theory, politics and psychology, from which the New Critics had amputated it. They envied the broader horizons and grander ambitions of European criticism. Writers like Auerbach, Spitzer, Lukács, Poulet, and Bachelard were expected to become guides in the struggle of American critics to pass beyond formalism, but they were far too idiosyncratic to offer any easy new method, and their approach made fools of less learned and nimble men who tried to imitate them too directly. It was only the arrival of structuralism and deconstruction in the late sixties and seventies that seemed to provide a way out of the formalist impasse with new critical techniques. For all their formidable difficulty, the works of Lévi-Strauss, Foucault, Lacan, Barthes, and Derrida collectively breached the resistance to theory endemic among English and American critics. Sympathetic expositors sprang up at key American universities who themselves began to provide a body of theory rivaling the work of the Europeans in its daunting complexity and elusiveness of style.

Marxism, Freudianism, structural linguistics, deconstructionism— American critics threw themselves into difficult and often contradictory conceptual systems with a reckless zeal as strong as their previous resistance. Yet the critical utopia that these theoretical breakthroughs once seemed to promise failed to materialize. Americans learned to handle big European ideas, but they have not really translated them into convincing critical practices. Literary theorists have had a greater impact on legal interpretation than on the way readers read or writers write. They've had no effect on journalistic criticism, which mediates between writers and readers. The test of a critic comes not in his ideas about art, and certainly not in his ideas about criticism, but in the depth and intimacy of his encounter with the work itself—not the work in isolation, but the work in its abundance of reference, richness of texture, complexity of thought and feeling. If the New Critics inhibited themselves by objectifying the text and putting it under glass, the deconstructive critics display their ingenuity by evaporating the text into an infinite variety of readings and misreadings. We grant that no two readers read the same book. But by scanting the degree to which different readings may overlap, and even coincide, the deconstructive critics undermined the communal basis of practical criticism, which is grounded in the possibility of common perception and mutual assent. The provisional (rather than definitive) character of any reading does not therefore condemn us to an anarchy of arbitrary subjective difference. Cut off from a text that he can manipulate at will, isolated from an audience whose agreement he deliberately es-

chews, the deconstructive critic creates an almost impenetrable bar-
rier—his style—which repels the uninitiated and becomes the self-
fulfilling prophecy of separation from the language of the tribe.

There is much to be said against the Arnoldian public style which
long dominated English and American criticism, especially for the air
of objective authority it arrogates to itself. T. S. Eliot's essays, for
example, don't bear examination as argument, despite his philosophical training; even his casual aphorisms read like dictatorial fiats. But
the plain style is at least a communal style, not a specialist's jargon,
and its transparency assumes that what matters about art is its relation
to life. The public style not only aims to communicate but presumes
what Jürgen Habermas calls a "public sphere," a liberal arena of
citizenship, public opinion, policy debate, and civic responsibility.
Deconstruction, on the other hand, especially among the imitators of
Derrida, gave rise to an intensely literary style, an artifact style, that
mimics the self-referential involutions of art's relation to itself. Sentences take a long, sinuous course before looping back upon themselves, donnish puns cascade over one another, hyphens separate
syllables to highlight dubious etymologies. Having decided that art is
not about life but only about itself, the deconstructionist then insists
that criticism can't really be about art but only about *it*self, about the
duplicities of language and representation. Life is a construct, a series
of fictions; art is a discourse which helps create those fictions; and
criticism is a competing discourse without genuine access to either art
or "life"—an illusion created by language. The style of deconstruction
reflects its rejection of the public sphere and the politics of liberal
humanism.

Writing some of these sentences, I feel myself falling into the very
jargon I have criticized. Words take on a life of their own, losing their
referential grasp and their power to communicate something precise
and concrete. In *Practical Criticism* I. A. Richards quotes Blake's
saying that "Virtue resides only in minute particulars," which could
stand as a justification for the whole enterprise of practical criticism.
To avoid dissolving into generalities, and to keep myself from fore-
closing the possibility that poststructuralist theory, for all its disbelief
in the idea of the individual author, will someday prove itself in the
criticism of actual works, I'd like to take a closer look at Richards's
book, which was a key influence on the New Criticism, and compare
it to structuralism's most ambitious attempt at practical criticism, Roland Barthes's *S/Z*. Before doing that, however, I ought to explain
at last what I mean by practical criticism, and sketch in some of the
background of its development.

Students of criticism can't help but notice that they almost never encounter detailed analyses of individual works or passages in criticism written before the twentieth century. Before the beginning of the nineteenth century, even essays devoted to individual authors are a rarity. Unlike the history of art itself, the history of criticism is progressive and cumulative. Criticism builds on past work as art need not. But until the early nineteenth century the history of criticism is really a history of aesthetics, not of critical practice. Though there is no reason to think that men of taste and perception in past ages read more superficially than we do, the comments they left us often seem distant and external. With a few remarkable exceptions, they had no framework or rationale for detailed interpretation and evidential analysis. The exceptions are notable, and usually have a purpose apart from criticism itself: philosophical treatises on other texts, such as the Neoplatonic commentaries on Plato or medieval discussions of Aristotle; handbooks of rhetoric from the ancient world through the Renaissance; biographies of artists, such as Vasari's lives of Renaissance painters or Johnson's great *Lives of the Poets,* which forms the effective beginning of practical criticism in English; polemical or didactic forays, such as Rymer's comments on *Othello* or Addison's papers on *Paradise Lost;* early legal commentaries, such as Blackstone; and above all, religious hermeneutics and biblical commentary, which provided the model for both literary scholarship (texts, annotated editions) and critical interpretation. (Later, when the "higher criticism" of the Bible developed in the nineteenth century, it repaid this secular scholarship the compliment of imitation.)

Occasionally, a work of aesthetic theory such as Lessing's *Laokoon* would shade off into close textual commentary of a surprisingly modern kind. But by and large, practical criticism developed in response to the immediate needs of expanding middle-class cultural activity. During the Romantic period, reviewing became the mediating force between an increasingly difficult literature and an increasingly diverse audience; and a reviewer, then as now, was prompted to confront the individual work as the aesthetician had not. Serious reviewing begins in England with the founding of the liberal *Edinburgh Review* in 1802 and its Tory rival the *Quarterly Review* in 1809, but there was an upsurge of reviewing in monthly magazines and newspapers as well, embracing not only literature but theatrical performances and art exhibitions. As Kean walked the boards, Hazlitt, Leigh Hunt, and their friends were there to record their reactions to his acting, and even Keats, inspired by Kean to write a play, could at times contemplate earning his living as a literary journalist. In the midst of this journalistic hubbub, much of its trivial and mediocre, the "Advertisement" in the first number of the *Edinburgh Review* sounded exactly the note that would later be heard from the modern quarterlies and the founders of the *New York Review of Books.* Unlike other reviews, the *Edinburgh Review* would "be distinguished, rather for the selection, than for the number of its articles"; rather than try to review everything, it would confine itself "in a great degree, to works that either have attained, or deserve, a certain portion of celebrity"; the articles would be fewer, longer, more reflective, and hence would not have to appear at just the time of publication. Lord Brougham, one of the prime movers, stressed in his memoirs that these were meant to be essays occasioned by books rather than strictly critical reviews of the books themselves.

Today the early stalwarts of the great reviews remain only sour footnotes to the history of English Romanticism. Jeffrey, Lockhart, Croker, and Gifford are largely remembered for their savage attacks on Wordsworth, Shelley, Byron, Keats, and Hazlitt. Francis Jeffrey, who edited the *Edinburgh Review* from 1803 to 1829, who contributed literally hundreds of articles (including at least fifty on contemporary English literature), whose pieces were collected into library editions after his death, has come down to us as the man who opened his review of Wordsworth's *Excursion* with the ringing words "This will never do." A look at Jeffrey's articles on Wordsworth shows us immediately what makes them both impressive and insufferable, even when they're manifestly right, as on *The Excursion.* Jeffrey's crisp, authoritative tone verges on bullying. His cold fury at Wordsworth is redoubled because he acknowledges real talent in the poet, and because the poet has had the temerity to refuse his earlier advice. The level of vituperation exceeds anything in twentieth-century criticism. *The Excursion,* for example, is "a tissue of moral and devotional ravings . . . such a hubbub of strained raptures and fantastical sublimities, that it is often extremely difficult for the most skilful and attentive student to obtain a glimpse of the author's meaning."

Just as the poetry of Wordsworth and Coleridge is one of the first examples of a conscious avant-garde, Jeffrey's reviews are perfect specimens of how critical theory, armed with precepts inherited from an earlier generation, interferes with practical criticism, especially during the time of a major revolution in taste. Jeffrey's obtuseness is partly rooted in snobbery, for the lower-class rural characters of Wordsworth reflected a social as well as poetic revolution. ("Why should Mr. Wordsworth have made his hero a superannuated Pedlar? What but the most wretched and provoking perversity of taste and judgment, could induce any one to place his chosen advocate of wisdom and virtue in so absurd and fantastic a condition? Did Mr. Wordsworth really imagine, that his favorite doctrines were likely to gain anything in point of effect or authority by being put into the mouth of a person accustomed to haggling about tape, or brass sleeve-buttons?") But Jeffrey's snobbery is really an aspect of poetic theory; he brings to bear a classical standard of *literary* decorum which rules out low-born characters entirely, or at least requires that they be depicted in a way that is consistent dramatically and consonant with their social standing. Jeffrey charges Wordsworth with "revolting incongruity and utter disregard of probability or nature." Wordsworth is "revolting" indeed, against the very notions of decorum and probability that blinker Jeffrey's criticism.

Before these passages make us complacent about our superior appreciation of Wordsworth and our more advanced critical subtlety, we ought to ask ourselves a small question. Are we really responding to the poet more deeply than Jeffrey did? Do our reverential commentaries really take in what is extreme and problematic about him? Can we even begin to understand his drastic affront to accepted taste? Aren't obtuseness and outrage the highest tribute conventional minds can pay to genius—particularly vanguard genius of the modern kind, which always *is* trying to "make it new"? This kind of sharp recoil wasn't limited to the bold, stylized products of Romanticism. The same obtuseness can be traced in reviews of Henry James later in the century, and in the initial responses to Beckett in our own time. I don't mean to elevate the angry rebuff of the offended philistine into the only true tribute to originality. As we follow the more positive reactions to Wordsworth from the comments of Ruskin and Mill, to the great statements of Arnold and Pater, along with the obligatory essays of the lesser Victorian critics like Leslie Stephen, Morley, Bagehot, and Lewes, we continue to feel the shock of recognition, the wrestling with the intractable that rarely intrudes into our modern academic assimilation of the poet. The plebeian sublimities that revolted Jeffrey became therapeutic and life-giving myths for Mill, Ruskin, and Arnold, but the personal stake of the critics never abates. The vitality of the poet radiates down through their work, as it rarely does in our academic discourses—despite the voluminous attention directed at Wordsworth by recent scholars.

Before we conclude that the discovery of close reading coincided with the loss of our ability to read, or at least to read deeply and feelingly, we ought to remind ourselves of James's response to his reviewers'

tribute of incomprehension and disapproval: "a periodicity of platitude and irrelevance." It would be hard to find a better phrase to
describe the work of those heirs of Jeffrey who populate I. A. Richards's modern *Dunciad,* oddly misnamed *Practical Criticism* (1929).
For several years in the late twenties Richards distributed a group of
anonymous short poems to his undergraduate audiences at Cambridge, giving them a week to compose written comments, on which
he subsequently lectured. Excerpts from these comments—or "protocols," as Richards calls them—make up the main part of *Practical
Criticism.* Richards introduces this material modestly, as an experimental survey and "documentation," and his own comments on the
protocols and the poems are spare and laconic. But others have followed his hints and asides to read recklessly large implications into
his evidence. According to Stanley Edgar Hyman, who is no enemy
of hyperbole, "what the protocols reveal, by and large, is probably
the most shocking picture, exhaustively documented, of the general
reading of poetry ever presented."

Published more than sixty years ago, *Practical Criticism* has always
been considered one of the landmarks of modern criticism, but like
many assumed classics it's more respected than read. After all, what
still shocked Hyman in 1948 could hardly surprise anyone who corrects
undergraduate papers today. Instead, we are likely to be impressed
by the technical sophistication and polemical eloquence with which
the protocol writers, like their ancestor Francis Jeffrey, pursue lines
of argument wholly irrelevant to any kind of fair-minded criticism.
Well equipped with information about meter, rhyme, and verse forms,
they unsparingly demolish poems whose rhythm departs even minutely
from a regular standard. Often able to piece out difficult thematic
configurations, they are quick to bully the poet with their own (irrelevant) point of view on the same subject. On one weak religious
poem a writer comments: "I don't like to hear people boast about
praying. Alfred de Vigny held that to pray is cowardly, and while I
don't go as far as this, I do think that it is rude to cram religious
ecstasies down the throat of a sceptical age." Such a brave agnosticism
makes clear that the writers are by no means hidebound and old-
fashioned, despite their aversion to poetic rudeness. Their stern up-
to-dateness is nowhere more evident than in their sharp attacks on
"sentimentality," even in great poems like Lawrence's "Piano" where
the sentiment is precisely qualified and vividly actualized.

Revealing much more than ignorance or the inability to read, the
protocols, like the reviews of Romantic poetry of a hundred years
earlier, demonstrate the drastic interference of critical theory with

critical practice. Richards's readers are caught in a backwater of Romantic and Georgian taste just when the tide is running out. Quite able to take the measure of decorous minor nature poetry, they're utterly lost with Donne, Hopkins, and Lawrence, all figures who, whatever their dates, belong to the new modern sensibility of the 1920s, poets whose verse forms all fail the late-nineteenth-century test of musical regularity and artful literary diction. One reader describes a delightful Hopkins poem as "a nonsensical agglomeration of words. Expressed in jerky, disconnected phrases, without rhythm." Another agrees that "there doesn't seem to be the least vestige of a metrical scheme." Others have equal difficulty with what the poem is saying: "I read this ten times without finding any meaning in it and very little attraction." Still others take a wild stab at what's happening in the poem, and then substitute their prose paraphrase for the poem itself, addressing all their subsequent comments to the paraphrase rather than the poem.

The main disability of Richards's readers is that they come to a poem with fixed ideas of what a poem ought to be, instead of attending to what is actually there. Richards is very amusing on this tendency of his readers to write substitute poems out of their own experience, which displace the poem on the page. This inattention to detail is matched in other readers by "dogmatic pronouncements on detail irrespective of the final result"; both approaches tend to ignore plain evidence of the poet's intentions. Richards demonstrates in great detail how "critical preconceptions" and "technical presuppositions" can blind readers to the whole point of a work, especially if it is original in form or meaning. "The blunder in all cases," says Richards, "is the attempt to assign marks *independently* to details that can only be judged fairly with reference to the whole final result to which they contribute. It is the blunder of attempting to say how the poet shall work without regard for what he is doing."

This emphasis on internal form and on the totality of the individual work was Richards's chief legacy to the New Critics. Richards had a great feeling for how poems are put together. His notion, developed in other books, of poetic statement as "pseudo-statement," emotive and provisional in character rather than cognitive and discursive, provided later critics with a rationale for objectifying individual works and isolating them from larger cultural contexts. Yet Richards himself, like the other great practical critic who emerged from the Cambridge English school in the twenties, F. R. Leavis, almost never confines himself to straight explication. Richards's work, for all the uses to which it has been put, offers a good deal that undercuts formalism and anticipates later developments, including structuralism. With his interest in psychology, linguistics, semantics, Basic English, literary theory, and Eastern thought, Richards is very much the nineteenth-century Professor of Things-in-General. Every page in *Practical Criticism* that tells us that works have a unity of form also tells us that they have a diversity of meaning, that people will read them in different ways, in different moods, using different codes and assumptions.

This is especially true when readers encounter literary works without the provenance and cultural authority of a known, brand-name author. Richards's experiment in anonymous reading foreshadows the structuralist interest in a science of literature, as well as its dream of a literature without authors, cut loose from the mystifying bourgeois idealization of the individual artist, bathed instead in the semiological glow of a staggering variety of semantic codes and potential meanings. Though New Critical exegetes like William Empson and Cleanth Brooks took from Richards a sense of the inherent ambiguity of all texts, they saw these contradictions as inherent in the object itself rather than in our different ways of reading it. Richards, on the other hand, anticipates the recent interest in literature from the point of view of the reader, which the New Critics ruled out under the heading of the Affective Fallacy. For Richards, a science of literature is a subdivision of a science of life, a psychology of behavior and emotion. He sees emotion as the fundamental element in literary response and, unlike the New Critics, makes short shrift of the critical charge of "sentimentality" when it is simply a cover for disagreement or simple contempt. His reaction to the protocols, which is usually so oblique and understated—we never learn what Richards thinks of most of the poems he presents to his students—rises to a pitch almost of indignation when they use their critical sophistication to rend the emotional fabric of Lawrence's "Piano." With his keen interest in emotion, and his sense that critical judgments are judgments about life as well as art, Richards is far from sharing the antiromantic, antisubjective bias Eliot and T. E. Hulme passed on to the New Critics.

I can't refrain from pointing out one other feature which gives *Practical Criticism* its contemporary feeling and keeps it a living work—its form. Cast as a report on a quasi-scientific experiment, "the record of a piece of field-work in comparative ideology," Richards takes pains to avoid the belletristic pontifications of a conventional man of letters. In *The Rise and Fall of the Man of Letters* (1969), John Gross described the gradual professionalization of criticism and its attachment to the university. But it is hard to understand, apart from some personal animus, why he makes Leavis the chief character in his demonology while hardly mentioning Richards. When Richards castigates "the attempt to assign marks *independently* to details that can only be judged fairly with reference to the whole final result to which they contribute," he is describing not only the hapless efforts of his untutored students but the whole line of attack of periodical criticism and book reviewing from Francis Jeffrey to his own day, and well beyond. Just as Leavis never tired of assaulting the cultural authority of the British weeklies and Sunday papers, one key element of *Practical Criticism* is its origin in the university classroom and its dedication to his student "collaborators."

The fissure opened up by the new modernist sensibility, into which those same students stumble and fall, is closely related to the growing gap in England between the conservative taste of the periodical reviewers and the more advanced literary thinking that was developing in the universities. What a reversal from the time, not much earlier, when not only modern literature but *English* literature were barred from the university, when Arnold could become the first Professor of Poetry in Oxford to lecture in English rather than Latin. It's in the context of this split between the middlebrow metropolitan culture of book clubs and consumer guidance and the advanced literary culture of Cambridge that we must see Richards's rejection of the essayistic mode, his unwillingness even to make explicit his own judgments of the works he presents for study, as well as Leavis's astringent critical judgments and knotty Jamesian cadences. For both of them, reading is a more searching process than the glib Sunday reviewers imagine. Their styles suggest steady work, the resistance of literature to easy assimilation.

What Leavis achieves through surly exactitude—his writing is both exact and exacting—Richards accomplishes by withholding: by restraint, understatement, and irony. *Practical Criticism* is not an essay but a palimpsest—multilayered and unstable. Richards's spare voice becomes the continuous bass line beneath a polyphonic display of more assertive critical voices, whose very diversity dramatizes the manifold range of reading and meaning. Richards is most intrigued by how differences in human psychology and background are reflected in the different ways we read. Even after we pare away those readings based simply on ignorance—on what Richards calls failures in "construing"—the exchange between text and reader remains mercurial and dynamic.

There are serious weaknesses in the analytical part of the book, where Richards is sometimes tempted to assume the role of the village explainer. But in the documentation section the interplay of different poetic texts, the voices of the protocol writers, and Richards's own oddly personal tone of subdued irony, learned objectivity, and donnish whimsy makes the book a uniquely instructive and entertaining work, as bold in its form as it is unusual in content.

It would be tempting to round off our excursion into practical criticism by saying that Roland Barthes's staggering book *S/Z* bears the same relation to structuralism (and poststructuralist "narratology") that Richards's book does to the New Criticism. Both are idiosyncratic works, in surprising ways more like each other than like the work produced by critics who share their approach. I have already underlined Richards's differences from the New Critics, not least of which were his strong theoretical interests, which found little echo in the busywork of explication that became the New Criticism. Of course there's a long, dreary tradition of "explication de texte" in the French school system, from which Barthes takes pains to distinguish himself, but the advanced part of French intellectual life is highly theoretical, grounded in philosophical training, with no equivalent of the Anglo-American empirical tradition to provide ballast. Deconstructionists have been much less eager to apply themselves to literary texts than to spin out pure theory, or comb earlier thinkers like Rousseau, Marx, Nietzsche, Freud, or Bataille for anticipations of their own views. In *S/Z*, even more than in his books on Racine and Michelet, Barthes sets out not only to confront a literary work but chooses one as alien to his own modernism and structuralism as can be imagined.

The quasi-scientific, quasi-dramatic form of Richards's book finds its unexpected complement in Barthes's equally polyphonic performance. The New Critics rarely ventured beyond the manageable confines of the lyric and had meager luck with narrative fiction, but Barthes's line-by-line commentary on *Sarrasine,* a little-known novella by Balzac, makes that story one of the longest secular texts ever analyzed so exhaustively. And since the book quotes the entire text of the novella, dividing it into 561 separate units, or lexia, there's a constant interplay between the voice of the narration and the voices of the critic. Like Richards, Barthes dedicates the book to his student collaborators, but their voices are never heard as in *Practical Criticism:* their views have been assimilated by Barthes, who intervenes with comments and miniature essays literally between the lines of Balzac's story. His goal is to dismantle the work, to demystify it, rather than to interpret it.

As an experiment in reading as disintegration and deconstruction, *S/Z* is unique. Barthes follows the linear sequence of *Sarrasine* from first sentence to last, but rarely has a critic interceded in a literary work, *interrupted* it, so aggressively or so possessively. Barthes's stated aim is to avoid doing a conventional "reading" of Balzac's story, one that would reductively transpose it into the prose and the argument of the critic. He wants "no *construction* of the text: . . . [T]he *step-by-step* method, through its very slowness and dispersion, avoids penetrating, reversing the tutor text, giving an internal image of it." Barthes's purpose is to preserve and extract the multiplicity of the text's meanings, the range of codes which make up a grid of interlocking significations. Like Richards he eschews belletristic continuity, preferring the appearance of a scientific analysis, and even constructs his title as a diagram, a symbolic paradigm, rather than a piece of writing.

But out of this very attempt to write an *open* book rather than a closed and seamless critical discourse, Barthes decomposes the Balzac story more thoroughly than any conventional exegete. A "reading" at least is a point of view, which we approach as argument, aware of its partiality; but the format of Barthes's interlinear commentary, like a page of the Interpreter's Bible, looks both exhaustive and official, for all its insistence on the text's inexhaustibility. Barthes even expresses annoyance that his readers are likely to want to read the Balzac story *first,* before turning to what he calls his "manhandling" of it. "Those who like a good story may certainly turn to the end of the book and read the tutor text first; it is given as an appendix in its purity and continuity, as it came from the printer, in short, as we habitually read it." That is to say, Barthes's book, like some specially formed creatures in nature, must be entered from the rear. But when we turn to that aperture, the appendix—perhaps already ashamed of our perverse reading habits, our unseemly appetite for the original— far from finding the text "in its purity and continuity," we see it interrupted by 561 numerical superscriptions, denoting Barthes's lexical divisions. The critic's blows have landed even in the despised appendix; the "original" text has been typographically deconstructed.

We need to consider the origin of the deconstructive critic's rage at what Barthes calls the classical or "readerly" text—the realistic narrative accessible to naive consumption—which shows up in his critical procedure and the never-explained fury of his slashing tones. As a literary journalist Barthes had come to prominence as a modernist, an exponent of Brecht, Robbe-Grillet, and the nouveau roman. Barthes had ingeniously expounded the critique of illusionism and verisimilitude made by both of these writers. But in *S/Z* he sets himself the task of commenting on a traditional narrative, while still holding to the view that its "realism" is a mystification and a deception. The alien character of the text, its remoteness from what he officially likes—yet also his unacknowledged fascination with its themes of castration and sexual ambiguity—bring out the best and worst in Barthes as a practical critic.

Barthes's very distance from realistic storytelling, his profound suspicion of its unreflective enchantments, enables him to describe the sheer mechanics of fictional construction more intricately than anyone since Henry James. If James aimed to make readers more conscious and respectful of the *art* of fiction, Barthes is eager to alert them to its mesh of appealing deceptions, its false continuity and lifelikeness, "the 'glue' of the readerly," which attaches "narrated events together with a kind of logical 'paste'." If an observant, articulate, highly cerebral Martian had arrived on Earth and had immediately been handed a novel to read, this is the account of it he might have produced. Who else could describe the ordinary sequence of cause and effect, the elementary consistency of character and motivation, in which "everything holds together," in the following terms?

> The readerly is controlled by the principle of non-contradiction, but by multiplying solidarities, by stressing at every opportunity the *compatible* nature of circumstances, by attaching narrative events together with a kind of logical "paste," the discourse carries this principle to the point of obsession; it assumes the careful and suspicious mien of an individual afraid of being caught in some flagrant contradiction; it is always on the lookout and always, just in case, preparing its defense against the enemy that may force it to acknowledge the scandal of some illogicality, some disturbance of "common sense."

Barthes transposes the concrete narrative into its abstract pattern and falls into overanalysis and wild hyperbole, yet somehow, quite wonderfully, he manages to create the frame of mind of a man reading a novel for the first time, amazed at the concatenation of "events" into the simulation of a story, of "life." In his very anger at this trompe l'oeil, Barthes has succeeded in pinpointing the almost indescribable feeling of wonder that lies at the root of our affinity for stories. But in doing this he also becomes the myopic viewer who stares too long and too closely at a painting, until it becomes just dots and patches of pigment. Finally, he projects on the narrative the very suspicion with which he himself greets and examines it.

The fear of "scandal," the conventionality that Barthes attributes to the classical narrative, may be news to those whose literary taste is guided by the Prix Goncourt, but most of us have long understood that realism is a set of literary conventions rather than a direct reflection of reality, that life rarely duplicates the pattern of a well-made plot, that dialogue is a stylized suggestion of the real, not naturalistic transcription, that realism, like all other conventions of discourse, has social and ideological presuppositions that should concern the critic.

It's disappointing that Barthes deals only with realism in its most naive sense—of art as a photographic duplication of "reality"—rather than with more subtle conceptions of social representation developed by Lukács, Auerbach, and others. Barthes's assault on realism, carried out within the textual terrain of one of its greatest practitioners, belongs with his demystification of the mythologies of popular culture, where he exposes images and texts that otherwise appear naive and natural as manipulative systems of signs. Performed virtually without reference to Balzac's other work, this reading is also an attack on the very idea of the Author, "that somewhat decrepit deity of the old criticism," who "can or could some day become a text like any other: he has only to avoid making his person the subject, the impulse, the origin, the authority, the Father." But by denying the personal element in both narrative and authorship, by concentrating so much on the mechanics of verisimilitude, Barthes virtually jettisons the human element in literature, which everyone but the Martian can recognize and appreciate. Far from passing beyond formalism, he simply dilates its concern with technique into grander and more subjective terms.

This self-conscious emphasis on mechanics, on formal engineering at the expense of theme and emotion, is one of the weaknesses which practical criticism and poststructuralism share. Barthes might retort (with Foucault) that this notion of the human is itself ideological, but this would not diminish his own disability in the face of what really moves people in literature, an obtuseness he himself tried to correct in later books like *The Pleasure of the Text*. Practical criticism is both the shame and the glory of criticism, shameful because it is merely practical and obsessed with technique, glorious when it really gets close to the work of art in a life-giving interchange of both judgment *and* interpretation, will and understanding.

Here Barthes shows his superiority to most of poststructuralist criticism. We all know that literature is written in language, but many recent theorists were obsessed with language and tended to give literature a wholly self-referential character.* Everywhere this

---

*As Barthes himself says in his autobiographical *Roland Barthes,* he "wants to side with any writing whose principle is that *the subject is merely an effect of language.*"

deconstructive critic turns, he or she finds writing about writing. In deconstructing the role of the author, the stance of the critic, and all naive assumptions about content and representation, poststructuralism represented another turn in the wheel of modernist self-consciousness, which arrived late in France but arrived with a paralyzing vengeance. And this critic's own involutions of style are a signal of his paralysis. Barthes, on the other hand, by grappling with the charms of the readerly, with the monster Balzac at his most lurid and exotic, with bizarre themes of sexual distortion and misplaced passion, undergoes the kind of unsettling confrontation that is the glory of practical criticism. (Before the end, in a chapter called "Character and Discourse," he even yields to the claims of the naive "realistic" reader.) In spite of himself he makes a neglected text vibrate with meaning, and develops a "reading" of it which can vivify and illuminate it even for someone who doesn't share his theoretical interests.

I myself take very little away from most deconstructive readings apart from the spectacle of a mind dancing on the head of a pin—if that kind of prose can be called dancing. The ingenious emphasis on minute details, framing devices, and conflicting subtexts, the rage to expose the mechanics and ideologies by which we are "taken in," can be numbing. It draws our attention to innumerable sideshows while we miss the main event. But because many brilliant critics have been attracted to structuralism, their work often tells us more about literature, peripherally, than their theory allows. Eliot once said that "the only method is to be very intelligent," and deconstructive critics are frequently more intelligent than their method. An elegant example is Jacques Derrida's essay on Nietzsche, "Spurs," which pretends to be about style but also manages to build up a fascinating pattern, almost entirely by quotation, of Nietzsche's notions about women. Gradually, however, the seductive distance and alluring inaccessibility of Woman modulates into Derrida's assertion of the distance and inaccessibility of Truth, and Nietzsche's texts on women are appropriated to confirm Derrida's view that "there is no such thing either as the truth of Nietzsche, or of Nietzsche's text." To demonstrate this point that "truth is plural," Derrida settles on a few strange words written in quotation marks in one of Nietzsche's unpublished manuscripts: "I have forgotten my umbrella." Derrida observes that this text may be trivial or highly significant. It may be an utterly casual notation of someone else's words. It may mean everything or nothing. As a text it is merely a "trace," a detached remnant of something which may be irrecoverable.

Because it is structurally liberated from any living meaning, it is always possible that it means nothing at all or that it has no decidable meaning. ...It is quite possible that the unpublished piece, precisely because it is readable as a piece of writing, should remain forever secret. But not because it withholds some secret. Its secret is rather the possibility that indeed it might have no secret, that it might only be pretending to be simulating some hidden truth within its folds.

From this exquisite miniaturization, however, Derrida leaps without warning to the largest generality: the possibility that "the totality of Nietzsche's text, in some monstrous way, might well be of the type 'I have forgotten my umbrella,' " since this illusory "totality," this whole body of work, is itself no more than a larger trace or remnant of what may also be irrecoverable. And the same may be true of Derrida's own "cryptic and parodic" text, which, he suggests, may be no more than a joke, a parody of his own ideas, and so on.

Derrida's aim, which he achieves beautifully, is to open up a vertigo of interpretation which forswears interpretation—by excess of interpretation to prove its very futility—so as to place a time bomb in the analytic baggage of all practical criticism. It's a brilliant performance, a feat of prestidigitation, but to agree with him we must abandon the plain evidence that a good deal more can be gleaned from Nietzsche's books, and even from Derrida's, than from the phrase "I have forgotten my umbrella" (though, as Derrida himself might say, the latter can be more important when it starts to rain).

With its emphasis on the subjectivity of interpretation, indeed, the impossibility of interpretation, poststructuralism was a deliberate affront to the empirical Anglo-Saxon tradition of the "common reader," what Leavis liked to call "the common pursuit of true judgment." The skeptical theorist dismisses evidence of what two minds can share to underline all that separates and eludes them.

By making criticism more technical, the New Criticism had opened a wide gap between the academic study of literature and periodical criticism, which understandably emphasized the *feeling* of a work rather than its form. The emergence of a new generation of younger reviewers in the fifties and sixties, trained in close reading yet also alert to the ambiguities of consumption in the literary marketplace, began to close this gap and to make periodical criticism more sophisticated.

The arrival of poststructuralism, with its impenetrable elite jargon, made this gap wider than ever. As academic criticism became more technical and theoretical, it generated the very split it posited between reader and reader, between reading and meaning, between reviewer and text. If the effect of recent theory on practical criticism has been limited, its effect on reviewing and cultural journalism has been nil; to their credit, the best reviewers continue to look on literature as experience, whatever the formal mediations.

What really damages deconstructionist criticism is not the questions it raises about the status of texts and the possibilities of interpretation but rather its remoteness from texts, its use of them as interchangeable occasions for a theoretical trajectory which always returns to the same points of origin, the same indeterminacy and happy multiplicity. For Nietzsche and his umbrella we could substitute Rousseau and his ribbon, or any other text, and the point would be the same. What wouldn't change is the use of texts as opportunities for self-display, the abdication of responsibility that Steven Marcus once aptly described as a "cheerful nihilism." From the New Critical text as object we have simply shifted to the deconstructionist critic as subject, seeking out either naive texts whose duplicities can be easily exposed, or self-deconstructing texts which have already done half the critic's work for him. Skeptical of interpretation, the critic remains faithful to the sound of his voice, the invitation some texts offer to his resourceful cleverness.

4

Journalism as Criticism

Even to link the words "journalism" and "criticism," as I have in the title of this chapter, goes against the grain of our tendency to think of criticism as an ever more specialized activity. The twentieth century has seen important advances in our technical understanding of how works of art are put together. This followed from the new kind of complexity and difficulty in the works themselves, and brought in its train a great many technical terms, refined concepts, and subtle strategies of critical attack. Literary criticism, which used to be the bastion from which the educated generalist held forth not only about books but about life itself—society, morals, politics, religion—has become so professionalized that even scholars in other fields like history and sociology complain that they can no longer understand it. This is a surprising reversal from the time when critics, priding themselves on their guardianship of the language and their access to a general audience, regularly attacked social scientists for their jargon-ridden obscurity, pseudoscientific aspirations toward system, and unduly narrow professional identification.

But even before criticism took on this special academic coloration, its difference from journalism was substantial. The word journalism suggests a day-by-day thing, as ephemeral as the paper it's printed on. Though journalists themselves often lead feverishly active, even adventurous lives, in their work they're expected to be passive conductors of the world's ongoing business. The critic, on the other hand, whose working life may be largely confined to an armchair, is engaged in an activity whose root meaning involves making judgments, and brings to bear criteria that are enduring rather than ephemeral. A critic is expected to intervene in his material far more drastically than the journalist. Strictly speaking, journalism is simply information, and cultural journalism, which has been with us since the eighteenth century, is information about books, performances, exhibitions, and other cultural events. The development of cultural journalism is interwoven with the growth of the press itself and the development of a large, anonymous reading public—new to culture, unsure of its own taste, and eager for guidance through a tangled maze of cultural artifacts.

"Modern journalism," writes Leonard Woolf, "saw its opportunity to meet this demand for information about new books and invented reviewing and the reviewer."[1] From early on, this reviewer was expected to make critical judgments about the books before him, and this is where journalism and criticism begin to intersect. Critical journalism becomes important when art leaves the court and the salon and enters the marketplace. The history of reviewing—a largely unwritten history, surprisingly—develops in tandem with the history of advertising, in a culture which depends less and less on patronage, more and more on publicity. Reviewers are key links in a commercial chain which connects the modern producers of culture with its potential consumers. Even today, books which are not reviewed in certain key periodicals like the *New York Times Book Review* are sometimes said not to exist: bookstores may not stock them, libraries will not order them, publishers will not advertise them, and other periodicals are less likely to review them.

With this kind of humble commercial origin, reviewing has generally been assigned a low cultural status. If even the better critic can be seen as a parasite on the body of literature, the reviewer is a parasite on the publishing industry and the miscellaneous public. Since most of what's published each year is worthless, the reviewer who begins with a sense of high purpose and a real love of books is quickly dispirited or reduced to a hack. George Orwell has described this demoralizing process in a chilling article called "Confessions of a Book Reviewer," where he notes that "the prolonged, indiscriminate reviewing of books is a quite exceptionally thankless, irritating, and exhausting job. It not only involves praising trash . . . but constantly *inventing* reactions towards books about which one has no spontaneous feelings whatever. . . . [The reviewer] is pouring his immortal spirit down the drain, half a pint at a time." His friend Cyril Connolly included regular book reviewing among the young writer's "enemies of promise."[2]

Connolly was writing in 1938, Orwell in 1946. The kind of professional reviewer they were describing, one who actually makes a meager living from reviewing a hundred or more books a year, is a vanishing breed. Connolly's composite critic, "Walter Savage Shelleyblake," belonged to another world. This is not simply because of the reduced importance of books in the postwar cultural scene. After all, Orwell's jaundiced remarks could as readily be applied to professional movie critics and drama critics. No doubt, inflation has made it much harder to live as a freelance writer. Reviewers have declined because so many reviewing outlets—newspapers especially—have disappeared and the producers of culture have developed high-powered forms of publicity, notably television, which involve no risk of criticism whatsoever. Instead of selling books themselves, publishers have learned to peddle the personalities of authors. The "Today Show" is the standard author's tour raised to the nth power and constricted to seven minutes. Only "quality" books with fragile commercial possibilities still depend on reviews.

Newspapers and magazines have responded to this *People* magazine climate by integrating reviews into their new Style sections and surrounding them with interviews, gossip, feature stories, ads, and listings. Accounts of book and movie deals, paperback sales, production problems, and the private lives of authors and performers have increasingly taken the place of critical judgments in the form of reviews. Nimble young journalists have learned to work their critical ideas into profiles and interviews, often between the lines. Reviews themselves often seem beleaguered. It is still possible, occasionally, to see a book or movie roasted in one column while being promoted uncritically as a glorious event on the other side of the page. But this schizophrenia has become too stressful even for reviewers to bear; it's far easier for them to join the chorus of celebration before passing on to the next undying masterpiece. Reviewers have become television performers themselves, peddling their personalities in bite-size chunks like actors on talk shows. Celebrity reviewers on television provide filler between the film clips; to the studios, their "criticism" is irrelevant as long as the clips go on. Even in print, reviewers can often be seen pleading for attention, pirouetting with factitious liveliness to hook the reader's elusive interest. The successful reviewer becomes a talked-about figure, like the people he writes about. (This has long since happened with the leading film critics.) The others remain mere appendages to the commercial scene. In this light, it's hardly any wonder that the status of reviewers remains low by any traditional standard.

But the overheated media scene of the present moment is not an accurate index to the underlying links between journalism and criticism. In "The Function of Criticism Today," Alfred Kazin reminds us how many of the greatest critics of the past did their best work for periodicals, provoked at times by bizarre occasions and harried by difficult journalistic pressures—lack of time and money, the specific demands of editors and audiences:

Have we forgotten under what conditions so much of the most powerful criticism orginated? Poe wrote his greatest critical essays for general mag-

azines, in the same way that Coleridge and Hazlitt wrote for newspapers.
... Sainte-Beuve wrote his greatest pieces week after week for newspapers.
Eliot wrote his best early essays as a reviewer for English weeklies. Proust
wrote his own first essays for frivolous Parisian papers.... Go back and
recall that Emerson's great essays were popular lectures, that Henry
James's famous essay on "The Art of Fiction" appeared in a popular
magazine, as did his best fiction, that Howells's essays on realism and his
marvelous essay on Mark Twain all came out first in magazines.... This
kind of critic sees himself not as a hack, but as a man seizing the largest
possible audience for his ideas, and in the weekly dialogue he holds with
his readers he establishes standards, and sets up a forum around which
ideas gather, where neglected important figures can be revived and new
writers recognized.[3]

In another essay, "Writing for Magazines," Kazin points to Chekhov
as a writer who especially enjoyed writing for magazines, where he
"was allowed to be *easy*.... [T]he classic style of the European *feuil-
leton,* the style of conversation, of intimacy, of pleasure and the cafés,
was Chekhov's delight and his genius."[4]

Since both these essays appeared in an immense collection of literary journalism, *Contemporaries* (1962), Kazin can perhaps be accused of painting an idealized picture or writing personal apologetics.
But his reminder is a timely corrective to the other picture we get
from academic histories of criticism, especially those written under
the influence of the New Criticism. The impression we get from Wimsatt and Brooks, from Wellek and Warren, and from most of Wellek's
multivolume history, is that modern criticism is indebted to everything
from Plato and Longinus to German idealism—everything, that is,
except the long tradition of critical journalism that began with the
founding of the *Edinburgh Review* in 1802; the *Revue des deux mondes*
in Paris; the *North American Review* in the United States; and the
great Victorian periodicals like the *Saturday Review,* the *Fortnightly
Review,* and the *Cornhill,* and continued down through all the modern
literary quarterlies and book-review organs like the *TLS* and the *New
York Review of Books.*

Though some of these early magazines were relatively popular,
others cultivated a reflective, highbrow mode deliberately different
from the hurlyburly of newspaper journalism. Many were edited in a
frank party spirit that added vinegar to their literary coverage. Though
writers like Wordsworth and Keats were violently assaulted, under
cover of anonymity, from meanly partisan motives, the results were
sometimes a significant contribution to the critical spirit. With the rise
of a Romantic avant-garde, with its emphasis on originality and its

sometimes revolutionary social agenda, a near philistine hostility became the fuel for a strenous new critical journalism, frankly antipopular. Francis Jeffrey's notorious attacks on Wordsworth and the Lake Poets were sometimes based on sheer snobbery, combined with an eighteenth-century sense of poetic decorum:

> The poor and vulgar may interest us, in poetry, by their situation; but never, we apprehend, by any sentiments that are peculiar to their condition, and still less by any language that is characteristic of it. The truth is, that it is impossible to copy their diction and their sentiments correctly, in a serious composition; and this, not merely because poverty makes men ridiculous, but because just taste and refinement are rarely to be met with among the uncultivated part of mankind.[5]

This is Jeffrey at his priggish worst, a hidebound representative of a timid Whig liberalism. But all Jeffrey's reviews make sharp and accurate points against the affected simplicity of some of Wordsworth's characters and language, points to which the poet responded with numerous revisions after they were echoed in the trenchant pages of Coleridge's *Biographia Literaria*. Unlike Coleridge, Jeffrey vitiates what he says by leaving out the other side of the picture. He saved his tributes to Wordsworth for drawing-room conversation, leaving himself open to a charge of hypocrisy. When he told Crabb Robinson many years later, "I was always an admirer of Wordsworth," the poet's friend couldn't resist replying, "You had a singular way of showing your admiration."[6]

What is not well understood today is that Jeffrey attacked Wordsworth not simply for political or strategic reasons or out of the limitations of his taste and judgment. Literary historians have collaborated with Wordsworth in conveying the impression of an enormous uphill battle for public acceptance, impeded by the obtuse reviewers who represented the reigning taste left over from the eighteenth century. In fact, Jeffrey attacked the Lake Poets because their revolution had quickly succeeded; Wordsworth had almost immediately been recognized as a great and moving poet, though an idiosyncratic one. Reviewing Wordsworth's *Poems in Two Volumes* (1807), Jeffrey admits that "the Lyrical Ballads were unquestionably popular; and, we have no hesitation in saying, deservedly popular,"[7] but it is clear that, in the main, he sees the mission of the *Edinburgh Review* as the correction of popular taste, which he *prides* himself in controverting. So sure is he that the new volumes confirm all of Wordsworth's worst faults that he announces, with great fanfare, that he is willing not simply to trust to the judgment of posterity—the usual court of appeal, evidently, for a highbrow quarterly—but to wager on the public opinion of his own time.

This is only one way in which the Edinburgh reviewers foreshadow the acerbic, dissident tone of Eliot in the twenties, *Scrutiny* in the thirties, *Partisan Review* in the forties and fifties, the *New York Review of Books* in the sixties, and neoconservative journals today. "Mass Civilization and Minority Culture," Leavis called it in an early polemical pamphlet, whose title was an emblem of the strange combination of conservative values and radical rhetoric in the highbrow culture of the modern era. (*Scrutiny* was explicit in tracing its lineage to the early nineteenth-century reviews.) The "Advertisement" in the first number of the *Edinburgh Review* contained many other elements which were prototypical of the later, fully developed quarterly mold. The magazine promised to be more discriminating than existing journals, to run fewer and longer reviews, really essays, and to allow books to ripen in the reviewer's mind without regard to the pressure of booksellers and the dates of publication.[8] Existing reviews like the *Monthly Review* and the *Critical Review* tended to be strictly informational and to publish large numbers of summaries and abstracts of new books. John Clive, the historian of the early years of the *Edinburgh Review,* has written that

> scores of hacks and penny-a-liners were completely dependent on the mercy of editors in their turn dependent on booksellers who financed the reviews in order to advertise the books they printed and sold. This meant that praise and blame were invariably bestowed on the basis of commercial rather than literary criteria. The venality that inevitably resulted put book reviewing as a profession into such bad odour that those who thought themselves gentlemen took it up only as a last resort.[9]

The Edinburgh reviewers, on the other hand, by and large middle-class professionals, were gentlemen in every way, down to their Whig prejudices and ambitions, their snobbish airs, and their enlightened liberal opinions on many social and political questions—enlightened, that is, in an England that still had a slave trade and an unreformed Parliament. The Whigs were out of power for nearly all the early period of the *Edinburgh Review,* and this helped give it a critical edge which its Tory counterpart, the *Quarterly Review,* mimicked in its ferocious attacks on liberals and radicals like Hunt and Hazlitt.

Thus a period of sharp political (and literary) polarization helped put criticism on an entirely new footing in England, far from the world of both Grub Street hacks and abstruse aesthetic speculation. Criticism became a hard-hitting enterprise deeply enmeshed with political pamphleteering and the emergence of new classes of readers, who were also new players in the political arena. This was a time when taxes and government-required stamps made the cost of newspapers artificially high as a way of depriving the restive working class of incendiary reading.[10] The kind of "impure" criticism produced under these volatile conditions evidently holds very little interest for modern historians and theorists of criticism. The New Criticism, despite its political origins among the Agrarians, was another step in the shift toward aesthetic criticism which had begun in the late nineteenth century but remained incomplete in Arnold, Pater, Wilde, and Yeats.

The New Criticism was also in its way a highly theoretical movement, despite its seeming aversion to theorizing; it aimed to overthrow existing notions of the literary text and prevailing habits of impressionistic, historical, and philological criticism. It was no mere method of explication, for all its influence on pedagogy. Writers like Ransom and Tate, Richards and Empson, Warren and Brooks, Wimsatt and Wellek, Blackmur and Burke were at once critical practitioners, historians of earlier criticism, and theorists who, early and late, tried hard to codify their own practical procedures. This is something that more journalistic critics, who aimed at a general audience, almost never tried to do, whether they wrote for newspapers or *Partisan Review,* for *The New Yorker* or the *New Republic.* A book like Stanley Edgar Hyman's study of modern criticism, *The Armed Vision* (1948), written under the influence of the more theoretical wing of the New Criticism, is a revealing document of its time—the same period when the academic histories of criticism were being written. Hyman's book begins with a set of villains—popular, historical critics like Van Wyck Brooks and Edmund Wilson—and gradually slides across the ideological spectrum toward a set of heroes, Blackmur, Empson, Richards, and above all Kenneth Burke, Hyman's mentor.

In many ways this is a refreshing set of emphases; Hyman is bracingly opinionated and fun to read, especially for his irreverence toward the sacred cows of middlebrow writing and academic system building. But one main thrust of his book is to eliminate cultural criticism, journalistic criticism, and personal, intuitive criticism—anything free of self-conscious "method"—entirely. This comes out most clearly in his furious attack on Edmund Wilson, which was later suppressed from the paperback edition. As far as I know, Wilson did not respond to Hyman directly. Instead he collected three decades of literary journalism into *Classics and Commercials* (1950) and *The Shores of Light*

(1952), which was far more devastating than any reply. There it was; he had done the work; his articles held up. His judgment, his eye for new talent, the crisp simplicity of his writing, were amazing. Taken together, the pieces formed a vast literary chronicle of the era—though, in the postwar climate of professionalization, it took some time for Wilson's standing as a critic to be restored and for him to become the reigning man of letters he was when he died in 1972.

By that time the world had gotten tired of the New Critical emphasis on interpretation rather than judgment, on the text rather than its contexts, on pedagogic Method rather than individual sensibility. The rising reputations of Wilson and Trilling after their deaths, the ascendency of successors like Howe and Kazin, Kermode and Donoghue—all of them writers who had figured only marginally in anyone's standard history of modern criticism—testified to their rare personal qualities of mind and style, yes, but also to many features of journalistic and cultural criticism which had begun to evoke new respect and attention. These were the qualities of the old-fashioned man of letters, the generalist—supposedly, according to John Gross, an almost extinct species.[11]

The modern version of this figure is not the same as the old pipe-smoking amateur spilling out his impressions on the page. Even a century ago this image was inaccurate, if we look at the prodigiously varied and productive lives of Victorian prose writers—not just the Carlyles, Ruskins, and Arnolds, but figures like G. H. Lewes, Frederic Harrison, John Morley, Walter Bagehot, and Leslie Stephen. Of course there were many genteel bookmen of a milder stamp, especially in America, as the angry young cultural radicals like Randolph Bourne and Van Wyck Brooks were fond of pointing out. The contemporary man of letters has been through the tempering furnace of Marx, Freud, the Holocaust, Sartrean existentialism, and the Kulturkampf of the sixties, just as the increasingly common *woman* of letters has been marked by the concerns of feminism and the tremendous growth of interest in women's writing, past and present. Yet their critical methods are likely to share many of the qualities of the great journalistic critics of the past, from Poe to Henry James to Edmund Wilson.

Journalistic criticism differs from academic or theoretical criticism in a number of crucial ways, some of which bring it much closer to the buried mainstream of the history of criticism—the very history from which it has all but been excluded by academic chroniclers. Journalistic criticism is practical criticism inspired by some timely and communal occasion, usually the publication of a new book. Sometimes it is victimized by the occasion: when the book is trivial, or minor, or below the author's own best standard. The good reviewer who wants to generalize about a writer and observe the shape of his career may feel that he's trapped inside the wrong book. Or she may be forced to give the reader so much information that little room is left for criticism or ideas. But in being obliged to meet the reader's immediate needs, the reviewer must create through his or her language what we often fear no longer exists: a community of shared literary values and social concerns. Good book reviewing is always relevant and contemporaneous, never merely antiquarian. Lionel Trilling was sometimes criticized for his use of the first-person plural; but at its frequent best his "we" spoke not for an in-group of the critic and his friends but for an acute sensibility attuned to the rhythms of the Zeitgeist and the nuances of the social mood.

Henry James in his journalism was a master of this kind of nuanced apprehension. Writing of Matthew Arnold, George Sand, or Anthony Trollope, James tells us exactly what made them seem so fresh twenty years earlier and why they have come to seem somewhat less so in the twilight of their careers. We understand from him that each book not only has its place in an unfolding career but interacts unpredictably with a cultural moment and an individual reader. Thus, at one and the same moment James describes the shape of a career, the history of his own reading, with its nimble shifts of generous enthusiasm, and the changing literary climate, which the subject himself, with his earlier work, may have done much to alter.

James's reviews demonstrate how the needs of the common reader encourage the journalist-critic to be especially vivid and dramatic. Writing constantly about new works to readers unlikely to have read them, the reviewer must try to flesh them out as effectively as a fictional character. James goes further; he tries, as all the great critics have traditionally done, to catch the essential flavor of a writer, to discern the figure in the carpet and lay bare the essential project. Of George Sand he writes:

> She was an *improvisatrice,* raised to a very high power; she told stories as a nightingale sings. No novelist answers so well to the childish formula of "making up as you go along." Other novels seem meditated, pondered, calculated, thought out and elaborated with a certain amount of trouble; but the narrative with Madame Sand always appears to be an invention of the moment, flowing from a mind which a constant process of quiet contemplation, absorption and reverie keeps abundantly supplied with material. It is a sort of general emanation, an intellectual evaporation.[12]

This is just the kind of writing that the New Criticism and academic criticism have shunned. It seems old-fashioned for being so impressionistic and lyrical. Yet James gets a great deal done here. This is a novelist's criticism, full of detail and atmosphere, but also a genuine *reader's* criticism, relaxed, intuitive, incisive. He characterizes the writer's essential stance toward the world in a suggestive, lively way, though one not easily subject to precise verification. As much by metaphor as anything else, he makes what Leavis would call an implicit limiting judgment of her work in the very act of praising it. He implies that there's something childlike and merely "natural" about her work; that it is meandering and, though perhaps inspired, not profoundly structured; and that its method differs as drastically as possible from his own more calculated procedures—a contrast which makes him feel both envious and superior. James's criticism is at once personal and detached, biased and objective.

James had before him the precedent of writers as different as Johnson and Hazlitt, Sainte-Beuve and Arnold, for this kind of experiential criticism. It depends on the accents of the personal voice, whatever its claims to impersonal authority, and centers on the interior drama of reading, responding, and apportioning praise and blame. Such critics' literary essays were rooted as much in the vibrations of sensibility as in any "objective" set of principles and standards. Even Sainte-Beuve, who was later attacked by the younger generation for his frigid biographical method, could rise to lyrical celebration in the presence of genius. One of his late *lundis*, "To Love Molière" (July 18, 1863), is a brief series of almost incantatory variations on the title phrase. What does it mean, he asks, to love Molière, or to prefer Racine or Corneille, or to respect Boileau (for "surely no one loves Boileau")? How would such affections, if we take them seriously, alter our whole outlook, not simply our literary judgments? In a mere three pages Sainte-Beuve provides a fine example of how literary journalism can reach epigrammatically toward the core of a writer's world and the heart of a critic's feeling for that writer. It tells us that to love writers is to be transformed by them, so that nothing else feels quite the same again, and each paragraph of the article is a brief inventory of a writer's unsettling intervention in our mundane lives: "To love Molière is to rid oneself of complacency and excessive admiration for man. . . . [T]o prefer Racine is to risk overindulgence in what in France we call 'good taste,' which in the end leaves such a bad taste."[13]

Much of modern criticism, by veering toward either the explication of themes or the analysis of formal structures, loses the intimate, experiential dimension that we feel in James and his forebears, and that survives best in journalistic criticism. Gerald Graff has described such interpretive criticism as "textual rationalization," the pyrotechnics of showing that—in a text, at least—whatever is is right. He points out that the early exegetes were reacting "against a crudely judicial criticism which especially condemned modern and experimental literature by arbitrary stylistic and doctrinal canons."[14] This description could apply very well to Francis Jeffrey and his colleagues, as well as to the early reception of modernism. Evaluative criticism can easily devolve into obtuse dismissal or hazy appreciation, as I. A. Richards showed so clearly in *Practical Criticism.* But interpretive criticism can turn just as easily into a mechanical process, a routinization of the imaginative. Critical journalism at its best combines the wide-ranging freedom, the gifted *un*professionalism of Victorian criticism, with a more modern textual attention and an awareness that a reading is not the Truth but only a quick take upon it, a singular perspective. Critical journalism is an epigrammatic shorthand awaiting completion by the reader, or a lone voice demanding an answering echo, which can come only from another reading. Sainte-Beuve's own metaphor for this in his article on Molière is striking: "I am only giving the key and the theme; it is up to the reader to carry on from here."[15] This is in keeping with the musical structure of the article itself.

Critical journalism is almost by definition partial, even fragmentary, taking shape in short flights rather than large, comprehensive works. Many modern critics, from Benjamin and Adorno to Trilling and Rahv—all weaned on the heroic phase of modernism—are attracted to the fragmentary dynamics of the essay for the way it accords with our fractured sense of contemporary reality. Literary journalism is criticism by fits and starts, bound to the moment, happily unable to systematize itself or break free from either its cultural setting or its very specific relation to readers and the marketplace. In newspapers— the cheaply printed anthologies which have been described as the verbal equivalent of the modern city—criticism must vie for attention with everything else, all the topical stimuli so characteristic of contemporary life. In "The First Edinburgh Reviewers" Walter Bagehot wrote that, because of the larger and more miscellaneous reading public, journalism and criticism had grown more rapid, lively, and instructive; but the very essay in which he said this was remarkably leisurely by modern standards.[16] Bagehot was partly sardonic about this development, as he was about almost everything, but he could also see its virtues. In our time, when the cultural scene often seems merely trendy and frenetic, it's much harder to strike that balance. The professionalization of criticism, heightened recently by the growth of specialized theory, has abridged the public space of literary discourse and made cultural journalism and the public style in criticism seem methodologically naive and academically suspect.

In reaction to this devaluation of public criticism, I have sketched perhaps a slightly idealized picture here, taking cultural journalism in its higher reaches rather than its mediocre norm. The best journalistic critics have always been properly scornful of the average performance of their colleagues and stringent advocates of more rigorous critical standards. Poe attacked publishers' reviewing cliques "which, hanging like nightmares upon American literature, manufacture, at the nod of our principal booksellers, a pseudo-public-opinion by wholesale."[17] (Apparently some things never change.) He mocked the reviewers who find an easy substitute for the labor of criticism "in a digest or compendium of the work noticed, with copious extracts."[18] On the other hand, he satirized the typical highbrow quarterly reviewer "who loves the safety of generalities" and "is a sworn enemy to all things simple and direct."[19] Poe held out for a criticism that would be both aesthetic and disinterested, "an absolutely independent criticism—a criticism self-sustained; guiding itself only by the purest rules of Art; analyzing and urging these rules as it applies them; holding itself aloof from all personal bias; acknowledging no fear save that of outraging the right; yielding no point either to the vanity of the author, or to the assumptions of antique prejudice."[20]

Like Poe fifty years earlier, Henry James described the criticism around him in the 1890s as a mass of vacuous fatuity. With bitter wit he castigated "periodical literature [as] a huge, open mouth which has to be fed" and assailed "the practice of 'reviewing' [as] a practice that in general has nothing in common with the art of criticism." In James's eyes, the eyes of a lifelong reviewer as well as an impassioned artist stung by obtuse reviews, "the critical sense is so far from frequent that it is absolutely rare, and the possession of the cluster of qualities that minister to it is one of the highest distinctions." James wanted the critic "to have perception at the pitch of passion and expression as embracing as the air, to be infinitely curious and incorrigibly patient, and yet plastic and inflammable and determinable."[21] Like Poe, James combined a grand vision of the potential of criticism with a jaundiced view of its current journalistic practitioners. In a similar vein, Edmund Wilson in 1928 wrote: "It is astonishing to observe, in America, in spite of the floods of literary journalism, to what extent the literary atmosphere is a non-conductor of criticism."[22] Herman Melville had uttered the same complaint in his essay on Hawthorne: "American authors have received more just and discriminating praise (however loftily and ridiculously given, in certain cases) even from some Englishmen, than from their own countrymen. There are hardly five critics in America; and several of them are asleep."[23]

These comments were written out of a sense of the value criticism could have, not as an academic specialty but as a contribution to the health of a culture and the well-being of writers. What Wilson wanted was the sight of "the intelligence fully awakened to the implications of what the artist is doing,"[24] and he called his prescriptive manifesto "The Critic Who Does Not Exist." Wilson, like Poe and James, was clearing a space for a reviewer-critic very much like himself. He saw around him a set of competing schools of writers and journalists, each pouring out scorn on the other and defending its own turf. He was sure "that our contemporary writing would benefit by a genuine literary criticism that should deal expertly with ideas and art, not merely tell us whether the reviewer 'let out a whoop' for the book or threw it out the window."[25] Merely judicial criticism is not enough; it must be a true practical criticism attentive to both the particulars of the text and the general questions it raises. Otherwise it defaults on what it can do for both writers and for the culture at large. Judicial criticism can never entirely be set aside without ushering in a narrow academicism. The almost forgotten journalism of a century ago remains a model of what criticism might yet become, a totality of response to works of art that is both scrupulous and committed, intensely private yet immensely public. In America a handful of academic critics whose work a decade ago was impenetrably theoretical, have turned more personal, essayistic, even autobiographical, substituting anecdote, atmosphere, and humor for interpretive abstractions. In the wake of feminism, many women especially have been reacting to books in a more personal and passionate way, though others have mimicked the worst excesses of literary theory. James in 1868 gave some of the purest formulations of the critic's function when he wrote that "the critic is simply a reader like all the others—a reader who prints his impressions." "Nothing will ever take the place of the good old fashion of 'liking' a work of art or not liking it. The most improved criticism will not abolish that primitive, that ultimate test."[26]

5

Criticism Among the Intellectuals: Partial Portraits

Lionel Trilling and *The Liberal Imagination*

When first published in 1950, *The Liberal Imagination* constituted far more than a collection of Lionel Trilling's best literary essays of the previous decade. It was one of the subtlest attempts to find a new political and cultural position for the generation that had passed through Marxism and then disillusionment in the thirties. In many ways the book is a belated obituary for a set of attitudes we associate with that period—Trilling seems at times to be beating a dead horse. But the book also became an intellectual credo for the fifties in ways Trilling himself may not have expected. Rereading *The Liberal Imagination* twenty-five years after I was first enthralled by it in 1959, I was most struck by the insistent argumentative thread that draws nearly all the essays together. Yet paradoxically the collection also gives an impression of abundance, elusiveness, variety. In a late essay in 1973 Trilling himself chose to underline the book's "polemical purpose" and its "reference to a particular political-cultural situation," though such overt polemics do not generally characterize his work. His animus was directed, he tells us, against "the commitment that a large segment of the intelligentsia of the West gave to a degraded version of Marxism known as Stalinism." In *The Liberal Imagination* the word "Stalinism" never appears, for Trilling was determined to avoid the sectarian debates that betrayed the very cast of mind he meant to bring into disrepute.

Trilling's "liberalism" is a code word for "Stalinism" that relocates the debate on higher ground and indicts a whole set of assumptions about progress, rationality, and political commitment. This has been a source of confusion for many readers, for "liberalism" as he uses it has very little in common with the usual economic, administrative, and electoral meanings. Yet the vagueness of Trilling's terms enabled many readers, myself among them, to nod with approval at arguments that would have seemed more dubious if stated in baldly political terms. Besides, by the time I read the book as a sophomore at Columbia in 1959, Trilling's positions—at least on Morningside Heights, and among New York intellectuals in general—had been canonical so long that they seemed self-evident, and one could attend without distraction to the superb play of mind by which he exemplified his call for "variousness, possibility, complexity, and difficulty." Though Trilling held out some hope for a politics that could also be subtle and discriminating, he appeared to be saying that only art and imagination, abetted by the critical mind, could truly do justice to the fullness of experience. This cultural hope, almost a civilizing mission, involved part of what made Trilling's own writing so attractive. To be a literary critic in this sinuous and elegant mode, to combine aesthetic sensibility with a sense of social urgency, to fuse intellectual analysis with so much moral awareness—this seemed a worthy professional calling. When I first read Trilling as a green undergraduate, I was astonished that criticism, which I took to be a secondary enterprise, could be pursued with such grace, immediacy, and moral seriousness. Trilling wrote about books the way the best writers write about life itself—as a vivid and pressing actuality, a personal challenge.

To Trilling all genuine criticism is a form of autobiography, a straining after self-knowledge. He conceives of an essay as an interior dialogue, the oscillations of a mind in motion working through its own ambivalence. According to excerpts from his journals which appeared in *Partisan Review* in 1984, he once considered writing an essay about the "ambivalent moments" we have as readers, "when we neither hate nor love what the author is saying but hate and love together: when our mind is poised over a recognition of a truth which attacks other truths, or when the author has brilliantly caught half the truth, and denies the other half. These are the most fertile moments. They are the moments of the critic." Trilling's ambivalence, like his emphasis on tragic realism, became one of the essential notes in the cultural register of the fifties—the sense that the genuinely discriminating mind, unlike the political or ideological mind, does not understand itself too quickly, and doesn't move easily from reflection to action.

This had been one of the main themes of Trilling's mentor Matthew Arnold, whose credo for critics had put a similar stress on poise and balance. "To handle these matters properly," Arnold had written in response to Francis Newman's attack on his Homer lectures, "there is needed a poise so perfect that the least overweight in any direction tends to destroy the balance." In the most neglected essay in *The Liberal Imagination,* one that comes closest to a self-portrait, Trilling applied virtually the same words to Tacitus: "Some essential poise of his mind allowed him to see events with both passion and objectivity." Trilling attributes this attitude in part to "the bitter division which his mind had to endure"—that is, his hopeless and tragic feeling for the vanished Roman republic, the burial ground of all his political ideals.

It is hard not to associate this portrait with the elegiac quality of some of Trilling's own writings* and his loss of utopian hopes in the thirties. The self-identification becomes even clearer when Trilling adds that "the poise and energy of Tacitus's mind manifests itself in his language." Trilling's style as much as anything else charmed and won me in 1959. A wonderfully supple and flexible instrument, a speaking voice at once formal and colloquial, it modulates easily from abstract ideas to anecdotes and epigrammatic asides. More playful than genteel, it answers to Arnold's demand that the critic "should have the finest tact, the nicest moderation, the most free, flexible, and elastic spirit imaginable."

In person Trilling seemed to exemplify the same values. By the time I first knew him, when he was already in his mid-fifties, he had an aloof but gracious amiability that did not make him particularly accessible. But there are similar accounts of him as a much younger man. Harold Rosenberg once described him as an Eliotic Cleric of Culture and mocked his formal demeanor, hedged with irony, as a case of advanced respectability. A longtime friend, William Phillips, speculates a little invidiously that he "was able to preserve his working self by dissociating himself from the draining and time-consuming entanglements of human relations," but no doubt he was more guarded with some people than with others. When I encountered him as a student in 1960, he appeared to stagger under the burden of his eminence, as if it were a solemn trust that had descended upon him. Despite his courtly Anglophile manner he showed anxieties and strengths that were distinctly Jewish. He weighed his words as though

---

* See, for example, in "Manners, Morals, and the Novel," his description of the stillness of the past as we experience it in the present: "Some of the charm of the past consists of the quiet—the great distracting buzz of implication has stopped and we are left only with what has been fully phrased and precisely articulated. And part of the melancholy of the past comes from our knowledge that the huge, unrecorded hum of implication was once there and left no trace—we feel that because it is evanescent it is especially human."

he were an institution, as if one thoughtless remark could make the edifice crumble, and he repelled would-be disciples on the Groucho Marx principle of not joining any club that would have him for a member. A deep streak of humility colored his self-importance, and a twinkling humor, perhaps defensive in origin, usually kept him from becoming too pompous. By the same token he had an ingrained and enviable habit of thinking against himself: he avoided taking hard-and-fast positions that would limit his freedom, and he would puck-ishly refuse to say whatever was most expected of him, to the con-sternation of his neoconservative admirers.*

Since Trilling's cast of mind was balanced, judicious, and highly mobile, the unremitting asperity of his critique of liberalism comes as a shock today. We can hardly be surprised by his hostility to the rigid ideological posturings of American Communism, with its subservience to Moscow and its bizarre turns of policy. But his antagonism in *The Liberal Imagination* is directed at the political mind in general, not simply at its progressive variant. If I read him correctly, his polemic is directed against any confirmed belief in enlightened planning and melioristic reform—not simply against totalitarianism, social engi-neering, or apocalyptic revolutionism. Trilling attacks the liberal im-pulse "to organize the elements of life in a rational way," noting that "organization means delegation, and agencies, and bureaus, and tech-nicians," which will inevitably incline to "ideas of a certain kind and of a certain simplicity." On the cultural side Trilling's attacks on old Marxist critics like Granville Hicks and Edwin Berry Burgum are also puzzling, for by 1950 the cultural policies of the Popular Front had long since been discredited. But here too Trilling is reaching for wider implications. When he attacks social realist writers like Dreiser for "naive moralizing" and a blind worship of "brute" reality, when he criticizes "the simple humanitarian optimism which, for two decades, has been so pervasive," he is subsuming the Popular Front in a long-standing American tradition of middlebrow boosterism, cultural na-tionalism, and a pragmatic faith in technology and democracy. In Trilling's view George Babbitt had become a Marxist by 1935, writing book reviews for the *New Masses,* attending the Writers' Congress, and helping to organize the fellow-traveling League of American Writ-

---

* See his deft undercutting of Norman Podhoretz and Hilton Kramer when they try to maneuver him into their own ideological camp in a round-table discussion of "Culture and the Present Moment" (*Commentary,* December 1974). After Trilling's death Podhoretz would accuse him of a failure of nerve for not joining *Commentary*'s no-holds-barred campaign against the remnants of sixties radicalism. Podhoretz is not one to allow honorable motives to his less militant friends, let alone to his adversaries.

ers. By the late forties Babbitt had grown completely respectable, writing a chatty column for the *Saturday Review,* doing occasional pieces for *Harper's* and the *Atlantic,* and reviewing frequently for the *New York Times Book Review.* You can easily guess which American authors were his favorites. I can assure you that Babbitt didn't think much of the gloomy ideas of the "advanced" intellectuals.

The Liberal Imagination is Trilling's only book that deals principally with American writers. Trilling's critical mission is to clear the cluttered scene of the Dreisers and Steinbecks and Sherwood Andersons to make room for a cosmopolitan European tradition that descends from Flaubert, James, and Conrad through the great modernists of the early twentieth century to Hemingway and Faulkner. This is an aesthetically intransigent line of writers strenuously hostile or indifferent to our own liberal pieties. The European modernists remain offstage in *The Liberal Imagination,* implied but only occasionally invoked; but Hemingway and Faulkner make a momentous appearance in the closing pages, where they are compared favorably with Dos Passos, O'Neill, and Thomas Wolfe, who were then among the reigning middlebrow favorites. Trilling finds that he can no longer "live in an active reciprocal relation" with most modern American writers—they present themselves to him only as passive objects of his attention—and in effect he trades them in for the European modernists, as he was soon to do in his teaching at Columbia.

Purely as literary judgments Trilling's have held up very well, despite the qualms he later developed about the modernists. But those judgments were not strictly literary: they were also social—as Trilling himself observed of Leavis's *The Great Tradition*—and they encouraged a generation of students and critics to neglect the strong native tradition of American naturalism. While insisting that the European social novel had never taken hold in America—a belief shared by observers of our fiction from Hawthorne and James to D. H. Lawrence to Richard Chase and Leslie Fiedler—Trilling managed to ignore or belittle our principal social fiction. The injustice was most flagrant in the case of Dreiser. Trilling's sweeping polemic against Dreiser in "Reality in America" was so persuasive that it kept me from reading Dreiser for years afterward. Trilling's watchwords of "variousness, possibility, complexity, and difficulty"—as embodied in writers like Henry James—became so canonical for the high culture of the fifties that seminal figures like Dreiser and Richard Wright were relegated to the shabby ghetto of propaganda rather than art. When I first read *Sister Carrie,* a novel not mentioned in Trilling's assault on Dreiser, I was surprised at how Jamesian it seemed, how subtle in its psychological insight as well as its social notation. Far from being an American primitive, Dreiser is, if anything, too analytical in this book, as James himself often became.

To attribute Trilling's strong animus against Dreiser solely to political differences would be foolish, for Dreiser's weaker novels do have many of the faults Trilling ascribed to them. Trilling's purpose is broader, more admonitory. By coupling his critique of Dreiser's naturalism with a dissection of Parrington's liberal historiography, Trilling seems bent on undermining a whole range of cultural attitudes. His constant emphasis on mind and ideas serves to counter the anti-intellectualism of the populist tradition. He has little use for the libertarian progressivism of the twenties avant-garde, with its muckraking reformism, its attacks on middle-class gentility, its bouts of primitivism, and its simplistic invocation of Freud and Lawrence as liberators of the instinctual life. These same attitudes, in his view, fed into the coarse and sentimental proletarianism of the literary culture of the Depression. Trilling's ploy, like that of Marx, Engels, and Lukács before him, is to rest his case on the deeper social and psychological awareness of more conservative writers like Balzac and James, as well as a Freud whose outlook is essentially stoical and tragic. Trilling mobilizes Freud to counter the "simple humanitarian optimism" of the progressive mind, a Freud who understands man not "by any simple formula (such as sex)" but rather as "an inextricable tangle of culture and biology," social demand and individual need. Freud's "tragic realism" does not "narrow and simplify the human world," as democratic liberalism tends to do, "but on the contrary opens and complicates it," as the best art does.

Yet Trilling remains ambivalent about the application of Freud's ideas to art, and this helps make "Freud and Literature" far superior to his one-sided account of Parrington and Dreiser. Trilling's cautious application of Freud to works of art paradoxically contributes to making him one of the best of all psychoanalytically oriented critics, the one most alert to the dangers of reductive and mechanical interpretation. Trilling sharply attacks the rigid determinism of most Freudian criticism, insisting on the inadequacy of Freud's own positivist conceptions of the nature of art. Anticipating the skeptical outlook of later deconstructionists, as well as their emphasis on the operations of language itself, Trilling argues that it is impossible to pin down any work to a single meaning. But he brilliantly demonstrates the profound compatibility between the formal operations of poetry and the mental processes described by Freud, especially in his psychology of dreams. In one particularly resonant passage, Trilling tells us that Freud dis-

covered "how, in a scientific age, we still think in figurative forma-
tions"; Freud therefore created "what psychoanalysis is, a science of
tropes, of metaphor and its variants, synecdoche and metonymy. . . .
Freud discovered in the very organization of the mind those mecha-
nisms by which art makes its effects." Trilling's ambivalence toward
Freud makes his final appreciation fresh and discriminating. As in the
fine Kipling essay—where politics and class prejudice are the issue
rather than art and psychology, and where the critic's own early love
of Kipling complicates his judgment—Trilling's criticism works best
when he is of two minds about a subject. This accords very well with
his belief that the best writers are those richest in contradictions, who
contain within themselves a large part of the dialectic of their culture
and their age.

Trilling's criticism is less successful with works like *The Princess
Casamassima,* which are too feeble to bear the weight of significance
Trilling attaches to them. This lengthy and much-celebrated essay
contains virtually none of the quotation that a critic like Leavis would
bring to bear so as to justify his high evaluation. Instead Trilling slips
away repeatedly from the book itself into wonderful divagations on
themes like "the Young Man from the Provinces," or else allegorizes
the characters of the novel into vehicles of his own defense of art and
imagination against radical politics. The essay is Trilling's sermon on
a text from James; with perversely misdirected brilliance it opens up
a whole vein of nineteenth-century fiction to which James contributed
only modestly. Fiction plays a key role in the moral economy of
Trilling's book: he sees it as the genre which best embodies the variousness and possibility that are most antithetical to the narrow idealism of the political mind. But this judgment is more true of the
novels James disliked—the "loose baggy monsters" and "fluid pud-
dings" of Tolstoy and Dostoevsky, for example—than of the ones
James wrote.

Trilling's case for James as a political novelist and for Hyacinth
Robinson as his aptly named protagonist is unconvincing, as Trilling
must sense, for when he writes about Hyacinth he drifts unconsciously
toward autobiography and apologetics. When Hyacinth discovers that
the glories of art have been erected on centuries of injustice, Trilling
turns him into a spokesman for the deradicalization of his own generation: "He finds that he is ready to fight for art—and what art
suggests of glorious life—against the low and even hostile estimate
which his revolutionary friends have made of it, and this involves of
course some reconciliation with established coercive power." Thus
James's credo becomes Trilling's own, with poor Hyacinth pumped

up as its spokesman. The character of the princess, on the other hand, calls forth Trilling's fiercest indictment of the liberal mind, "the modern will which masks itself in virtue, . . . that despises the variety and modulations of the human story and longs for an absolute humanity." To Trilling she is the very type of the ideologue, symbolizing "the political awareness that is not aware, the social consciousness which hates full consciousness, the moral earnestness which is moral luxury."

This essay exemplifies one of Trilling's limitations: his relative indifference to form as against theme, and his rapid translation of literary elements into ideas.* This essay's dithyrambic conclusion is typical of several pieces in the book which, in their last few pages, leave their immediate subjects behind and rise to a prophetic intensity that irresistibly recalls Trilling's Victorian forebears. They too wrote secular sermons on literary texts and freely enmeshed literary commentary with social criticism and cultural diagnosis. Norman Podhoretz has praised Trilling's "highly developed sense of context," but of course one man's context can be another's pretext, as Podhoretz's own coarsening of Trilling's themes repeatedly demonstrated. Podhoretz argues that Trilling's work was "drenched in politics," regardless of his own hesitations; but "drenched" is just the kind of hyperbolic word Trilling himself would have avoided, for he was acutely aware of the general loss of precision that would follow if the case against ideology itself turned sharply ideological.

Nevertheless a passage like the concluding description of the princess shows us why Trilling's collection became one of the important documents of the fifties, influential for its subtle and ingenious attack on ideology, its arguments for the saving power and complexity of art, and its Niebuhrian emphasis on tragic realism as opposed to utopian idealism. Trilling's own sensibility was strongly antiutopian, but he felt an undeniable attraction to the extreme, the romantic, and the apocalyptic that he never abandoned; that attraction gave his work its dialectical poise, and kept his mind from taking its ease in any comfortable certainties. It is instructive to watch his stories and essays for the moment when the Anglophile mask cracks, when Trilling turns

---

* Compare Leavis's "E. M. Forster" (1938), reprinted in *The Common Pursuit*, with Trilling's short book-length study (1944). The Leavis account is aggressively evaluative and judgmental, while Trilling's work is a generous, finely wrought series of thematic appreciations which Forster himself very much welcomed. The difference may remind us of John Stuart Mill's powerful comparison of Bentham and Coleridge: "By Bentham, beyond all others, men have been led to ask themselves, in regard to any ancient or received opinion, Is it true? and by Coleridge, What is the meaning of it?"

upon himself to question his carefully cultivated pose. (His first story, "Impediments," ends with a twist that undermines the aloofness and snobbery of its autobiographical protagonist.) These pendulum shifts were not simply personal: Trilling had a remarkable nose for cultural change, and as a critic he understood acutely how contexts alter texts.

This sense imbues his essays with one of their most appealing qualities: their highly nuanced strategies for bringing virtually any subject ancient or modern into a tense dialectical relation with contemporary concerns. His historicism was based on a sense of the present as much as a sense of the past. The idea of "relevance" was no creation of sixties radicals: it was practiced instinctively by Trilling and his nineteenth-century predecessors; to a student in the fifties it made them far more attractive models than their academic rivals, with their dull, fussy, antiquarian interests, or the New Critics, who sacrificed context to texture and achieved virtuosity as close readers. Trilling's work had a long tradition behind it, but it was hard to imitate, for it was eccentrically grounded in his own sensibility. At best his followers learned that the intricate filiations between literature and culture resisted easy formulations; at worst they aped the surface mannerisms of his style. In general he held himself apart, offering encouragement to many, approval to few. He was a sorcerer who took on no apprentices.

If Trilling's manner suggested the Victorian man of letters or the more relaxed essayists of the *Edinburgh Review,* his central theme— the conflict between the political mind and the literary imagination, between a faith in progress and a tragic awareness of man's limitations—had an even longer lineage that Trilling revitalized in contemporary terms. In the background of Trilling's argument one hears the undersong of Burke's attack on the "sophisters, economists, and calculators" behind the French Revolution; of Hazlitt's great discussion, apropos of *Coriolanus,* of why great art tends to be antidemocratic and why "the language of poetry naturally falls in with the language of power"; of Blake's dialectic of reason and energy and Keats's antithesis of poetry and truth; of Coleridge, Carlyle, and the running Victorian critique of the practical, reforming spirit of Benthamite utilitarianism; and especially of the many ways Arnold found to contrast Hellenism and Hebraism, being and doing, culture and conscience. This nineteenth-century tradition of cultural criticism, which F. R. Leavis revived and Raymond Williams studied, shows itself most plainly in Trilling's witty demolition of the crude social and psychological assumptions that underlay the first Kinsey Report, with its quantitative mechanical standard of sexual health.

Whatever else in the fifties can be linked with Trilling's work, sexual repression certainly forms no part of it. He was one of the first to praise Marcuse's unjustly neglected *Eros and Civilization* (1955), and he virtually sponsored Norman O. Brown's *Life Against Death* (1959) when it was published to no fanfare by a small university press. He anticipated their radical reinterpretation of Freud in *Freud and the Crisis of Our Culture* (1955). Yet he recognized that Brown was "nothing if not Utopian" and therefore a problem for his own "thoroughly anti-Utopian mind." To understand Trilling correctly means not to pin him down to this or that position but to grasp the dialectical quality of his temperament, his attraction to minds drastically different from his own, and his impulse to restore the balance upset by whatever the prevailing cultural mood. When the Romantic poets—or later romantic writers like F. Scott Fitzgerald—were being dismissed as immature, antirational, or technically faulty, Trilling offered different readings that re-created them as writers growing up, learning from politics and experience, and developing a tragic sense of the complexities of life. Even an essay as culturally detached as the one on Wordworth's Immortality Ode fed directly into the mood of the fifties, with its premium on maturity and a chastened adult sobriety. Bypassing the strict formal concerns and stern emotional hygiene of the New Critics, with their distaste for romantic sentiment, Trilling helped created a sense of Wordsworth, Keats, Fitzgerald, Dickens, and other romantic writers that a new literary generation could readily accept.

Trilling was such an engaging and seductive writer, with such a shrewd sense of the cultural moment, that many of his dissenting opinions not only prevailed among intellectuals but hardened into a new consensus. Some of these positions were already being widely established, at least among intellectuals, by the time *The Liberal Imagination* appeared. Trilling's arguments against radicalism and liberalism gave way to a thorough depoliticization, a premature celebration of the "end of ideology." In literature his favorite romantics and modernists eventually triumphed completely over the native middlebrows and muckracking naturalists. Anticommunism became the official creed of a cold-war society and its most influential intellectuals. Thus by the end of the gray fifties Trilling was drawn to extreme and apocalyptic figures like Norman O. Brown and R. D. Laing (when few others had heard of them), only to turn against them in the next decade, when their sensibility became, in his view, a new and dangerous orthodoxy. (Similar oscillations can be observed from decade to decade in Matthew Arnold's work between the 1840s and the

1880s.) If the ideological critic is always promoting a fixed set of values, and the academic critic has turned literature (in Trilling's terms) into an "object of knowledge" rather than a source of power, then the Arnoldian critic—the historical critic, the critic of sensibility—offers his own inner dialogue to dramatize the cultural contradictions of the moment.

As R. P. Blackmur noted in reviewing the *The Liberal Imagination,* Trilling's mind, his famous "we," was always at least partly a mind not his own, the "public mind" that he highlighted as a way of thinking against himself. His way of paying tribute to writers or dramatizing social tendencies was to call them into question, or at least to bring them into high relief, by finding their antitype. His attempt to rehabilitate the reputation of William Dean Howells in 1951 was an extreme example. When this essay first appeared in *Partisan Review,* it caused something of a scandal, for it was understandably taken as apostasy to the creed of modernism that the magazine had nurtured since its inception. Trilling put all his emphasis on a Howells entirely devoted to the quotidian and the commonplace, for whom "the center of reality was the family of the middle class." But Trilling's feelings about Howells and the middle class were no more clear-cut than his feelings about modernism.

Before most of modern art, Trilling wrote in an unfinished memoir shortly before his death, "I stood puzzled, abashed, and a little queasy. . . . I took the view, pious and dull enough, that the advanced art of one's own age cannot possibly be irrelevant to one's own experience, and that one is under the virtually moral obligation to keep one's consciousness open to it." Howells does not nullify modernism, but his values put it into question, for Trilling's image of Howells is not arbitrary or accidental: it is fashioned precisely as a dialectical foil to the modern temperament. When Trilling writes of the Victorians or earlier writers, he half shows them to be more modern than we ever dreamed they were, but half makes them proleptically critical of everything modern that haunts and fascinates him.

Writers who have labeled Trilling a conservative go astray here, as do others like Podhoretz and William Barrett who are disappointed that he proved, to them at least, insufficiently firm and militant in the war against the political and cultural Left. Trilling's distinctive style is rarely noticed by commentators who try to give his work a strongly ideological character. When they cut through his rhetoric to the Archimedean point of his belief or commitment, they are cutting away nearly everything we are likely to value about him—not his certitudes, which were few, but his way of arriving at them; not his ideology, but the undulations of mind that ran counter to the fixities of ideology. This genuinely dialectical movement of mind was Trilling's deepest contribution as a critic, more than any fixed positions he was ever tempted to take. The campaign against Stalinism, the founding experience of the whole *Partisan Review* circle, was the last good war; but by 1950 Trilling saw that this war was essentially over and that nothing could ever be quite so simple again.

Feeling "the virtually moral obligation"—the solemn yet playful duty—"to keep one's consciousness open," Trilling wielded irony as a way of both exploring his inner uncertainties and playing on the expectations of the audience. "Jane Austen's irony," he once wrote, "is only secondarily a matter of tone. Primarily it is a method of comprehension. It perceives the world through an awareness of its contraditions, paradoxes, and anomalies. It is by no means detached." Trilling's irony was frequently misunderstood, especially in his most pervasively ambivalent book, *Beyond Culture,* where one poignant footnote announces that "it will perhaps save trouble if I explain that the sentence is ironic." Unfortunately this did nothing to protect other sentences, so that, in a new preface added to the paperback edition, he observed that "the ironic mode has lately become riskier than it formerly was"—an opening sentence that is itself ironic. In his later work Trilling possibly lost control of the ironic mode and became the victim rather than the master of his own method. But perhaps Trilling's more simpleminded readers violated his intentions, even betrayed his spirit, when they turned his subtle doubts about the "adversary culture" into a full-scale onslaught on modernism, the counterculture, and the "new class."

Readers of a book like *Beyond Culture* rarely understand Trilling's way of building up polarities such as self and culture as a magnetic field hospitable to the play of mind, or as an almost musical play of categories and antitheses. To write this kind of fluid criticism must have been nerve-wracking; surely it was a difficult role for any intellectual to sustain. No one was ever comfortable being Hamlet, of two minds about everything; once positions are taken in print, they can turn into a rampart that demands to be defended. Yet such a role was particularly congenial in the fifties, a contemplative rather than an activist period. But Trilling's work may have suffered from the complete rout of his radical adversaries. An aura of stoical quiescence, even depression, hangs over several of the essays in *The Opposing Self* (1955), an abeyance of the will and an emphasis on "the conditioned life" that bespeak a crisis of middle age. It was perhaps then—

and during the Kulturkampf that followed—that Trilling in his chosen style and role risked seeming ineffectual.

The Liberal Imagination concludes with a eulogy of Keats's idea of negative capability, the power to remain open to mysteries, uncertainties, and doubts. Once Trilling had used fiction to dramatize his own inner dialectic, his buried feelings of attraction and repulsion toward characters outwardly different from himself, like Hettner, the "scrubby little Jew" in "Impediments," Tertan, the mad and brilliant young student in "Of This Time, Of That Place," and the charismatic Gifford Maxim, the Whittaker Chambers figure in *The Middle of the Journey*. But Trilling's modest fictional gifts, like Matthew Arnold's poetic powers, were gradually sublimated into the drama of his critical voice, and he published no more fiction after the success of *The Liberal Imagination*. Trilling's constitutional ambivalence is related to his ordeal of being a Jew in a gentile world, teaching English literature in a gentile university. This problem of identity was a theme in Trilling's early stories, but he turned away from it in his mature fiction, with fateful results.

Behind a mask of civilized irony his essays thrived but his fiction grew discursive and vague. Darker personal feelings he confined to his journals: the selections that have appeared in *Partisan Review* are frequently touched by self-doubt and self-loathing as well as self-affirmation. These ruminations take a literary turn when Trilling is visited by his former student Allen Ginsberg, now convalescing at a psychiatric institute (the year is probably 1949): "We spoke of Kerouac's book. I predicted that it would not be good & insisted. But later I saw with what bitterness I had made the prediction—not wanting K's book to be good because if the book of an accessory to a murder is good, how can one of mine be?—The continuing sense that wickedness—or is it my notion of courage—is essential for creation." A great deal of Trilling coalesces in this passage. On the surface he belongs entirely—defensively—to the party of gentility, the camp of the superego. But an equally strong personal pressure drives him toward self-criticism—and to an association of art with criminality and moral adventure. I hope I have not overstressed Trilling's ambivalence and irony, the angular movements of his mind. He turned self-questioning from a personal habit into a principle of criticism. The form of the journal suited him as well as the form of the essay, of which it is a more intimate crystallization. In complicated remarks such as this passage about Ginsberg and Kerouac, Lionel Trilling's life and work merge in a lacerating gesture of introspection that is also a source of impersonal strength.

R. P. Blackmur: The Last Book

The literary criticism of R. P. Blackmur has suffered some strange reversals of fortune in this country. In the thirties and even moreso in the forties—heyday of the New Criticism—he was a living legend while still young, commonly described as the ideal critic. By the sixties, however, his work was often rejected as tortuous and unreadable. The late seventies and eighties saw yet another turn of the wheel. There was an uneven biography by Russell Fraser in 1979, which told the story of Blackmur's strange marriage and literary relationships. But Blackmur and his wife also figured significantly in one of the most vivid memoirs of the forties generation, Eileen Simpson's *Poets in Their Youth* (1982). Discerning critics like Edward Said and Denis Donoghue wrote impressive tributes to Blackmur, while others began to see him not as a murky, aberrant New Critic but as a prescient forerunner of literary theory.

The last collection Blackmur himself published, *Eleven Essays in the European Novel,* appeared not long before his death in 1965 but received almost no attention, though it reprinted some extraordinarily good work. Lionized but not much appreciated at Princeton, where he taught, dismissed or respectfully ignored by the literary world at large, Blackmur gathered together in that book what he called "fragments of an unfinished ruin," the shored-up remains of a number of separate volumes he had planned to devote to the novel. It was a sad end, and the book did nothing to recapture the audience that had long since deserted him. In 1967 a posthumous collection appeared, *A Primer of Ignorance,* titled and partly planned by Blackmur himself and edited by his distinguished literary executor, Joseph Frank. It was not really a good book, and it suffered an even chillier fate than its predecessor. Yet it is a dense, almost a rich book, which should have enabled readers to take stock of the later Blackmur in a more complex way.

If most readers judged Blackmur's later work harshly, it was partly because he himself established so high a critical standard. Though the essays that he wrote in the thirties on the modern poets lost some of their force as the ascendancy of Eliot and Pound gave way to the romanticism of Whitman, Stevens, Crane, and the Beats, they still constitute one of the notable critical projects of the century: a frontal assault of an elusive, demanding, and arrogantly new body of literature, an adventure not only in exegesis but in evaluation. Both poetry and the climate of taste have changed a great deal since the thirties, but Blackmur's individual essays on Eliot, Yeats, Pound, Stevens, and Hart Crane for a long time had more to tell us than most book-length studies of these poets.

It would be misleading to say that Blackmur never again found a subject so congenial to his powers. Henry Adams, Henry James, and the European novel all were to evoke great work from him after 1940, and in fact two superb examples of this work were collected belatedly in the last section of *A Primer of Ignorance:* a study of James's artist fables, "In the Country of the Blue," and a brilliant discussion of Henry Adams's novels. But both these essays—included by the editor, it seems, largely to fill out the volume—are quite early, dating from 1943, and one comes upon them only after 175 pages of prose alternately murky and brilliant, gnomic and pompous, contorted and eloquent. They seize their subjects with a directness and lucidity, a sense of communicable purpose, that was all too often absent from Blackmur's work after 1950 or 1951.

This is especially true of the writings of the late fifties reprinted in the middle section of this volume, most of them ostensibly travel essays but actually personal meditations on European and American cultural style. No reportage could be less journalistic than Blackmur's. In most journalism we get many facts, but recorded discretely, shapelessly, incoherently, so that their meanings remain enshrouded. In Blackmur the opposite is true: meaning is everything, but meaning is vitiated by the paucity of fact, the weak grasp upon the actual. His method is poetic rather than discursive: he turns objects into emblems and recurrent images, slight narratives into allegory, and elusive phrases into choruses and leitmotivs. Strange juxtapositions lead to gnomic observations and conclusions, a wisdom that often seems arbitrary and self-reflexive.

The Jamesian obliqueness of these essays is very much a part of Blackmur's design. He listens for the timbre of a culture and watches its small, revealing gestures, seeking to put himself in touch with that culture's momentum and energy rather than to be taken in by its ideas about itself. This, I think, is the key to the book's title: the sense of "intimacy," Blackmur tells us in an obscure passage, is a "primer of ignorance." It is clear that "ignorance" is no more a pejorative word for the later Blackmur than for Karl Shapiro in his polemical, neo-romantic collection *In Defense of Ignorance* (1960). In *The Lion and the Honeycomb* (1955) Blackmur had adopted for himself Santayana's plea that he is "an ignorant man, almost a poet." Ignorance to Blackmur means the poet's way of knowing, knowledge that is in the ear, the eye, and the fingertips as well as in the mind. It is precisely the quest for intimacy—and perhaps at the same time a lingering embarrassment at intimacy—that makes these travel essays intuitive and haphazard in style as well as substance.

Paradoxically, it is the critic's sense of style that sometimes redeems the essays and makes Blackmur's intuitions convincing. In the best of them, "The Swan in Zürich," a comparison of American and European ballet companies, of brilliant technical precision versus human warmth and vibrancy, he moves effortlessly from observations on styles of dance to generalizations about national style. Much to his own surprise, he opts in the end for intensity of life and plenitude of content over perfection of form. Watching a Spanish company "reputed to be very low stuff indeed as ballet goes," he is overcome:

> The "aesthetic distance" was there all right, but something in you crossed the distance, into the living unity that flowed in face and voice and body. . . . I was withdrawn into them and their clamor: into intimacy which was also access of knowledge.

In such a response—and these moments are the didactic texts in Blackmur's primer—we see a Blackmur very different from the skeptical rationalist and formalist of the thirties. This is Blackmur echoing, of all things, D. H. Lawrence's famous poem "Piano," with the speaker's inner reserve giving way to a clamor of emotional intensity. In the thirties this autodidact rehearsed his education in public (like his hero, Adams), and the resulting primer taught everyone how to read. In the fifties he undertook to teach a generation of trained explicators to be ignorant again, for the sake of intimacy and a deeper access of knowledge.

Much of the strength and weakness of Blackmur's later work can be attributed to this undertaking, which seems to have been provoked not only by cultural changes but by a deep, perhaps unconscious disaffection with his own previous positions. It may perhaps be misleading to call the early Blackmur a formalist, for nowhere does he separate form from content or reduce his discussion simply to elements of structure, imagery, or meter. Yet no one could have been more committed to "aesthetic distance," to an art which transmuted the chaos of personal emotion into order and objective form. Blackmur, like the rest of his generation, had gone to school with Eliot and learned from him the doctrine of the "objective correlative," learned from him that "poetry is not a turning loose of emotion, but an escape from emotion . . . not the expression of personality, but an escape from personality." It is no wonder that both Blackmur and Eliot felt so strong an antipathy toward Lawrence. Blackmur's early essay on Lawrence's poetry—where he accused Lawrence of the "hysteria" of disproportionate emotion, expressed in "language commonplace for everything except its intensity"—was one of his most tendentious and wrongheaded pieces, derivative of Eliot at his most austere.

In the forties when Blackmur turned from poetry to the European novel, particularly to Dostoevsky and such modern masters as Mann and Joyce, he did more than change subjects. He moved to investigate the genesis of order in the chaos of immediate experience and to broaden his notion of form by studying writers who more closely reflected that disorder. Beyond the well-wrought urn loomed the loose and baggy monsters which seemed to embody so much of our turbulent inner life, and our public life as well. At the same time he began gingerly to distinguish himself from his friends, the New Critics, among whose number he had once often been counted. He criticized their emphasis on analysis over judgment and showed how it tended toward a more narrow preoccupation with form. In an essay on Tate, Ransom, and I. A. Richards in *A Primer of Ignorance,* he finds in their work "a tendency to make the analyzable features of the forms and techniques of poetry both the means of access to poetry and somehow the equivalent of its content." Of Ransom's essay on "Lycidas" ("A Poem Nearly Anonymous") Blackmur observes that

> there are no statements of importance in it as to what "Lycidas" is about; only statements about formal aspects of texture and structure. . . . There is no sense at all of that side of Milton which made the poet a builder of cities and maker of men or which made a good book the precious life blood of a master spirit.

Much of Blackmur's later project shines through here, in words that shade off characteristically toward rhetoric. One can see that his travel to foreign cities is as much a part of the project as his meditations on Dostoevsky and his increasingly revisionist essays on criticism. His transformation becomes most decisive, however, in the four lectures on modern literature which make up the first section of *A Primer of Ignorance.* The very titles suggest the extent to which Blackmur is willing to relax his commitment to order and give sway to the irrational and demonic explosions in modern writing: "Reason in the Madness of Letters" (the subtitle of the whole), "The Great Grasp of Unreason," "The Techniques of Trouble," "Irregular Metaphysics." Blackmur remains what he calls a "bourgeois humanist," but only by redefining bourgeois humanism into the broad and subversive doctrine it may once have been: "the treasure of residual reason in live relation to the madness of the senses." He is, as he says of Mann's heroes, a bourgeois humanist tainted by art, and this double perspective enables him to give so inward and yet so ambivalent an account of modern literature. Here we have no academic embalming but a testimony from within, the culmination of a lifetime of practice and contemplation and struggle. Blackmur grew up with these books; his new understanding of them had a special claim to be heard.

Yet hearing him clearly is far from easy. The style is ruminative, the thought condensed but far from tight; as in travel essays, he eschews consecutive reasoning for odd confrontations and elusive paradoxes, in a language at once eccentric and exact, epigrammatic and quirky. He aims not to explicate these books but to prove them upon the pulses, to be intimate with them. But the avoidance of normal discursive procedure all too often turns intimacy into obscurity, and we are left merely puzzled when we should be amazed. The lecture on the poets, the third and weakest of the four, is a collection of page-long comparisons, at first obvious (Crane and Stevens; Pound and Whitman) but growing gradually more playful and arbitrary to the point of weirdness (Cummings and Dryden; Auden and Tennyson; Lord Byron and William Carlos Williams; Rilke, Herrick, and Emily Dickinson.) By the end we feel trapped in a morass of intellectual gymnastics and merely verbal ingenuity—and this talk was delivered for the edification of an audience at the Library of Congress! The more Blackmur sought intimacy and "the great grasp of unreason," the more clotted his channels of communication became, the more he resigned himself to a soliloquy in a void. As a brilliant formalist Blackmur was limited but perfect; as an avatar of intimacy and the chthonic powers of art his rhetoric grew diffuse. His growth as a critic took him away from his intrinsic strengths.

This is not true of the fourth and best of these lectures, a quiet coda aptly titled "Contemplation," in which Blackmur for once allows himself the old luxury of extended observation, first of *Ulysses,* then of the criticism that accompanied the modernist upheaval. But on the whole, despite all the passages and formulations that deserve our own extended contemplation, these lectures are unsatisfying in both content and style. Even as his procedure foregoes rational design, Blackmur's reading of modern literature leaves too little room for the irrational. Thus we find him quoting once more Eliot's attack in "East Coker" on "the general mess of imprecision of feeling / Undisciplined squads of emotion," without noting the repressive cast of mind on which it is based. Instead, he sees Eliot "finding reason in the madness that grasps him all about." For all his invocations of the demonic and the chthonic, there is a fundamental Wasp civility about Blackmur that makes one feel he is only slumming in the lower depths. Reading Kafka could not have been easy for a man who had so closely identified himself with Adams and James, albeit with versions of these writers a good deal more subversive than their stereotyped academic images.

But though art to Blackmur is necessarily subversive—providing "images of the deep anarchies out of which the order of the state must be remade if that order is to be vital"—in the end it was the commitment to order that remained paramount; Blackmur's attempt to be "ignorant" and to encompass unreason and anarchy was part of his intellectual growth, but his ultimate aim was to domesticate them and put them at the service of culture rather than of individual fulfillment.

This bias leads to some valuable emphases. Blackmur tells us that the irrational elements in modern literature were not ends in themselves but were pursued by writers with deep roots in the humanist tradition, with the hope—Blackmur's hope as well—of fulfilling rather than abolishing that tradition. The neohumanist critics of the twenties found Joyce's work chaotic, immoral, and scarcely intelligible. But to Blackmur it was only lesser writers like the dadaists who renounced form and critical perspective, capitulating to "pure behavior," producing a fragmentary art which deified "things as they are." But he goes on to level the same charge in different ways at a number of greater writers as well. He creates a kind of classicist line in modern letters which enshrines Joyce, Mann, and Gide (perhaps even James), but which excludes not only the dadaists but Kafka, Lawrence, Faulkner, and Proust. *Ulysses* alone, he says "is the book that *made* an order out of the substance of the dadaist imagination." One is reminded at moments of another bourgeois humanist, Georg Lukács, who wrote a book to prove that only Thomas Mann—but not Kafka—might be admitted to the Great Tradition. The controlling animus of Blackmur's 1935 essay on Lawrence is softened in these lectures, but not rescinded.

This classical conception of form, though untenable as a critique of Lawrence or Kafka (whose work is no less organized for being organized uniquely), does raise serious questions about some later art, starting with sixties phenomena like pop art, happenings, theatrical assaults like *The Brig,* or Burroughs's "cut-up" method, in which the syntax of significant organization does really suffer under the often random domination of "things as they are," much in the manner of dadaism. Are we to understand these developments as postmodern and posthumanist, or as radical continuations of the modernist movement of the twenties? Blackmur was deeply concerned about this question. He saw the continuity between American art and American society and feared our tendency to give way to our own momentum and be mindlessly dominated by sheer behavior. (The bombing of North Vietnam began in the same month he died.) By the time Blackmur died in 1965, the modernism he defended had begun to seem old-fashioned, replaced by an avant-garde that often championed the New at any cost. In a post-Warhol era, when art is "anything you can get away with," he comes to us as a voice from an old-fashioned literary culture, demanding of both our art and our conduct the critical exercise of a humane intelligence. For all his late Nietzschean moments, he is finally a classicist in the turbulent, disorderly pantheon of modern letters.

The Critic as Sage: Northrop Frye

Northrop Frye's 1967 book of lectures, *The Modern Century*—not one of his major books, but one of his most distinctive and far-reaching—came as a surprise, for it was not mainly a critic's book about modern literature, but an individual—I do not say personal—survey of the whole "modern century." Frye—North America's answer to structuralism—had long been accused of ignoring history and society in his criticism, and of immuring literature in a timeless vacuum of archetypal myths. This book perhaps was his answer, a consideration of the culture of the previous hundred years, *our* culture, especially in terms of the intricate role of literature within it. It is a work of high commitment, diagnostic and prescriptive rather than professorial, a tract for the times. It showed the Frye of the sixties quietly moving down the path laid out by Marshall McLuhan, Herbert Marcuse, and Norman O. Brown, from scholar to sage, from his own discipline to the politics of culture.

As a sage, however, Frye failed to provide any new and compelling doctrine. He turned out to be an old-fashioned liberal humanist, fearful of mass culture, contemptuous of nationalism, basically committed to the life of disinterested reason that the modern century had done so much to undermine. This results in a peculiar tension between Frye and his material, as if Bertrand Russell had solemnly undertaken a short life of Saint Theresa or Rimbaud. In Frye's first book, on Blake, a similar tension helped produce a masterpiece; by writing a brilliant schoolman's paraphrase of Blake's system, he demonstrated its utter sanity and coherence for the first time. He was understandably less successful in his *Anatomy of Criticism* (1957), when he tried to elicit an equally strict design from the whole of literature. That corpus proved less rational than Blake's, and stubbornly miscellaneous in the face of Frye's staggering powers of original synthesis. This conflict resulted in too casual and tendentious a treatment of individual works, so that the theoretical categories remained skeletal and amounted to little more than a private mythology, inferior to Blake's, rather than a synoptic ontology of literature. Later theorists and cultural historians like Hayden White (in *Metahistory*) and Paul Fussell (in *The Great War and Modern Memory*) ran into trouble when they applied Frye's categories too literally, as if they constituted some elusive science of literature—the dream of structuralism. Modern literature provides similar resistance to Frye in the critical part of *The Modern Century,* and he mostly retreats from system to mere summary—at times illuminating but otherwise marred by intellectual slackness and the absence of any discernible argument.

Frye's summary of modern literature, however, because it deals with a single period, allows for a sharper focus than what we find in the *Anatomy,* for in the years that followed that magnum opus Frye began atoning for his sins by writing some of the practical criticism which, as he himself admitted, was glaringly absent in that book. (Frye suggested it needed a companion volume of actual literary discussion, which he tried to supply in collections of essays like *Fables of Identity,* 1963.) Yet even on single writers or periods, his method remains synoptic and generalizing. Surprisingly, in his last important book, *The Great Code* (1982), he does this even with the Bible, perhaps the work closest to him. Frye always establishes a distance, at once heuristic and self-protective, between himself and any subject. Unlike R. P. Blackmur, he aims at precision of outline rather than intimacy or concreteness of detail. The second of the three lectures which make up *The Modern Century* is called "Improved Binoculars"; for the New Critical microscope Frye substitutes archetypal binoculars; but both optical devices turn criticism into pseudoscience, both enable the observer to see without being seen, almost without being there. For the gain in clarity and access we lose all depth of feeling, all writerly passion.

Frye's detachment can be unearthly. Here is a typically summary sentence from *The Modern Century:* "Whatever is progressive develops a certain autonomy, and reactions to it consequently divide: some feel that it will bring about vast improvements in human life by itself, others are more concerned with the loss of human control over it." How many disorderly, passionate commitments are crudely (but not uselessly) put in their place by such a schematic résumé! The prose is unmistakably Frye's, a medium conveying its own distinctive message. Frye always had a deserved reputation for writing "well" (read: clearly and fluently), but there is something passionless and cerebral about his very lucidity, something machinelike in his unflappable evenness of tone. His style is so free of mannerism that in itself it became a recognizable manner. It proclaims a detachment and intellectual purity, a resilience against existential doubts and confusions. Its message is Only Disconnect, in return for which it offers knowledge without pain or risk.

Frye's work was academic in the best and worst sense, clear-sighted, learned, and comprehensive yet also unexpectedly hedged by caution, despite its enormous range. A certain idea of the university was central to Frye's plan for society as a whole. He sees the university both as an achieved model of community and as a center of that disinterestedness and "spiritual authority" which enable us to see the "real form of human society" as "revealed to us through the study of the arts and sciences" (as he writes elsewhere). He follows a number of modern writers (and the later Blake) in seeing society as a "repressive anxiety-structure" which can be undermined only by a revolution in human consciousness, not through political activity. Frye is therefore sanguine about the growing intimacy between contemporary art and the university. He envisions a university, energized by the modernist consciousness and the modernist antagonism to contemporary life, becoming an instrument of social change. Along with the communications media (much of it unfortunately in enemy hands), our artistic and educational institutions, he says, form a "leisure structure" which could eventually rival the power of the economic and political structures, since it can "fulfil the entire range of non-material human needs"; he hopes this will create "a system of checks and balances which will prevent any one of our new three estates from becoming too powerful."

It would be hard to disentangle possibility from fantasy here. If *The Modern Century* gives us Frye's politics of culture, it should be evident from this brief glimpse how apolitical he really is. For Frye, despite the determined impersonality of his work, the only genuine avenue of change is individual, not social or institutional; he asserts "that no improvement of the human situation can take place independent of the human will to improve, and that confidence in automatic or impersonal improvement is always misplaced." What distinguishes Frye from Dwight Eisenhower or a doctrinaire conservative is his Blakean vision of unfallen man, his liberal faith in the individual will to change,

which he discerns beneath the rubble of alienation and social manip-
ulation, just as he can see the "buried or uncreated ideal" of
America—embodied in "Thoreau, Whitman, and the personality of
Lincoln"—beyond the machinations of a superpower pursuing its
Asian war. In a book published soon afterward, *A Study of English
Romanticism* (1968), he would see the Romantic revolution as a rad-
ical break in Western consciousness. His politics were at once blind
and visionary.

Frye's emphasis on the autonomous and self-critical individual made
him as sensitive as Marcuse to the prevailing forms of manipulation
in a supposedly free society, such as advertising and propaganda. (The
first, the diagnostic lecture, is easily the best thing in the book.) It
also made him a pungent critic of the technological determinism of
McLuhan and, more platitudinously, of the crude historical determinism of some Marxists. But he took no account of the revisionist,
Hegelian Marxism that became so influential in the sixties, which
sought to reconcile individual agency with historical change. Such a
unity was anticipated by Blake in his figure of Orc, who embodies
what many of the Romantic poets first saw in the French Revolution:
not only political emancipation but a renewal of human nature, a
liberation of the mind from the trammels of repression.

But Blake himself grew disenchanted, and the hero of the later
prophetic books is no longer the rebel Orc, who now becomes trapped
in a cycle of revolution and reaction, but the artist Los, the visionary
who will preside over an apocalyptic transformation of human consciousness. Frye follows this later Blake, but though there are some
moving utopian moments in *The Modern Century,* what he gives us
in the prescriptive parts is often no more than a dreary and pallid
version of Blake's faith in art as an instrument of salvation. His projected alliance between art and the universities, itself a far cry from
apocalypse, does a grave disservice to both of them. Were the universities ever the strongholds of Arnoldian disinterestedness that he
imagines? Long before Vietnam, civil rights, and the student rebel-
lions, there were always strong political forces at work in academic
life—forces of overt advocacy, forces which defined the organization
of knowledge, forces which inducted the young into society by in-
culcating certain accepted values. Though writing in 1967, Frye largely
ignored the ferment agitating the universities. He refers to those manifestations of campus activism as a sort of benevolent and pardonable
"trahison des clercs," but otherwise he is content to write about an
abstract idea of the university rather than what is actually happening.

Moreover, he demands a similarly abstract disinterestedness from art, and seems willing to emasculate it if he should detect impure gestures of advocacy. He is confident that the "reactionary and anti-social attitudes" of so much of modernist writing will lose their force when turned into course assignments:

> [W]hen contemporary authors are assigned for compulsory reading, and when they are taught in a way that relates them to their cultural heritage, a certain detachment comes into the attitude toward them. Not all the detachment is good, but one thing about it is: the social attitude of the writer is taken over by the social attitude of education itself, and loses its crankiness by being placed in a social context. Study, as distinct from direct response, is a cool medium, and even the most blatant advocacy of violence and terror may be, like Satan in the Bible, transformed into an angel of light by being regarded as a contribution to modern thought.

Here the message of Frye's style becomes his explicit message as well. It is a bad but not an uncharacteristic moment, when Frye seems to embody so much that is complacent and devitalizing in our universities and in the liberal culture to which they belong, so much that the modern writers set out to destroy. How chillingly ironic that they themselves, trimmed of their "crankiness," should finally be skewered and served up to the next generation as "contributions to modern thought."

Up from Alienation:
The New York Intellectuals

Intellectuals cherish the right to scrutinize everything with a critical eye. But one subject they commonly ignore is the position of intellectuals. All too often they take the status of the observer for granted, as the deconstructionists of the seventies—who rarely questioned their own vantage point—were fond of pointing out. In the United States in recent decades, a handful of writers and intellectuals began to enjoy the kind of celebrity more typical for writers in France. A few authors like Gore Vidal and Norman Mailer became frequent television performers, while others—Susan Sontag, for example—grew adept at provoking controversy with sensational formulations on sensitive issues. Meanwhile the appetite for gossip and anecdote, once confined to stories about movie stars and society scandals, contributed to the success of William Barrett's engaging memoir *The Truants: Adventures Among the Intellectuals* (1982), though its cast of characters had only a minuscule audience in their heyday in the forties. In the twilight of their existence as a recognizable group, the New York intellectuals threatened to be taken up as an American Bloomsbury, more famous for their witty sallies and outlandish personalities than for anything they wrote. Memoirs by Irving Howe, Lionel Abel, William Phillips, and Sidney Hook soon followed Barrett's, rekindling old quarrels and fighting current ones, evoking the past as a way of intervening in the present. The New York intellectuals were probably the closest thing America had to a Russian or French intelligentsia, a group of deracinated writers in rebellion against their social origins, passionate about ideas, marginal to political and economic power yet subtly influencing the mind and character of future generations. A look at the trajectory of this group of writers from the thirties to the present may give us some insight into the status of mind in America and the position of intellectuals as a social type.

What is an intellectual? By my definition, most academics and professionals do not qualify, despite their constant commerce with ideas. An intellectual is someone concerned with general principles, devoted to thinking things through, moving beyond the confines of any single field. Most do have a field of special authority—sometimes they have even gained academic respectability—yet typically they were unable to resist enmeshing their field in what Carlyle called Things-in-General. By this standard most professionals, including lawyers, doctors, and scientists, are certainly no intellectuals, unless they begin to reflect on the first principles of what they're doing and on its implications for society at large. Paul Goodman even went so far as to define this as the essence of professionalism. But Goodman knew very well that he was flying in the face of ever-increasing specialization, the explosion of technical knowledge, and the modern cult of the expert. In "Plaidoyer pour les intellectuels," lectures delivered in Japan in 1965, Sartre takes the opposite tack and describes the intellectual, in his opponent's terms, as someone "who mixes into things that are none of his business" (*qui se mêle de ce qui ne le regarde pas*). Both Goodman and Sartre avoid the fallacy of many present-day humanists who treat the intellectual as a specialist in "values," as if values were an external monitor of conduct rather than the inherent relation of any field or idea to the social whole.

America has not often had a class of intellectuals in this sense. In its early years, before the Revolution, Things-in-General were usually the province of religion. Powerful minds like those of Cotton Mather and Jonathan Edwards worked within an intense but narrow exegetical tradition. Modern intellectual life begins in the struggle with dogmatic and doctrinal constraints. It stands for the secularization of the clerical mind, as Coleridge recognized in calling his ideal elite a "clerisy." Under the influence of English libertarian pragmatism and the French Enlightenment, Jefferson, Hamilton, and Madison formed the nucleus of a genuinely secular group of intellectuals. The Federalist papers brought the principles of the founding fathers to a high order of general reflection. But the Transcendentalists—rooted, like Coleridge, in Unitarianism—present the clearest example of the secularization of the religious mentality. Even apart from his direct influence on many writers, Emerson remains to this day the prototype of a certain kind of American intellectual: not a social critic, like his Victorian counterparts, but the prophet of a new social order and a whole new order of consciousness. Writers as different as Lewis Mumford and Norman O. Brown have played the role of utopian visionary, the voice in the wilderness, directly echoing some of Emerson's higher flights.

The crude, robust growth of the American economy after the Civil War underlined the abstractness of the Emersonian rhapsody and increased its remoteness from practical life. *The Education of Henry Adams* is a portrait of the intellectual in the Gilded Age, tinged with the bitterness of an old patrician elite now shunted aside and cut off from political power. The grubby materialism of the Gilded Age proved as hostile or indifferent to the free play of mind as the old evangelical religion. As society developed an ever-growing need for technicians and practical minds, the reformers and intellectuals grew more isolated, more attracted to older cultures in preference to their own. Toward the turn of the century the lure of Europe, the Far East, and even the Middle Ages took hold of many intellectuals, increasing their distance from the world of business and boosterism that horrified them. While novelists and muckrakers could look to the example of Zola and naturalism to galvanize their relation to the American scene, many intellectuals turned instead to travel and expatriation.

World War I brought this period to an end. The old genteel tradition was virtually exhausted and could provide no realistic basis for a new cultural synthesis. The new intellectuals came not from the universities but from the ranks of progressive reformers like Herbert Croly and Walter Lippmann or were literary radicals like Van Wyck Brooks and Randolph Bourne. Brooks's work from 1915 to the midtwenties was typical of the new mood. Though based on a deep antipathy toward the whole culture of the 1865–1915 period, though grounded in alienation and an admiration for European culture, it was fundamentally a search for positive goals and ideals, for a new patriotism and a new basis for community and common action. "If we are dreaming of a 'national culture' today," wrote Brooks in *Letters and Leadership* (1918), "it is because our inherited culture has so utterly failed to meet the exigencies of our life, to fertilize its roots. . . . We, whose minds are gradually opening to so many living influences of the past, feel as it were the chill of the grave as we look back over the spiritual history of our last fifty years."

Brooks himself suffered a prolonged emotional crisis in the late 1920s which made it impossible for him to sustain the critical edge of his earlier work. By the mid-1930s his search for a usable past led him to become the celebrant and chronicler of all of America's cultural history. He became a bitter enemy of European modernism and a fierce critic of those intellectuals who, under its influence, had adopted the very posture of alienation which he had left behind. The grinding poverty and misery of the Depression radicalized many writers, just as the soulless prosperity of the Gilded Age had radicalized Brooks and his contemporaries. But the impact of Europe was far greater on the young intellectuals of the thirties than it had been on Brooks. Since many of them were Jewish and the children of immigrants, their instinctive roots were more in European than in American culture. Their literary sensibility was more comfortable in the Russian novel, with its emotional and spiritual intensity and its imagination of disaster, than in the Anglo-American traditions of civility, gentility, and class consciousness.

Yet the Jewish writers were doubly alienated, not only from America but from their own Jewish traditions, which they, like their Frankfurt School counterparts, tried to forget just as the Nazis were trying to make them remember. Formed by two apparently conflicting European currents, modernism and Marxism, passionate about ideas in a way that was alien to the pragmatic, upbeat, problem-solving bent of the American mind, the New York intellectuals contributed a marginal but deeply cosmopolitan strain to the culture of the thirties, which otherwise reacted to the Depression by turning inward. Their alienation was partly a fact of their daily lives, for not only were jobs scarce but the universities, the publishing houses, and other centers of cultural power were still bastions of gentility which had little use for the children of immigrants, whatever their brilliance. Thus, relatively few of the first generation of New York intellectuals, among them Lionel Trilling and Meyer Schapiro, went on to advanced degrees, teaching positions, and eventual academic recognition. Others received university posts only decades later, long after their books had made them famous. They especially admired a critic like Edmund

Wilson, partly as a man who earned his living from his writing, without entangling academic attachments, partly as a native-born American who, unlike Brooks, was a cosmopolitan figure who had responded deeply to modern writing, to European ideological currents, and to the ongoing American crisis. When all other models failed, Wilson was one who left an enduring mark.

Though they were deeply affected by Wilson's example, few of the New York intellectuals actually wrote like Wilson. The mark of Wilson's style is an almost Augustan transparency, the no-nonsense directness of a man who knows his own mind. His critical appetite manages to assimilate a vast range of material with the same unswerving common sense, whether he is writing a chapter of a book, a short review, or a personal letter. Echoes of Wilson may occasionally be heard in a few New York writers with highly developed critical sensibilities, men like F. W. Dupee and Alfred Kazin, who became exceptional stylists and prided themselves on a certain novelistic element in their criticism. But the typical tone in *Partisan Review* was much more nervous and mercurial, a kaleidoscopic style of almost neurotic dazzle and intensity. This was not true in 1934 when the magazine was first founded as a literary organ of the Communist John Reed Clubs. But its principle editors, Philip Rahv and William Phillips, broke with the party three years later, and by the end of 1937 they revived the magazine as an organ of independent radicalism. It had vague Trotskyite sympathies and an affinity for the avant-garde and for modern literature that was quite alien to the conservative cultural line of the Popular Front.

Within a few years *Partisan Review* had assembled a group of brilliant writers, many of whom had also broken with the Communist Party, including Wilson, Dupee, Dwight Macdonald, Harold Rosenberg, Delmore Schwartz, Clement Greenberg, Mary McCarthy, James T. Farrell, Sidney Hook, James Burnham, William Troy, Paul Goodman, and Lionel Trilling. Others who came aboard in the forties included Kazin, Irving Howe, William Barrett, Elizabeth Hardwick, Robert Lowell, Hannah Arendt, Randall Jarrell, Saul Bellow, Isaac Rosenfeld, and Robert Warshow. Among the European and emigré writers who appeared frequently were George Orwell, T. S. Eliot, Ignazio Silone, Nicola Chiaromonte, and Arthur Koestler, with some contributions from the new French existentialists, Sartre, Camus, and Malraux. Along with Dwight Macdonald's *Politics* from 1944 to 1949, *Commentary* after 1945 (first under Elliot Cohen, then from 1960 under Normal Podhoretz), Irving Howe's social democratic *Dissent* after 1953, *The New York Review of Books* after 1963, and Philip

Rahv's short-lived *Modern Occasions* from 1970 to 1972, *Partisan Review* was the chief forum for the New York intellectuals, though its peak circulation in the late forties and early fifties, at the height of its influence, never exceeded twelve to fifteen thousand.

The *Partisan Review* writers had many striking personal qualities, but I have no room in this group portrait to portray them individually. Instead I want to suggest a few ways in which their careers dramatized the situation of the modern American intellectual. I have already emphasized their internationalism, which is a typical response to somewhat provincial national cultures that have a high degree of political freedom. (Eastern European and Third World intellectuals demonstrated the opposite pattern before their liberation in 1989: insurgent nationalism in the absence of political freedom, under the heel of oppressive foreign cultural domination.) Another striking feature is their exclusion from the universities and their distance from the levers of cultural as well as political power. Most academics, like other professionals, are essentially technicians. Education and scholarship are their practical goals, but as purveyors of ideas they are sharply constrained by the parameters of their discipline, its accepted categories and hierarchies, and its well-rehearsed rewards and punishments. When Irving Howe, who eventually became a highly regarded critic and professor of literature, was asked why his generation had contributed little to the theory and methodology of criticism, he replied that they had scarcely thought of themselves as critics at all, but rather as writers and men of letters. They had little facility with abstractions, and their social and political interests—fostered by Marxism, the Depression, World War II, and the break with Communism—made it difficult for them to be concerned with literature for its own sake. Though they differed from the Communists in their respect for the integrity of the arts and the freedom of the artist, they had far less interest in form than their Southern agrarian counterparts. Instead they saw literature as an adjunct of morality and right conduct; they were more interested in what it *said* than in what it *was*. Their sensibility was planted near what Lionel Trilling called "the dark and bloody crossroads where literature and politics meet."

Nevertheless, despite the exemplary impurity of their interest in the arts, the New York writers exhibited the tendency of intellectuals not only to form groups but to crystallize their views in relation to some great movement in the arts. Their fascination with the difficult works of modern literature, with Joyce, Kafka, Proust, Eliot, and Mann, separated them drastically from the more middlebrow, more insular critics who held forth in the *Saturday Review of Literature* and the *New York Times Book Review* or selected the books for the Book-of-the-Month Club and the Literary Guild. The modernist aesthetic of fragmentation even affected their own writing; like the Frankfurt critics, who shared their affinity for modernism at a higher level of abstraction, they specialized in essays and epigrams, in isolated aperçus, rather than in comprehensive or definitive tomes. Their very marginality, which gave way gradually to acceptance, influence, and eventual lionization, was itself a perfect demonstration of the modern workings of the avant-garde. Matthew Arnold had hopefully described the process of gradual dissemination by which "the best that is known and thought in the world," at first the province of the militant few, eventually affects the wider culture and society. After World War II, American isolation ended dramatically. Retroactively, the New York critics became accurate prophets of the new international culture and the widespread diffusion of modernism. At the same time, the vast expansion of higher education shattered the power of the old genteel tradition, centered in a few elite universities and blinded by its own nativist bias.

Though they lacked academic credentials, men like Kazin, Howe, Phillips, and Rahv were eventually welcomed into the universities and the influential book-reviewing organs, even during the heyday of New Critical formalism. Lionel Trilling, whose credentials were impeccable, saw his work at first gain only grudging acknowledgment from his academic peers, who thought it too journalistic and impure, too belletristic and well written. But by the late sixties and early seventies, when Trilling was invited to deliver the prestigious Norton Lectures at Harvard and the first annual Jefferson Lecture in Washington, his preeminence was assured, and it continued to grow after his death in 1975. Even *Partisan Review* itself finally left New York and accepted university sponsorship, first at Rutgers after 1963, then at Boston University after 1978, still under William Phillips, one of its founding editors. But by then the *New York Review* had stolen some of its fire and many of its writers, providing them with a format of more popular academic journalism which achieved a much wider readership.

The *New York Review* was not simply "*PR* on newsprint," as it was first dubbed, but *Partisan Review* for the hip new academic scene of the sixties, minimizing the centrality of literature and cutting across generations, disciplines, and geographic regions. With its strong, sometimes overwhelming leaven of English reviewers, it was also *PR* with a distinctly Brahmin tone, far from the cafeterias off Union Square and the coffee houses of the old Village. And with its militant political line in the sixties, it was a throwback to the radicalism of the early years of *Partisan Review,* which had slowly given way to a more aesthetic, more literary emphasis in the depoliticized atmosphere of the fifties. The New York intellectuals won acceptance not simply because the world changed in their direction and American culture grew more enlightened, more cosmopolitan, but also because they themselves changed and assimilated, diluting their Marx with Freud, their radicalism with "the tragic sense of life." *Partisan Review's* famous symposium on "Our Country and Our Culture" in 1952 is often cited as a turning point in the intellectuals' shift from alienation to accommodation, a ratification of their homeward-bound itinerary in the America of McCarthy and Eisenhower, the cold war and suburbia. But as early as 1940 *Partisan Review* considered changing its name to *The Forties,* though it desisted in the face of its readers' protests. As the magazine grew less political, a recurrent joke expressed nostalgia for the days when *"Partisan Review* was really partisan," even though its Trotskyism had been short-lived.

A deeper loss of identity took place after World War II, when the magazine's dissident anti-Stalinism was swallowed up in a broad national anti-Communist crusade. Up until 1960, only a few of the New York writers were able to sustain their old posture of independent radicalism. Their opposition to McCarthy was hobbled by their own long-standing anti-Communism, for McCarthyism was like a mischievous parody of their deepest beliefs, a lumpen burlesque of the cause on which they had staked their honor. A handful of intellectuals who still considered themselves socialists and who thought of the fifties as an "age of conformity" joined to found *Dissent* in 1953, while the more militant anti-Communists gravitated toward *Commentary, Encounter,* and the Congress for Cultural Freedom, which soon drew the attention and support of the CIA. This was the first sign of a political split which ultimately shattered the rough unity of the New York intellectuals and continues with unabated animosity down to the present moment.

The revival of radicalism in the sixties deepened this split and gave it focus. Some of the intellectuals who had suffered a failure of nerve in the face of McCarthyism and the cold-war consensus felt rejuvenated. The civil rights movement, the New Left, and the antiwar agitation propelled them back into a critical relation with American society, whose economic and political successes they had but recently been ready to acclaim. The mantle of the thirties seemed to descend on them and they stood ready to prophesy. But for their opponents on the right, history was repeating itself in a quite different and more horrible way. In the rise of the New Left, for all its anarchic individualism, they could see only the specter of Stalinism and totalitari-anism—or a know-nothing populism that would level all cultural and academic values. And in the counterculture they could see only a mindless irrationalism that parodied their own youthful enthusiasm for modernism and Bohemia. A severe and thundering strain of Jewish moralism took hold of these aging intellectuals as they contemplated the lurid spectacle of drugs, sex, rock, protest, and the rejection of authority. In the radicalism of the young they saw only an Oedipal psychodrama which pitted the sons against the fathers, though the story of Oedipus actually begins with the anxious father's attempt on the life of his infant son. A few intellectuals tried to give marching orders to the New Left, only to discover that it did not share their overriding concern with Communism; others were annoyed that the young did not pay more attention to them. If they could not lead the New Left they were determined to destroy it, out of a sneaking sus-picion that it might otherwise destroy them.

The New Left eventually destroyed itself, though its spirit survives, amorphously but tenaciously, in the generation that passed through it or was touched by it. Even before this happened, a segment of the New York intellectuals had drifted into the right wing of the Dem-ocratic Party, and finally toward Nixon and Reagan. They came to be known as neoconservatives, and in some cases developed a very cozy relation to governmental bodies, large foundations, powerful corporations, and influential institutions like *The Wall Street Journal* and the *New York Times*. They convinced corporations and foun-dations to fund journals, buy ads expressing their views, and support research, enlisting them in a war of ideas they had always dismissed as inconsequential. The trajectory of these old New York intellectuals from their original socialism and anti-Stalinism was long but direct, and though they had come far from alienation, a long way from the corridors of City College to the corridors of power, their old habits of mind persisted. As their influence grew, they still loved to portray themselves as a beleaguered, dissident minority within a vast left-wing intellectual consensus. But in fact most of them had become "policy intellectuals," servants of power, technicians and publicists rather than thinkers and critics. Their obsession with the Left was the last trace of ideological fervor they could muster. Intellectuals had finally won at least a shadow of power, but only by inverting everything they had formerly believed.

The intellectual Left found *its* niche in the world of communication and information rather than in the direct exercise of power. Tamed radicals could get jobs in universities, on magazines, in publishing houses, in the social service professions. For them, manifestations in the streets gave way to manifestos in little magazines, arcane theorizing in scholarly journals, all assimilated into the business of education. The tenured Marxist, the radical journalist, became fixtures in American culture. The expansion of higher education had created a vast semi-intellectual mass with a great hunger for entertainment and information. The younger generation of intellectuals learned to teach them history and literature, to write articles and movie scripts and even advertisements for them, and was rewarded with stable employment and even occasional moments of celebrity. A culture that was once resistant to innovation came to thrive on novelty and change. Learning to ingest everything, it ingested its critics; right and left became different ways of joining the social establishment.

Once the business world and the government had ignored intellectuals as marginal and irrelevant. Now they learned to buy them instead, with think tanks, fellowship grants, expense accounts, lavish conferences, and slick, well-fed periodicals. We naively think intellectuals are naturally subversive and fall readily into oppositional roles. In fact they have always been fascinated with power; when they are noticed and cultivated, they tend to go where money, fame, and influence call. Because they have been educated above their class, intellectuals tend to develop the tastes of the rich—for good art, travel, fine food, expensive vacations—without having the means to satisfy them. Success and acceptance work to undercut the ultimate critical function of the intellectual—to take ideas to their limit, wherever they lead. The legacy of the New York intellectuals was in their style of pugnacious irreverence, their speculative freedom. Obscure in their origins, uncertain of their influence, they thrived on their own anxiety, their marginality. Our knowledge industries today have a continuous need for fresh talent, but they risk turning intellectuals into technicians and "kept" minds revolving in narrow orbits, in line with the old American emphasis on practical, positive thinking rather than destructive or utopian speculations. On the surface, the history of American intellectuals over the last sixty years has been a success story, a saga of inexorable acceptance despite an ingrained tradition of anti-intellectualism. But as intellectuals become an official band of educators, policy advisers, publicists, popularizers, and celebrities—catering to, and enlarging, the semi-intellectual mass—this may leave genuine intellectuals as small, isolated, and marginal a group as ever.

How much will have changed, then, since the 1930s?

A Precious Anomaly: F. W. Dupee

The death of F. W. Dupee in January 1979 deprived the literary community of one of its most elegant and playful minds. A warmly admired figure from the first generation of New York intellectuals, Dupee was neither a prolific critic nor a typical academic, though he reviewed many books and taught at Bard and then Columbia for many years. Like Edmund Wilson he was simply a man of letters, a nearly extinct species. He had an eye for "character," for the eccentric and individual; he was a writer who happened to write about books and authors. His finely crafted pieces belonged to a waning tradition of serious belles lettres: the lost art of the literary essay, swamped by decades of "practical" criticism and turgid theory. When he sent off letters of recommendation for students and colleagues, department chairmen wrote back to compliment him on his style. I can't believe he ever wrote a bad sentence.

Style meant a great deal to him, both in life and in art, but he was neither a dandy nor an aesthete. Fred Dupee was a dapper and dignified man, but his puckish side could turn good form into a comedy of manners. He didn't value form or artifice for their own sake, though he relished the sheer verbal bravura of a Gertrude Stein or a Nabokov. He praised Gide's "tireless habit of self-cultivation," which was also his own. In an oblique self-portrait, he said that Gide "helped to rehabilitate the word *amateur,* which has been made disreputable by the modern pride in pure creation and unremitting professionalism." Dupee's writing was not confessional and introspective, as Gide's was, but both of them still showed traces of the eager adolescent who could never quite decide what to *do.*

Like many intellectuals, Dupee flirted with politics without being a political person. Born in Chicago in 1904, educated at the University of Illinois and Yale, he spent the early thirties playing the adventurer in Spain, North Africa, and Mexico. When I tried to imagine his life then, which I knew nothing about, I could only think of movies like *The Treasure of the Sierra Madre* or *Only Angels Have Wings,* or stories I'd heard about gunrunning in Cuba and Palestine. He too had trouble conceiving the person he had been. As he looked back at his journals thirty years later, he said he felt they belonged to someone else.

Back in New York in the mid-1930s, Dupee joined the Communist Party and made some comical forays as an organizer on the waterfront. For a brief period he was literary editor of the *New Masses,* but by 1937 he helped refloat *Partisan Review* as an anti-Stalinist journal devoted to independent radicalism and modernist aesthetics. On the whole he had too much joie de vivre for politics, just as he had too much fellow feeling for *l'art pour l'art*; he later wrote tellingly of one writer's split between the "citizen" and the "wanderer." By the time I got to know him at Columbia more than twenty years later, he was more the civilized wit and raconteur than a veteran of the turbulent thirties.

At Columbia and to the world at large he was a little overshadowed by Lionel Trilling, a close contemporary, whose interests and sensibility overlapped with his. But Dupee habitually attracted an ardent undergraduate following distinct from Trilling's. Preeminently a man of ideas, Trilling appealed most to the budding intellectuals, the bright, aggressive overachievers hungry for cultural authority, while Dupee attracted the poets, aesthetes, and campus wits, hedonists more eager to please themselves. As a militant intellectual myself, I was late in appreciating how much thought he could distill into a sentence without noticeable strain or effort. Yet writing did not come easily for him. Reviewing *The King of the Cats,* his superb 1965 collection of essays, Elizabeth Hardwick observed that he seemed to wait upon inspiration to fulfill even the most casual commission.

Lightness of touch was crucial to his writing—a feeling for nuance and tone, the evocation of atmosphere. He was as much in thrall to the comic spirit as Trilling was to the tragic, and his best sketches were devoted to great comedians, Dickens, Nabokov, Beerbohm, Chaplin, the New York poets, even Thomas Mann. He rebuked critics for being "engulfed by Mann's own omnivorous critical intelligence" and for making heavy weather of his metaphysics, and he was wonderfully attuned to the social comedy in Henry James, another writer whose work has driven critics to excesses of abstraction.

Dupee's point of view was not anti-intellectual, but he was against criticism that milked art for its "ideas" and themes without being alert to its relation to lived experience. He believed that "culture was founded in experience" and that "knowledge is always primarily personal." Here, on the subject of Chaplin's tramp character, is a specimen of his lively, concrete, and sinuous literary style:

> Charlie is a dream—but a dream that much solid stuff is made of. In the way he twitches a property mustache or slices with a knife a derby hat doused in a creamy sauce, believing the hat to be a real pudding, there is a multitude of all too human suggestions. Twitched mustaches are implausible by nature. All dinner party embarrassments approximate to the impact of cold steel on creamed felt, setting the teeth on edge.

This is compact writing and eloquent, demonstrative thinking, but above all it is sensuous and immediate in its feeling for art, for life. Dupee's prose can be almost voluptuous in its fluidity and critical refinement. Yet he had an Augustan epigrammatic wit and a born ironist's seismic sensitivity to cant or pretension. Chaplin's childhood, he remarks, "was made to order to destroy a waif or foster a genius." Dupee paid tribute to artists and intellectuals more single-minded than himself but he disliked humorless moralists and ideologues. "A student did once tell the present writer that Chaplin's style lacked 'moral reference' and was a little dated. It is the unfortunate student who seems a little dated now—if such things matter."

Among the few negative pieces in *The King of the Cats* are reviews of F. R. Leavis's intensely partisan book on D. H. Lawrence and of James Baldwin's eloquent sermon *The Fire Next Time.* He finds Leavis's pages "acrid with the smoke of old feuds" and complains that Baldwin, after his first two books of essays, "has exchanged criticism for prophecy, analysis for exhortation." Dupee's attack on Baldwin dismayed me when it first appeared in an early issue of the *New York Review of Books;* it seemed to reveal the limitations of his Apollonian civility. It looks more defensible today, as the prophetic mode has run its course and sometimes left chaos in its wake. We can see what it did to Baldwin's later work, and what it still does to some discussions of race. But Dupee's recoil from Leavis and Lawrence—like Edmund Wilson's from Kafka—shows us the Achilles heel of his catholic sensibility. His receptivity was enormous, but it closed down before the passion of an evangelical temperament bent on a consuming mission, burning for conversion and salvation.

In the range of his taste and the stylishness of his writing, Dupee resembles another English critic very different from Leavis—V. S. Pritchett, like Dupee a cultivated comic ironist adventuring among the world's classics. Both of them treat criticism as a contribution to literature as well as a comment upon it; both write exquisite prose and manage to strike a delicate balance between aesthetic appreciation and moral seriousness; both are exceptionally novelistic critics who love to tell stories and sketch characters, who love variety and vivacity and are drawn to literature out of an interest in life, not a recoil from it. Dupee's curiosity made him an avid traveler, though, unlike Pritchett, he wrote few travel pieces. He saved his tourist lore for his friends. He jotted down pages of notes on the French provinces which my wife and I used in 1969 along with our Michelin guides. Only once did they steer us wrong: In St. Céré in Périgord we became the victims of a henpecked hotelier and his grasping wife, comical snobs out of

French provincial novels, who kept asking unctuously after their great friend Monsieur Dupee, who scarcely knew them. Dupee loved the French for their zest for life and even their bombast, and he relished their language, which he pronounced appallingly.

At Columbia Dupee's openness and his perpetual curiosity were translated into an unusual accessibility to students and junior instructors. Later in California he said what he missed most was having students come by, though quite a few old ones managed to drop in. In the late sixties, in his own sixties, he had the venturesome temperament of a man thirty years younger. Unlike some of his colleagues, he bore his reputation lightly, with a twinkle of irony that may have concealed a sadness about the things he might have done but knew he never would. Once I remarked that his discussions of Henry James's novels had the freshness of contemporary reviews, the responsive kind James almost never received in his lifetime. Unexpectedly he seemed a trifle hurt, for *Henry James* was his only "real" book. "I suppose I've always been a journalist," he said ruefully. In fact no journalist was ever more of a real critic, whatever such a distinction might mean. The same tender nerve was touched when I wrote in a book that his mock-heroic account of the Columbia student disorders in the *New York Review* in 1968 was "an almost novelistic evocation." "But true," he wrote to me, with unusual emphasis, as if either of us thought of "novelistic" as the opposite of veracious!

Dupee may have felt impaled by that time on the horns of the Yeatsian dilemma—perfection of life *or* of work—for he had chosen to savor the moment rather than make full use of his literary gift. Had he been more ruthless or ambitious, he would never have given as much of himself to his friends or students. His wit was legendary. We heard it crackle after he was selected by students at Columbia to receive their Mark Van Doren Award for great teaching. The presentation dinner could have been a solemn affair, except that the guest speaker was Dwight Macdonald, an old college friend, and Dupee kept interrupting him with barbs from the other end of the dais. Macdonald shot back in kind—it was a vaudeville routine they must have been improvising for forty-five years, and one of the funniest acts I'd ever seen.

As a student a decade earlier, I had observed Dupee do a series of turns almost as hilarious in Columbia's august colloquium on great books. The other instructor was Sidney Morgenbesser, the university's most quick-witted philosopher and kibitzer, whose analytic ability could devastate any statement into its logical (or illogical) components. Dupee was all nuance and sensibility, Morgenbesser all intellect and argument: two more mismatched minds—and evenly matched wits—could hardly be imagined. For several weeks the duel raged, with tongue-tied students enjoying the spectacle too much to intervene. Once, after one innocuous student observation, Morgenbesser began a surgical dissection of the hapless speaker's "thesis." Dupee erupted with exasperation: "That wasn't a thesis," he fumed, "it was just a remark, a comment, an aperçu." With that remark hostilities ended and the course began in not-quite earnest. I think they later became good friends.

Dupee thought of his own essays as "remarks," impressionistic shafts of illumination rather than formal commentaries. This put him at odds not just with philosophers but with most academic students of literature. But the English Department at Columbia had its own strong undergraduate teaching tradition, once exemplified by men like John Erskine and Raymond Weaver, later by Mark Van Doren, Trilling, and Andrew Chiappe, for whom the professionalism of modern criticism was like Swift's "mechanical operation of the spirit." Their approach was thoroughly unacademic: Victorian in its impulse to direct celebration of great books and writers, classical in its appeal to an older idea of the academy. Dupee had no doctoral degree and no "field"—he taught everything from "Modern Writers" (which he initiated) to "Shakespeare" (which he undertook shortly before retirement)—but here at Columbia he found a suitable niche and some very sharp students.

During the campus uprising in 1968 he was far more sympathetic to the students than most of his contemporaries. He spent untold hours with much younger faculty trying to avert a police showdown, which came anyway. He was a genuine liberal, usually a quiescent one, but Vietnam revived in him the political indignation of the thirties. Plagued by a lung condition resembling emphysema, he returned from the big Washington demonstrations looking more dead than alive.

Dupee retired from Columbia in 1971, sold a house he loved in upstate New York, and moved to a spectacular site overlooking the Carmel Valley in California, where he hoped to breathe better air. To my astonishment he retired as a writer as well. He imagined he was facing death and could not go on as he had been. As his health improved he continued to read, to think, to travel, to write long, amusing letters to friends, even to teach for short periods at Berkeley and Stanford. But for reasons of his own, like an actor unwilling to return to the boards, to try yet another impersonal audience, he refused to write for publication.

Inevitably, as his silence continued, his reputation—never very firmly rooted in academic circles—began to decline. A posthumous, much-enlarged edition of *King of the Cats* had little impact, but ensured that his essays would remain available. He wrote too well to be long neglected; though his body of work is not large, his perfectly sculpted pieces should survive as both mandarin prose and keenly discriminating criticism. As he said himself of the unclassifiable Max Beerbohm, another writer who insisted on retiring, "he is still a wonder, a precious anomaly, at once great and small, easy to forget but delightful to remember."

Alfred Kazin's America

Maxim Gorky compared Tolstoy's relations with God to two bears in a cage. The same could be said of Alfred Kazin's powerful engagement with American literature. The fur has been flying for half a century, ever since Kazin published *On Native Grounds* in 1942, an astonishingly precocious, mature (for a young man of twenty-seven), and brilliant study of our modern prose writers. The son of poor Jewish immigrants in Brownsville, Kazin was unique in his generation of New York intellectuals for the lyrical fluency of his critical style and the ardor of his fascination with the American past. As he later showed in three passionate, turbulent volumes of memoirs, *A Walker in the City* (1951), *Starting Out in the Thirties* (1965), and *New York Jew* (1978), Kazin always saw himself as a writer, not just a commentator on other people's books.

Like his mentors Edmund Wilson and Van Wyck Brooks, journalist-critics with a strong sense of culture and history, Kazin aimed to make his readers see and feel and touch, not simply think and agree. While his friends were overdosing on European modernism and sniffing at most American writing for its provinciality, Kazin stole American literature from the genteel academics (who never forgave him) and reshaped it into something dangerously modern.

On Native Grounds begins in 1890, when the literary center shifted from New England to New York; a later and more circumscribed study, *Bright Book of Life* (1973), continued the story of our fiction into the postwar period; finally, in *An American Procession* (1984), he ambitiously completed the trilogy by circling back to 1830 to embrace all the American classics firmly canonized by 1930: Emerson, Thoreau, Hawthorne, Poe, Whitman, Melville, Dickinson, Twain, Henry James, Henry Adams, and the key modern writers who emerged in the twenties. The book is a critic's version of the Great American Novel, a grandiose summa of a lifetime of wrestling with one culture and many books.

Even the style is strikingly American, oscillating between the rhapsodic and the acerbic, between Emersonian celebration and modernist sarcasm. His remarkably sharp sketch of T. S. Eliot, for example, is balanced masterfully between irony and empathy. Kazin has been criticized for not including writers like Frederick Douglass and Harriet Beecher Stowe, let alone the "mob of scribbling women" who wrote sentimental fiction in Hawthorne's day. These writers have been highlighted by recent work in American Studies, but Kazin's list is a frankly personal one: these are the authors he has read with pleasure all his life, the ones *his* generation discovered or utterly transformed. *An American Procession* is just what its title suggests: not a restrictive, definitive canon but a stunning parade of idiosyncratic cases—separate profiles that melt down both the life and the art of these figures to expose the imaginative core. Kazin is fundamentally an essayist who loves to apply his scalpel to individual genius. At least half the chapters, like the one on Eliot, would work extraordinarily well as independent essays on each of these writers, which was how some of them no doubt originated.

This is not a book with a single key or theme, and no minor authors need apply. Not for Kazin the affirmative-action approach to literature, invoking "interesting" authors as fodder for cultural history. But neither does he confine himself to finished masterpieces—no American critic can. The Great Books ideal fits no American writer easily. In his method, Kazin is more phenomenologist than formalist, looking at the grain of the wood rather than the shape of the building, listening for the rhythm of a writer's perception before it crystallizes in finished "works." The relentless inwardness of Kazin's readings can seem oppressive, repetitious. Not content to explicate, unwilling to simplify, he provokes his readers to pluck at the heart of a writer's mystery.

Fifty years in literary journalism gave Kazin an eye for the telling detail and a marvelous feel for dramatic irony. To the terseness and limpidity he learned from Edmund Wilson he added an aphoristic compression almost explosive in its sense of impacted energy:

Item: Everything Whitman wrote about the war shows what it did to age him, ripen him, and perhaps finally kill him. To kill him not through the paralysis the boastful man previously in "perfect health" felt he had incurred in the hospitals, but through the mass suffering that was smashing its way past all the pretenses of his lonely ego. . . . War was the concussion of young men on each other, a terrible parody of the dreamy love play Whitman had celebrated. . . .

Item: Whatever Eliot's reasons for staying on in wartime London, his defiance of his family in St. Louis seems to have surprised him. This was the first significant *act* of his bookish and highly introverted character. Though Eliot turned out to be more traditionalist than his family, a great believer in institutions so long as they were British, his move to England was a rebellious American action that parallels the "infidel" Emerson's leaving the church.

Kazin's intensity in such passages can be startling. Every word takes a position, detonates an idea. (His explosiveness as a critic brings to mind the agonizing stammer he once described as the "secret ordeal" of his youth.) He fuses biography and criticism to treat books as evidences of character, the written traces of a writer's personal destiny. This is relentlessly personal criticism, focusing on character as enacted in language. What he says of Emily Dickinson he aspires to himself, that "the voice of her poetry is peculiarly immediate, exclamatory, anguished, and antic in its concern; it is the most concentrated cry for life we are to hear from an American in her time." He praises Henry James in surprisingly similar terms. "James's scene-drama succeeds," he says, "because he . . . is unrelenting in his attention. Everything must point, point all the time. James bears down hard on a scene. We feel his excitement." A line he quotes from Emily Dickinson sums this up: "Dare you see a Soul *at the White Heat?*" This is criticism at white heat, with little of the "relaxed will" writers like Lionel Trilling worked hard to sustain.

An American Procession is finally, as the title indicates, a journey through the national identity. Nearly all the titles of Kazin's books allude to travel, to sightseeing, or to the sense of place. He is the critic as *flâneur,* a walker in the city of literary classics. He has a painter's skill at portraying local color and a seasoned traveler's ability to convey keen sensory impressions. He is a storyteller of ideas, a connoisseur of authorial landscapes. He sees all writers in terms of origins, flow, movement. His very style is restless, kinetic, propulsive. His autobiographies, especially *A Walker in the City,* helped initiate the quest for "roots" at a time when most intellectuals were eager to forget where they came from. His deepest affinity in *An American Procession* is for Henry Adams, who hovers over the book not just as a student of his own origins—and American origins—but as the spirit of the historical imagination, the very sign under which Kazin writes.

By the time of World War I, Adams's historicism had turned into a kind of nihilism, a belief that (in Kazin's words) "the modern world was meaningless, insane, out of control," a vision that Kazin ingeniously compares to *The Waste Land.* (He even unearths Eliot's little-known review of Adam's *Education.*) Thus a period that began with Emerson's doctrine of self-reliance and "the infinitude of the private mind" ended in bloody carnage on the fields of Flanders, a catastrophic irony that informed the bleak vision of modernism. For Adams, as Kazin presents him, the refuge from ugliness and chaos was always to find a pattern, impose an artistic order, and achieve a style. Kazin, too, is a pessimist who feels trapped in a grim, murderous century. Like the great works of Adams's later years, *An American Procession* is a momentary stay against confusion, a stylish group portrait that will endure.

6

The Critic and Society, 1900–1950: The Counter Tradition

Criticism: The Transformation

In the first half of the twentieth century, criticism in the English-speaking world went through a momentous, dramatic, and far-reaching transformation. Surveying the state of criticism in 1891, Henry James wrote: "If literary criticism may be said to flourish among us at all, it certainly flourishes immensely, for it flows through the periodical press like a river that has burst its dikes. The quantity of it is prodigious. . . . Periodical literature is a huge, open mouth which has to be fed—a vessel of immense capacity which has to be filled." Filling this maw, James found, was a great deal of uninspired chatter of a generalized, mechanical kind, a deluge of "reviewing" that "in general has nothing in common with the art of criticism": "What strikes the observer above all, in such an affluence, is the unexpected proportion the discourse uttered bears to the objects discoursed of— the paucity of examples, of illustrations and productions, and the deluge of doctrine suspended in the void."

Besides this periodical literature there was also a significant quantity of academic scholarship that was either genteel-Arnoldian, concerned with preserving certain moral and social values, or historical-philological, oriented toward the establishment of literary facts, mainly biographical, and exact texts, some of which—the poems of Donne and other Metaphysical poets, for example—would prove highly useful in the critical revolution that followed. But especially in America, there was little that we today—with our long habituation to close reading, with our paradoxical tendency to treat literary commentary as professional discourse yet also as a political and social force—would describe as criticism. Two longtime antagonists, the humanist Paul Elmer More and his iconoclastic opponent, H. L.

Mencken, could agree on one thing: the sheer paucity of genuine aesthetic criticism in the first decade of the twentieth century, when each began writing. "When I did most of my work," wrote More, "there was almost a critical vacuum in this country and in England. . . . It was something of an achievement—I say it unblushingly—just to keep going in such a desert." Mencken said much the same thing. "When I began to practice as a critic, in 1908, . . . it was a time of almost inconceivable complacency and conformity."

By midcentury, complacency and conformity were again a problem, but no one could complain, as James had, of a criticism that failed to take account of the concrete literary fact. In a 1949 lecture on "The Responsibilities of the Critic," F. O. Matthiessen described how Eliot and other modern writers, in the face of their wrenching experiences during and after World War I, had set out "to use a language that compelled the reader to slow down," a more difficult, more densely physical, more disjunctive language that also demanded a different kind of reading. I. A. Richards called it "practical criticism" in his famous book of the twenties that had an especially strong impact on American critics. "What resulted from the joint influence of Eliot and Richards," noted Matthiessen, "was a criticism that aimed to give the closest possible attention to the text at hand, to both the structure and texture of the language."

F. O. Matthiessen had mixed feelings about this emphasis on language, technique, and close reading, which was rapidly establishing itself as a new orthodoxy in American universities. He himself had given great impetus to the academic study of American literature with his epochal *American Renaissance* (1941), a book which applied a variety of analytic approaches—mythic, psychological, linguistic, and social—to a sharply defined canon of five of our greatest writers. Though Matthiessen was a leftist and Christian socialist who insisted on his subjects' "devotion to the possibilities of democracy," his influence was pedagogic, not political. Just as D. W. Griffith had invented cinematic narrative by perfecting the close-up, Matthiessen scanned the physiognomy of his writers through a lens borrowed from the study of difficult modern literature.

But by 1949 he was disenchanted: "As we watch our own generation producing whole anthologies of criticism devoted to single contemporary authors and more and more detailed books of criticism of criticism, we should realize that we have come to the unnatural point where textual analysis seems to be an end in itself." A movement which had come to challenge the old undiscriminating journalism, caught up entirely in the hubbub of the present, and the old historical scholarship, which left the writers of the past safely immured in the past, had itself become pedantic, mechanical, predictable. The little magazines, which had raised the banner of criticism against the journalists and the scholars, had declined into "a new scholasticism" and were "not always distinguishable from the philological journals which they abhor. The names of the authors may be modern, but the smell is old."

Matthiessen's ambivalent discontent highlights many of the changes that had occurred in criticism since the twenties, and their limitations. His essay is itself part of the flood of "criticism of criticism" that began in the forties with John Crowe Ransom's *The New Criticism,* Stanley Edgar Hyman's *The Armed Vision,* and René Wellek and Austin Warren's *Theory of Literature.* The shift from general commentary to close reading reflects the overall turn from periodical journalism and belles lettres to academic criticism, which in turn resulted from the great expansion of higher education all through the twentieth century, but especially after World War II. Few modern writers had much use for democracy; they treated the extension of literacy as the degradation of art, the precipitous decay of language. Indeed, the difficulty of their work can be seen as a reaction against their predecessors, the Victorians, but also against the hackneyed conventions of a readily consumable mass culture still Victorian in its idiom. The New Criticism built an exegetical bridge between the modern writers and their rejected audience, but it did so at the expense of some larger, less instructional aims of criticism.

The Generation of 1910

If the prevailing criticism of 1950 was analytical, the criticism of 1900 was predominantly social, moral, and historical, whether it dealt with older writers or with the new realists who challenged them. From Hegel and Marx to De Sanctis, Taine, and Brandes, history was the secular god of the nineteenth century. It was natural for a critic like Matthew Arnold to shape his criticism into a narrative of periods and generations, to think in loosely Hegelian terms of "epochs of expansion" followed by "epochs of concentration," and to say that "for the creation of a masterwork of literature two powers must concur, the power of the man and the power of the moment."

In the eyes of the Young Turks who appeared on the scene before World War I, the social and historical vision of those great critics had decayed, among their followers, into a fussy moralism hard to distinguish from the ordinary prejudices of their compatriots. "We have done with all moral judgments of art as art," said Joel Spingarn in his once-famous manifesto "The New Criticism," a lecture delivered at Columbia University in 1910. "It is not the inherent function of poetry to further any moral or social cause," he added. "The historian, the philosopher, the legislator may legitimately consider a work of art, not as a work of art, but as a social document. . . . The poet's only moral duty, as a poet, is to be true to his art, and to express his vision of reality as well as he can." Spingarn considered American critics especially prone to confuse moral and aesthetic judgments. "Critics everywhere except in America have ceased to test literature by the standards of ethics."

Spingarn followed Croce in insisting that every work of art was the unique expression of an individual vision, not a document of its times or the manifestation of a certain genre, convention, or style. To the scholar he said, "We have done with all the old Rules. . . . We have done with the *genres,* or literary kinds. . . . We have done with the comic, the tragic, the sublime, and an army of vague abstractions of their kind." To the rhetorical critic he announced, "we have done with the theory of style, with metaphor, simile, and all the paraphernalia of Graeco-Roman rhetoric. They owe their existence to the assumption that style is separate from expression . . . instead of the poet's individual vision of reality, the music of his whole manner of being."

Spingarn continued his litany of rejection until he reached the Tainean historical critic: "We have done with the race, the time, and the environment of a poet's work as an element in criticism. To study these phases of a work of art is to treat it as an historic or social document, and the result is a contribution to the history of culture or civilization, with only a subsidiary interest in the history of art."

The generation of 1910 was an iconoclastic one, deeply influenced by English critics of Grundyism and Victorianism like Shaw and Wells, impressed above all by their sparkling manner, their attacks on puritanism, their faith in progress. It was a much more cosmopolitan generation than its Victorian predecessors, whose idea of a European writer was a classic figure like Dante or Goethe, or a minor one like Sénancour or Amiel. The new generation in America had been introduced to Ibsen and Wagner by Shaw, to Zola by Howells and Norris, to impressionism and the fin de siècle by James Gibbons Huneker, to Nietzsche by H. L. Mencken, to Freud by G. Stanley Hall, who had invited Freud and Jung to visit the United States in 1909. Much of the acquaintance with these radical figures was superficial but, with the added impact of new ethnic voices just beginning to be heard, it made Anglo-Saxon insularity much harder to sustain.

One typical history of a young rebel was written by Randolph Bourne in his third-person "History of a Literary Radical," published posthumously in 1919. Bourne describes how his alter ego, called Miro, a young man with a strict classical training, was stunned and converted after hearing a lecture on modern writers by—of all people—William Lyon Phelps. After reading some of them, including Turgenev, Tolstoy, and Hardy, "Miro returned to college a cultural revolutionist. His orthodoxies crumbled. He did not try to reconcile the new with the old. He applied pick and dynamite to the whole structure of the canon. Irony, humor, tragedy, sensuality suddenly appeared to him as literary qualities in forms that he could understand. They were like oxygen to his soul."

Miro joins a group of young radicals who start a new college paper.

> Social purpose must shine from any writing that was to rouse their enthusiasm. . . . Tolstoi became their god, Wells their high priest. Chesterton infuriated them. They wrote violent assaults upon him which began in imitation of his cool paradoxicality and ended in incoherent ravings. . . . The nineteenth century which they had studied must be weeded of its nauseous moralists. . . . In a short time Miro had been converted from an aspiration for the career of a cultivated "man of letters" to a fiery zeal for artistic and literary propaganda in the service of radical ideas.

Eventually Miro comes to a more balanced position. He learns to develop critical discriminations even among the radical writers—the naturalists, the muckrakers, the pamphleteers—making judgments his perplexed teachers are unable to provide. "Miro had a very real sense of standing at the end of an era. He and his friends had lived down both their old orthodoxies of the classics and their new orthodoxies of propaganda." He looks to critics henceforth to be as boldly unconventional as the writers they discuss, just as Spingarn had called for a criticism as creative and expressive as literature itself ("a unity of genius and taste"). "To his elders," writes Bourne, "the result would seem merely anarchy. But Miro's attitude did not want to destroy, it merely wanted to rearrange the materials. He wanted no more second-hand appreciations. No one's cultural store was to include anything that one could not be enthusiastic about."

Spingarn and Bourne were two versions of the young radical intellectual of 1910. Though Spingarn attacked literary scholarship, he himself was a superb scholar of Renaissance criticism. Though he appeared to renounce politics and society for aesthetics, he was a founder and for three decades a leading figure in the NAACP. Bourne, who seemed, during World War I, to leave literature behind for political controversy, was a forerunner of the kind of cultural radical who brought aesthetic concerns into politics itself. Progressivism, notes Christopher Lasch, "was for the most part a purely political movement, whereas the new radicals were more interested in the reform of education, culture, and sexual relations than they were in political issues in the strict sense." If Spingarn was the prophet of a recoil into aesthetics which, as his later essays show, he came partly to regret, Bourne was the forerunner of the adversary intellectual alienated from the temper of American culture, determined to put it on a wholly new footing.

The Attack on the Gilded Age: Van Wyck Brooks and H. L. Mencken

Neither Spingarn nor Bourne made their effect strictly as critics; neither pursued much extended commentary on contemporary writers. For members of this generation, the line between literary criticism and social or cultural criticism was hard to draw. They saw writers and artists as exemplary figures—allies or enemies in their struggle for cultural renewal; they saw them as representing either the wave of the future or the dead hand of the past. Other members of the class of 1910 were more directly political, including Greenwich Village radicals like John Reed and Max Eastman, who put out *The Masses* (founded in 1911), and the progressive intellectuals who began publishing *The New Republic* in 1914, among them John Reed's Harvard classmate Walter Lippmann. (T. S. Eliot was another Harvard contemporary, but that belongs to a different part of the story.)

The two men who eventually had the greatest impact as socially oriented critics were H. L. Mencken and Van Wyck Brooks— Mencken as editor of *The Smart Set* from 1914 to 1923 and the more widely read *American Mercury* from 1924 to 1933, and Brooks for a decade after the publication of *America's Coming-of-Age* in 1915, perhaps the single most influential diatribe against the culture of the Gilded Age. The following year, in one of a series of essays in *The Seven Arts,* Brooks sounded the keynote of a generation and an entire era: "How does it happen that we, whose minds are gradually opening to so many living influences of the past, feel as it were the chill of the grave as we look back over the spiritual history of the last fifty years?"

Everything about this passage is typical of the early Brooks: the doleful prophetic note sounded more in sorrow than in anger; the sinuous poetic flow of the sentence itself, appraising an entire culture in a single interrogative nod; the emphasis on spiritual history rather than material life, since Brooks, far from rejecting the past, insists on its quickening influence—this was the "usable past" that he would spend his life trying to recreate. *America's Coming-of-Age* is best known for its attack on the division between highbrow and lowbrow in America, but where these terms have come down to us as aspects of an entertainment culture, a putative hierarchy within the arts, for Brooks they stood for a grievous split in the American mind, in the culture as a whole. Though Brooks tags one with the name of Jonathan Edwards (calling it puritan) and the other with the name of Benjamin Franklin (and calls it practical), his real subject is the business civilization of post-Civil War America, with its division between a brash entrepreneurial culture resourcefully bent on acquisition, and a rarefied intellectual culture that has devolved from puritanism and transcendentalism to a thin-blooded gentility.

Brooks took his main argument and even some of his examples from George Santayana's seminal 1911 lecture on "The Genteel Tradition in American Philosophy." (Other notable sources include Carlyle's exhortations to Emerson to be less abstract and more worldly; Henry James's 1879 study of Hawthorne, with its stress on the thinness of American life; and Matthew Arnold's contrast between the practical, activist spirit he calls Hebraism and the more reflective, aesthetic mode he labels Hellenism.) In his lecture Santayana found America "a country with two mentalities, one a survival of the beliefs and standards of the fathers, the other an expression of the instincts, practice, and discoveries of the younger generations." He suggested that "one half of the American mind, that not intensely occupied in practical affairs, . . . has floated gently in the backwater, while, alongside, in invention and industry and social organization, the other half of the mind was leaping down a sort of Niagara Rapids." While the American *mind* looked back toward Europe and to the secular remnants of its own Calvinist past, American energy was hurtling forward into the modern world.

As Brooks develops this argument, he comes close to the spirit of Max Weber's and R. H. Tawney's work on the Protestant Ethic and the Spirit of Capitalism. (Weber, of course, also uses Benjamin Franklin as his prime exhibit.) Brooks writes that "the immense, vague cloud-canopy of idealism which hung over the American people during the nineteenth century was never permitted, in fact, to interfere with the practical conduct of life." But it's not enough for him to invoke the split between culture and society, mind and practical life. To him, as to any nineteenth-century historicist, the great writer is not simply an individual but a crystallization of his time and place. He is concerned, for example, with the relation between Emersonian individualism and America's economic individualism. For him Emerson's thought reflected the spirit of the pioneers. It went back to a period of genuine mobility in American life: "It corresponded to a real freedom of movement and opportunity; pioneers, inventors, men of business, engineers, seekers of adventure found themselves expressed and justified in it."

Though Emerson himself eventually traveled west on the new transcontinental railroad, to Brooks he presides over this new world like a rarefied spirit, hovering above it but scarcely part of it. Here Brooks follows Santayana, who had found "a certain starved and abstract quality" in Poe and Hawthorne as well as Emerson. ("Life offered them little digestible material," said Santayana, "nor were they naturally voracious. They were fastidious, and under the circumstances they were starved.") Brooks too insists on the abstractness of Poe and Hawthorne, which flies in the face of Hawthorne's abundant historical detail and Poe's richly embroidered Gothic fantasies. Brooks may also have been influenced by John Jay Chapman's brilliant account of the "anaemic incompleteness of Emerson's character," with its astonishing peroration: "If an inhabitant of another planet should visit the earth, he would receive, on the whole, a truer notion of human life by attending an Italian opera than he would by reading Emerson's volumes. He would learn from the Italian opera that there were two sexes; and this, after all, is probably the fact with which the education of such a stranger ought to begin."

Brooks himself was a man whose inhibitions, grounded in his own genteel upbringing, drove him to identify with Emerson as well as to criticize him. (According to Brooks, a typical American grows up "in a sort of orgy of lofty examples, moralized poems, national anthems and baccalaureate sermons; until he is charged with all manner of ideal purities, ideal honorabilities, ideal femininities.") Chapman, a severe, idiosyncratic moralist as well as a cultural critic of great distinction, thought Emerson dangerous reading for the impressionable young, for "his philosophy, which finds no room for the emotions, is a faithful exponent of his own and of the New England temperament, which distrusts and dreads the emotions. Regarded as a sole guide to life for a young person of strong conscience and undeveloped affections, his works might conceivably be even harmful because of their unexampled power of purely intellectual stimulation." Like Brooks's treatment, this attack is also a rare tribute, and undoubtedly an autobiographical one.

Edmund Wilson, a literary heir to both Chapman and Brooks, wrote a striking study of Chapman's personality in *The Triple Thinkers* as well as several shrewdly balanced reviews of Brooks's later work. Brooks himself was subject to recurring bouts of depression, which no doubt impelled him toward the psychological approach of one of his best books, *The Ordeal of Mark Twain* (1921). But the position of the alienated outsider critical of American culture, which finds its fullest expression in his treatment of Twain, was personally difficult for him to sustain. It led to a nervous breakdown later in the twenties, which kept him from working for five years—significantly, just as he was completing a biography of Emerson.

As he recovered, Brooks abandoned criticism and social prophecy for a more anecdotal kind of literary history—a "pageant of genius," he later called it. His biography of Emerson turned lyrical. He celebrated much about American life that he had once denounced, and, in his best-selling "Makers and Finders" series (1936–52), wove a richly detailed tapestry of the usable past he had once been so hard-pressed to discover. By the early forties he was attacking Eliot and other modern writers and critics in vituperative terms as "coterie-writers," as if only the past had produced any literature of value. As Wilson drily noted, for Brooks the "modern" writers were still the writers of the Wells and Shaw generation who had excited him before World War I. The man who had once looked to Europe as a standard now became an uncritical promoter of American literary nationalism. The aging Young Turk wrapped himself in the Great Tradition. "A homeless generation has obvious needs," he wrote in a 1934 preface to his earlier work. "It needs to be repatriated. It needs to find a home."

Like the Marxist critic Georg Lukács, Brooks criticized his early books without entirely renouncing them. In his later preface he attributed their pessimism to the Oedipal vivacities of youth. Puritanism, he says with some justice, "has ceased to menace any sentient being; and, properly apprehended, it stands for a certain intensity that every writer values." The bold new scholarship of Perry Miller was just over the horizon, and the rebel causes of 1915 seemed remote. In *America's Coming-of-Age* he had followed Santayana in finding this special intensity in Whitman. In Emerson he then saw only the vaporous idealism of someone "imperfectly interested in human life." Looking for a writer more grossly embodied, a writer with more *mud* on him, he settled on Whitman, who, though "saturated with Emersonianism, . . . came up from the other side with everything New England did not possess: quantities of rude feeling and a faculty of gathering humane experience almost as great as that of the hero of the Odyssey. . . . He challenged the abnormal dignity of American letters. . . . Whitman—how else can I express it?—precipitated the American character."

Can any writer ever really do this much, or even stand for this much? Brooks's early books, beautifully written, remain of permanent interest, yet it's hard to escape the impression that he is using a method inherited from Matthew Arnold to work out his own inner conflicts—Arnold's "dialogue of the mind with itself." Like Arnold he turns writers into cultural emblems, projecting the divisions of his sensibility into a historical dialectic. He was no practical critic; he never got close to writers in the intense formal way the New Critics would teach everyone to do. Despite his fame and influence, his name goes unmentioned in W. K. Wimsatt's and Cleanth Brooks's hefty history of criticism (1957). At the end of his essay "On Creating a Usable Past," he writes, rather lamely, that "the real task for the American literary historian . . . is not to seek for masterpieces—the few masterpieces are all too obvious—but for tendencies." Even more than Arnold, he turned criticism into a form of cultural diagnosis, an examination of the national mind.

H. L. Mencken was older than Brooks, but his vogue came afterward, when the young men of the twenties devoured *The American Mercury* and lived by his cynicism, wit, and satiric gusto. Mencken was protean, he was a force of nature. He learned to write not among pale Harvard aesthetes like Brooks but in the hurlyburly of Baltimore journalism and at smoke-filled national conventions. If Brooks's weakness was a poetic vagueness, as if he were sometimes mesmerized by the soulful flow of his own voice, Mencken's writing was almost too clear and sharp. Like all great caricaturists, he sacrificed nuance for vivid exaggeration. He could be blunderingly unsubtle, elephantine, ponderously Germanic. But like his master, Shaw, Mencken was never vague, never in doubt. In a perfectly Shavian put-down of the man he calls "the Ulster Polonius," Mencken writes that much as he enjoys reading Shaw's works, "so far as I know, I never found a single original idea in them." No, he says, Shaw is an immensely entertaining set of rhetorical tricks. Shaw is "quick-witted, bold, limber-tongued, persuasive, humorous, iconoclastic, ingratiating. . . . It is his life work to announce the obvious in terms of the scandalous."

In other words, Shaw, like Mencken himself, is a style: a dazzling high-wire act, an endlessly resourceful iconoclasm: "He has a large and extremely uncommon capacity for provocative utterance; he knows how to get a touch of bellicosity into the most banal of doctrines; he is forever on tiptoe, forever challenging, forever *sforzando*. His matter may be from the public store, even the public junk-shop, but his manner is always his own. The tune is old, but the words are new."

Mencken was not primarily a critic, though he wrote a great deal of criticism between 1910 and 1920. But as these scintillating lines on Shaw demonstrate, Mencken wrote about books with exactly the same kind of sweeping brush strokes he used to attack politics, morals, and manners. His portrayal of Shaw, supposedly the most intellectual of writers, is simply a piece of Shavian paradox: just the way Shaw might have eviscerated anyone who dared influence *him*. Mencken's style is his rhythm; he repeats himself, courses his theme through endless variations, but he can never be boring. As a satirist he relishes strut and pretension, adores folly and stupidity on a grand scale. No one would say he's "fair" to his subjects, but outsized characters like William Jennings Bryan, Anthony Comstock, or Henry Cabot Lodge offered themselves to him as vivid cartoons the way no literary subject could; unlike merely bad writers, these men cut a figure in the world. They unwittingly synthesized the prejudices and pomposities of others, conveying a great deal about the mood of the moment.

Despite this turn toward social satire, Mencken did his work as a critic. He took up the causes initiated in Howells's and Norris's campaign for realism by tirelessly promoting the work of Dreiser and Conrad. He shared his friend Huneker's cosmopolitan taste and loved to lampoon American provinciality. He was a working editor as well as the key adviser to Knopf, one of several new publishing houses that began to bring out new European writers along with young, unconventional Americans. As Edmund Wilson later wrote, "The publication of Mencken's *Book of Prefaces* in 1917, with its remarkable essay on Dreiser and its assault on 'Puritanism as a Literary Force,' was a cardinal event for the new American literature." As late as 1950 Wilson would pay tribute to Mencken's old battle against "the genteel-academic culture that had done so much to discourage original American writing from about 1880 on," adding, "he was without question, since Poe, our greatest practicing literary journalist."

Yet even his essay on Dreiser is more vivid on Dreiser's faults, such as his style, than on his virtues. He offers up a small anthology of

Dreiser's sins with the note that "every reader . . . must cherish astounding specimens." Dreiser's worst novel, *The "Genius"*, sends him building toward a Homeric riff: "There are passages in it so clumsy, so inept, so irritating that they seem almost unbelievable; nothing worse is to be found in the newspapers." The book's structure fares no better: it "is as gross and shapeless as Brunnhilde. It billows and bulges out like a cloud of smoke, and its internal organization is almost as vague. . . . The thing rambles, staggers, trips, heaves, pitches, struggles, totters, wavers, halts, turns aside, trembles on the edge of collapse." Yet Dreiser is not to be dismissed. Mencken, a great stylist himself, never mistakes style for greatness. Keeping his balance, he criticizes Dreiser's vision of the world without confusing the philosophy with the fiction.

Along with Brooks and Wilson, Mencken was one of our last true men of letters. He takes us back to a world where newspapermen could be more literate than most academics and could write far more intelligently about American literature and the American language. He loved baiting professors, especially heavy-handed moralists like the New Humanists, and in a piece called "Criticism of Criticism of Criticism" he praised Spingarn's demolition of all the usual academic ways of pigeonholing writers, especially troublesome and innovative writers. He attacks most critics for "their chronic inability to understand all that is most personal and original and hence most forceful and significant in the emerging literature of the country." "As practiced by all such learned and diligent but essentially ignorant and unimaginative men, criticism is little more than a branch of homiletics." If the writer is "what is called a 'right thinker,' if he devotes himself to advocating the transient platitudes in a sonorous manner, then he is worthy of respect."

Warming to his theme, Mencken writes that "we are, in fact, a nation of evangelists; every third American devotes himself to improving and lifting up his fellow citizens, usually by force; the messianic delusion is our national disease." Mencken, of course, cannot resist intensifying, exaggerating; settled into his pulpit, caught up in the swell of his surging prose, he exemplifies the very evangelism he loves to pillory. Moreover, though he detests moralism, he cannot accept a purely aesthetic attitude: "Beauty as we know it in this world is by no means the apparition *in vacuo* that Dr. Spingarn seems to see. It has its social, its political, even its moral implications. . . . To denounce moralizing out of hand is to pronounce a moral judgment."

We remember Mencken the entertainer rather than Mencken the critic. He had a plain bluff way with books, as with everything he wrote about, but his mind was never so simple or so eager for effect that it left no room for qualification. The serious issues of the Depression plowed Mencken under, made him seem cranky and irresponsible, and he subsided gracefully into autobiography, like Edmund Wilson in his final years. As a critic he had no role to play in the Age of Eliot, when terms like "beauty" and "sincerity" lost their meaning, and modern literature became Hemingway, Joyce, and Proust rather than Ibsen, Shaw, and Wells. The struggle against Victorianism was over; the battle for modernism had hardly begun.

As Americans became less provincial, more cosmopolitan, Mencken lost his subject. He has had some imitators but no successors. Perhaps the many-sided work of Dwight Macdonald came closest. He too was a sharp critic of language, a witty and destructive polemicist, a brave editor, a political gadfly, and a ruthless but entertaining mocker of cultural sham and pomposity. But he was more purely the intellectual, a nemesis of middlebrows and a critic of ideology, in a style that originated with the thirties generation. Like Mencken he could be obtuse and unsubtle; he could simplify for effect. But he lacked Mencken's wider interest in the whole American gallery of rogues and fools.

The New Critics hated Mencken for his mockery of the South and his refusal to take literature with their kind of gravity, as a special, complex realm of aesthetic discourse. The radical intellectuals of the thirties, not notable for their sense of humor, followed the model of Brooks and Bourne and the cultural radicals of *The Masses,* not Mencken. (Macdonald wrote perhaps the sharpest attack on Brooks for his defection from the highbrow camp.) The younger critics were as theoretical, as remote from the cynical *Front Page* world of daily journalism, as any of the professors. The work of Edmund Wilson and Malcolm Cowley bridged the yawning gap between the Mencken world of the teens and twenties and the radical thirties.

The Critic as Man of Letters:
Edmund Wilson and Malcolm Cowley

In a career that spanned five decades, Edmund Wilson became the paradigm of the twentieth-century literary intellectual in America. He came of age in the twenties, a friend and contemporary of F. Scott Fitzgerald—"my literary conscience," Fitzgerald once called him. He earned his living as a book editor and literary journalist, first for *Vanity Fair,* then for *The New Republic,* then for *The New Yorker.* Wilson's work was rooted in the historical criticism of an earlier era. In *Axel's Castle* (1931) he had written: "The old nineteenth century criticism of Ruskin, Renan, Taine, Sainte-Beuve, was closely allied to history and novel writing, and was also the vehicle for all sorts of ideas about the purpose and destiny of human life in general." In contemporary criticism he found too much of "a detached scientific interest or a detached aesthetic appreciation which seems in either case to lead nowhere." By "nowhere" he seems to have meant, nowhere beyond the text itself. Yet Wilson's advance over Brooks and Mencken lay precisely in his ability to get much closer to books and writers without detaching himself from a larger social and intellectual framework. In the fewest, clearest words, he could tell you exactly how a book was put together, could compare it effortlessly to other books of its kind, to other things that weren't books. He practiced the New Criticism without taking any notice of it.

By our standards today, Brooks and Mencken seem to be pursuing their own special agendas when they write about literature. Their critical personalities are too strong, their prose too unbending, their prescriptions for the culture too urgent and pressing. Lewis Mumford's 1926 book on the American literary tradition, *The Golden Day,* shows how the diagnostic Brooks approach could lead a potentially strong critic astray. Though Mumford strikingly anticipates the canon Matthiessen would later carve out in *American Renaissance,* he canvases the major figures all too briefly and distantly before wielding them as a club against the writers of the Gilded Age. It was not until he dealt with architecture in *The Brown Decades* (1931) that his own feeling for the city landscape and its designers—men like Olmstead, the Roeblings, Sullivan, and Wright—could break free of Brooks's abstract polemic against the post-Civil War period, which altogether missed the ruggedly expansive energy of the era.

Reviewing Brooks's book on Henry James in 1925, Wilson complained that "Mr. Brooks has completely subordinated Henry James the artist to Henry James the social symbol, with the result that James's literary work, instead of being considered in its integrity on its own merits, has undergone a process of lopping and distortion to make it fit the Procrustes bed of a thesis." Determined to protest "the spiritual poverty of America and our discouragement of the creative artist," Brooks "cannot help expecting a really great writer to be a stimulating social prophet." In a later review Wilson expressed amazement that Brooks had been able "to develop into one of the first rate American writers of his time" without learning to appreciate "other writers save as material for cultural history." For Wilson, as for the New Critics, some notion of aesthetic autonomy is essential, even for the cultural historian. Brooks's appropriation of James shows evidence of "the critic's failure to be fully possessed by his subject."

It may be significant that *Axel's Castle,* the only critical work of Wilson's that feels dated today, is also the only book of his driven by a thesis: the origins of modernism in the French symbolist movement. Moreover, Wilson was converted to radicalism in the course of writing the book, and this obliges him ultimately to condemn the aesthetic ideas he had first expounded sympathetically. This gives some individual chapters—those on Valéry and Proust, for example—a slightly schizophrenic quality. (Besides undergoing a political conversion, Wilson was recovering from a nervous breakdown as he composed this book; the text reflects some of the unresolved tensions of his personality.) In addition, Wilson had little feeling for verse, which he had already begun to consider "a dying technique." Though Wilson was never fully committed to modernism—his chapter on Gertrude Stein is at best perfunctory—his engagement with Proust and Joyce, writers who speak to his strong social interests, was far stronger than his limited empathy for Yeats or Valéry.

Like the nineteenth-century critics he praises in the book, Wilson writes criticism closely allied to history and biography. But his crystalline narrative method, the very hallmark of the public critic and literary journalist, is refined by his acute literary judgment. He had a feeling for art as art that Brooks never had—a feeling which, in Eliot, excluded all other critical considerations. Wilson was a great reader; as an evaluative critic, his literary taste holds up better today than that of any of his contemporaries except F. R. Leavis. But he was a far more catholic reader than Leavis, whose strength lay in selection, exclusion, canon formation, certainly not in wide-ranging curiosity or enthusiasm. And Wilson, in his longer works, aimed at panoramic effects and social visions that belonged more to the critics of the nineteenth century.

In the opening essay of *The Bit Between My Teeth* (1965), Wilson described how enthralled he was at the age of fifteen by Taine's *History of English Literature,* impressed above all by Taine's scenic and dramatic method: "He had created the creators themselves as characters in a larger drama of cultural and social history, and writing about literature, for me, has always meant narrative and drama as well as the discussion of comparative values." And Wilson adds: "I had also an interest in the biographies of writers which soon took the bit in its teeth." But "the bit between my teeth" also alludes to the specific writer, the particular book, that he must chew over, that he can neither swallow nor spit out. Though his sensibility scarcely resembled Wilson's, Eliot was one such writer he could not put by; the chapter devoted to him in *Axel's Castle* is balanced between cultural history and Wilson's very personal kind of literary judgment. (One example: "I am made a little tired at hearing Eliot, only in his early forties, present himself as an 'aged eagle' who asks why he should make the effort to stretch his wings.")

In "The Critic Who Does Not Exist," a virtual manifesto written in 1928, Wilson reviews the critical scene in acerbic terms reminiscent of James's 1891 screed: "It is astonishing to observe, in America, in spite of our floods of literary journalism, to what extent the literary atmosphere is a non-conductor of criticism." What he finds instead are separate schools that pursue different methods and collect adherents but have nothing to say to each other. (He gives the school of Mencken and the school of Eliot as two examples.) Wilson's essay is a prescription for a critic very much like himself: a writer who practices criticism for its own sake, who can write knowledgeably about the past in terms of the present, a professional reviewer who can "deal expertly with ideas and art, not merely tell us whether the reviewer 'let out a whoop' for the book or threw it out the window." Unfortunately he finds that, although many people write criticism with their left hand, "no such creature exists as a full-time literary critic— that is, a writer who is at once first-rate and nothing but a literary critic."

Wilson himself should have been an ideal candidate—in one sense this was just the critic he ultimately became. But in 1928, when his literary ambitions still covered a wider field, this limited future would have been a bitter pill for him to swallow. A year later, about to publish his first novel, *I Thought of Daisy,* a portrait of the Village bohemian scene and his friend Edna St. Vincent Millay, Wilson rereads *The Great Gatsby,* "thinking with depression how much better Scott Fitzgerald's prose and dramatic sense were than mine. If I'd only been able to give my book the vividness and excitement, and the technical accuracy, of his!" (Wilson, *Letters on Literature and Politics,* 1977, p. 173). Though he tries to reassure himself that "writing, like everything else, is partly a matter of expertness"—as if technique were separable from talent—the honest critic in him, holding to high standards, is beginning to tell him he's not really a novelist. Nevertheless, his journals of the thirties are largely composed of material he was collecting for his second novel, *Memoirs of Hecate*

County, which he perversely singled out, much later, as "my favorite among my books—I have never understood why the people who interest themselves in my work never pay any attention to it."

Socially oriented critics are often blocked novelists, just as formal critics, critics of language especially, tended in this period to be moonlighting poets. Lionel Trilling's ambition was to write great novels, but he published no more fiction after *The Liberal Imagination* fully established his standing as a critic in 1950. In his journals in 1948 he complained that he paid for his professorial life "not with learning but with my talent . . . I draw off from my own work what should remain with it." At moments he envied wilder, more "irresponsible" writers like Hemingway and Kerouac for their lack of balance, inhibition, decorum. Fifteen years earlier, while still a young man, he had already lamented "how far-far-far- I am going from being a writer—how less and less I have the material and the mind and the will. A few—very few—more years and the last chance will be gone." His criticism, as he recalled publicly in 1971, had begun as a something "secondary, an afterthought: in short, not a vocation but an avocation."

George Orwell was a failed novelist who later returned to write political fables more closely related to his critical essays than to his earlier fiction. On the other hand Eliot, Pound, Ransom, Tate, Blackmur, Winters, Warren, and Empson wrote about poetry as practicing poets. The first kind of critic shows an elective affinity not only with fiction but with the social and political issues that often animate fiction. The other critic is more often drawn to questions of form and structure that turn literature in upon itself, that sunder it from its social matrix.

A concern with technique, with methodology, is a major theme of twentieth-century thought, from post-Newtonian science and post-Weberian social science to analytic philosophy and modernist art, which searchingly interrogates the forms it inherits. The advanced criticism that responded strongly to modern art sometimes became the discursive projection of its self-consciousness, its anxiety, or its technical ebullience. Toward the middle of the twentieth century, a few critics tried to apply the same formal approach to fiction that had dominated the new poetry criticism. They found antecedents in the letters of Flaubert and the late prefaces of Henry James, which R. P. Blackmur assembled into an influential book in 1934, as well as in the Russian formalists and the Chicago Aristotelians. One well-known example from a modernist viewpoint was Mark Schorer's 1948 essay "Technique as Discovery," which appeared in the first issue of the *Hudson Review.* But there was a brilliant rebuttal from a historicist viewpoint in Philip Rahv's 1956 essay "Fiction and the Criticism of Fiction," which expressed the viewpoint of the socially oriented critics of the *Partisan Review* circle.

Schorer argued that unlike the naturalists, who struggled aimlessly within received fictional forms, modern writers like Joyce, Faulkner, Lawrence, and the early Hemingway *were* their styles: books like theirs are "consummate works of art not because they may be measured by some external, neoclassic notion of form, but because their forms are so exactly equivalent with their subjects, and because the evaluation of their subjects exists in their styles." (Fresh from a study of Blake, a strongly historical study, Schorer might have been more skeptical about this fearful symmetry, this "fitting & fitted" that Blake decried in Wordsworth.) Rahv, on the other hand, argued for a looser, more open, more Bakhtinian sense of the novel, insisting that formal rigor was often less important than the work's interactions with a wider world. He pointed out that inferior or unimpressive stylists like Dreiser, Tolstoy, or Dostoevky could still be great novelists, since their effects "are achieved not locally, in the short run, but in the long run, by accumulation and progression."

The New Critics were generally in Schorer's camp, while the social critics were allied with Rahv. The New Critics, when they wrote about fiction at all, were drawn to patterns of metaphor, myth, and symbolism, while their antagonists often made fiction their vehicle for writing social and cultural history. The work of certain writers became a virtual battleground. F. R. Leavis—who published a continuing series of essays in *Scrutiny* on "The Novel as Dramatic Poem"— excluded all but one of Dickens's novels from his Great Tradition. Echoing Henry James's disparagement of Tolstoy and Dostoevsky, he found most of Dickens too abundant with "irrelevant life." When Leavis later reversed this judgment, or when R. P. Blackmur turned his attention from the close analysis of poetry to the modern European novel, it marked a significant shift from formal criticism to social prophecy. Long before Leavis changed his mind (without acknowledging he had done so), Wilson, Orwell, and Trilling wrote signally important essays on Dickens reclaiming him as a social critic but also, in Wilson's and Trilling's case, as a modernist whose dark, neglected later novels achieved depth and intensity through a profound symbolic organization.

Thus Dickens became a meeting ground between historical criticism, focused on social conflict in Victorian England, and modernist poetics, which emphasized radical departures from strict realism. At about the same time, Erich Auerbach's *Mimesis,* combining philology with a European tradition of *Geistesgeschichte* going back to Hegel, demonstrated that style itself was socially and historically conditioned. Just as Montaigne had argued that each man bears the whole form of the human condition, Auerbach showed how local details of syntax, description, and dialogue could be understood in historical terms, for writers of each period constructed reality in different configurations of language.

It was the call of history that kept Edmund Wilson from becoming either the exponent of modernism implied by parts of *Axel's Castle* or the purely literary critic conjured up in the manifesto of 1928. Thanks to the Crash and the onset of the Depression, by 1931—when Frederick Lewis Allen published *Only Yesterday,* when Wilson finished *Axel's Castle,* when Fitzgerald wrote "Babylon Revisited"—the twenties already seemed like another world, an unimaginably distant time. The Depression enmeshed many writers, including Wilson, in the larger world beyond the arts. It brought most of the expatriates home; it interested them for the first time in what was happening in the American heartland; it made journalism and politics feel more pressing than aesthetics; it made the Menckenite cynicism and sophistication of the twenties seem thin and brittle.

Even before the Crash, writing early in 1929, Wilson had praised his friend Dos Passos—one of the first of his contemporaries to be radicalized—for keeping his eye trained on the larger social picture, not simply on his own small corner of the field. Wilson contrasted this not only with other writers of their own generation but with the reigning wit, Mencken. Despite Mencken's brilliance as a social critic, Wilson complained, "the effect of Mencken on his admirers is to make them wash their hands of social questions. Mencken has made it the fashion to speak of politics as an obscene farce." Dos Passos, on the other hand, "is now almost alone among the writers of his generation in continuing to take the social organism seriously." Yet he complains that Dos Passos gives far too monolithic a picture of life under capitalism. Dos Passos's own characters are deformed by it, their lives are too unrealistically constricted by it. "No human life under any conditions can ever have been so unattractive. Under however an unequal distribution of wealth, human beings are still capable of enjoyment, affection and enthusiasm—even of integrity and courage." Instead, Dos Passos's "disapproval of capitalist society seems to imply a distaste for all the beings who go to compose it."

This 1929 article shows that before the Depression Wilson's social interests had already prepared him to favor a radical shift. But it also shows the limits of that radicalism as applied to literature. As he later discovered, he would always remain a man of the twenties, would always believe that people were capable of enjoyment, affection, courage—whatever the larger public forces affecting their lives. Nevertheless, the thirties were a turning point for Wilson. In "An Appeal to Progressives," a widely discussed manifesto written early in 1931, he found a striking change not only in the economy but in the national psyche. The Horatio Alger belief in enterprise and opportunity had waned: "American optimism has taken a serious beating; the national morale is weak. The energy and faith for a fresh start seem now not to be forthcoming: a dreadful apathy, unsureness and discouragement is felt to have fallen upon us." He urged radicals and progressives to "take Communism away from the Communists" but to take it seriously, for some form of socialism seemed the only solution. By 1932 he joined a group of intellectuals endorsing William Z. Foster, the Communist candidate for president.

Wilson's days as an agitator and organizer were short-lived; so was his enthusiasm for the Soviet Union. He was a genuinely independent radical, with little affinity for movements and causes. Wilson was transformed as a writer—in the subjects he chose, the way he approached them—not as a political activist. The same cannot be said about Malcolm Cowley, his successor as literary editor of *The New Republic,* who was an ardent fellow traveler all through the thirties and an early victim of red-baiting when he was appointed to a minor government job in 1942. In the thirties Cowley was perhaps the most influential literary critic in America, thanks to his limpid and beautifully crafted weekly reviews in *The New Republic.* Except for Wilson himself, no one could say so much, so gracefully, in so brief a compass. His literary judgment was good; he kept a remarkably even temper through a tumultuous era; collections of his articles still hold up as literary chronicles of their time.

But by the second half of the thirties he also became a functionary of the literary Left, signing petitions, chairing front organizations, and learning to tell less than the whole political truth in his weekly articles. In several stinging letters, his friend Wilson accused him of "plugging the damned old Stalinist line . . . at the expense of the interests of literature and to the detriment of critical standards in general," and even, on one occasion, of writing "Stalinist character assassination of the most reckless and libelous sort" (Wilson, *Letters,* pp. 311, 358).

Cowley later made some attempts to come to terms with his "sense of guilt" about this unhappy period, most notably in *—And I Worked at the Writer's Trade* (1978). His memoir of the thirties, *The Dream* *of the Golden Mountains* (1980), stops short in the middle of the decade, and its promised sequel never appeared. Apart from this lamentable episode, Cowley's long career must be seen as a remarkable chapter—some would say the last chapter—in the rise and fall of the man of letters in America. Despite his productivity over nearly seven decades, his body of work was a less adventurous version of Wilson's. If Wilson was the literary journalist and public critic par excellence, Cowley, like many English reviewer-critics, was *only* the journalist, without Wilson's breadth and range as an intellectual historian, travel writer, and restless student of other cultures, languages, and literatures. Yet Cowley was also a cultural critic of considerable importance whose first book, *Exile's Return,* published in 1934 and revised in 1951, remains our most revealing portrait of the Lost Generation.

Cowley's book is deeply indebted to *Axel's Castle,* a book it praises, imitates, criticizes. Cowley takes note of Wilson's shift of attitude midway through the book, yet *Exile's Return* is also a divided, ambivalent work—part recollection and celebration, part demolition—which views the modernist writers of the twenties through the political prism of the thirties. Where Wilson, playing the Poundian role of the village explainer, had taken the whole sweep of international modernism as his field, Cowley stays closer to the bone, confining himself to the expatriate writers of his own generation. And where Wilson took the symbolists as prototypes, Cowley looks to the influence of the French Dadaists, the ones he himself knew in his Paris years.

In his chapters on Joyce, Proust, and Eliot, Wilson, despite his growing political commitment, had managed to strike a balance between sympathetic exposition and stern criticism. Cowley is more heavy-handed. His main theme is the self-destructive madness, the social irresponsibility, of the bohemian writers of the teens and twenties. Wilson, though alert to the risks of decadence, the pitfalls of the purely aesthetic attitude, had been attuned to the social basis of modernism. He saw Proust, for example, as "perhaps the last great historian of the loves, the society, the intelligence, the diplomacy, the literature and the art of the Heartbreak House of capitalist culture." Wilson could be amusing on his own apostasies to modernism. As early as 1925 he wrote to Cowley, "I am contemplating myself experimenting in a vein so journalistic and optimistic that admirers of Eliot will never speak to me again" (*Letters,* 127). Cowley, on the contrary, is determined to condemn the writers of the twenties for their pessimism and escaptism, for taking refuge from real life in a "religion of art."

Bohemianism and Dada are Cowley's emblems of rebellion, escape, *épater le bourgeois;* his book culminates in the suicides of Hart Crane and Harry Crosby—the dead end to which such movements inexorably lead. Even earlier, in Flaubert's Paris, "the religion of art very quickly expressed itself as a way of life, and one that was essentially anti-human." Later, "the Dada manifestations were ineffectual in spite of their violence, because they were directed against no social class and supported no social class." For all his essential identification with this generation, which would last a lifetime, Cowley was by temperament a survivor, a man who moved with the times: he had signed on for the new puritanism and moral uplift that thirties Marxism offered. From this new vantage point, Dada violence could only be seen as futile and self-destructive. Cowley insists on a social ethic, an ethic of responsibility, not the values of the lone romantic artist. "The young man who tried to create a vacuum around himself would find in the end that he could not support it. He would find that the real extremes were not that of Axel's lonely castle, or Gauguin's Tahiti, or Van Gogh's fanatical trust in the Sun: they were inertia, demoralization, delusions of persecution and grandeur, alcohol, drugs or suicide."

There is drama in watching Cowley play sober Polonius to Hart Crane's wild, erratic Hamlet, trying to convince the poet, as he tells us, to give up "the literature of ecstasy" for "the literature of experience, as Goethe had done." Instead, Hart Crane chose the path of Werther, not the Apollonian course of the elder sage. Rather than taking Cowley's advice he ran off with his wife, Crane's first heterosexual lover, who was with him on a ship from Mexico in 1932 when he took his leap into the sea. Meanwhile, back home, Cowley became the superego to the Lost Generation.

As cultural history, *Exile's Return* propagates a myth of social responsibility that belongs strictly to the thirties, but this shouldn't obscure the book's enduring value. Cowley's ambivalence gives the book its personal anchor and internal drama. His description of bohemianism could be applied with few alterations to the counterculture of the sixties. So could the book's remarkably original account of how easily this rebellion was commercialized into a toothlessly hedonistic culture of consumption. Indeed, Cowley's account of the way a *"production* ethic" gave way to a *"consumption* ethic" has been widely accepted by historians of the twenties (such as William E. Leuchtenburg in *The Perils of Prosperity*). And Cowley's finely wrought pattern of exile and return is axiomatic for any understanding of the cultural history of the years between the wars. Even his insistence on a "literature of experience"—on the social and personal basis of all art—

must, in a more subtle way, remain essential to the historical critic's understanding of the relations between literature and life, between a writer and his books, and between art and its audience. These were the communal themes to which critics like Cowley and Wilson returned all through their careers.

Wilson spent most of the decade dealing with political and economic issues rather than literary matters. While Cowley took over his duties at *The New Republic,* Wilson took to the road to report on how ordinary Americans were coping with the Depression. The results were collected in *The American Jitters* (1932), one of the best of many valuable volumes of Depression reportage, which included books by older writers like Dreiser and Sherwood Anderson and others by newcomers like John Steinbeck, Erskine Caldwell, and James Agee. In 1935 Wilson traveled to Russia to do the research for a history of Marxism and revolution that proved to be his masterpiece, *To the Finland Station* (1940). Though written and published like all his books as a series of essays, this was his most unified work, which dramatically extended his critical range.

Marxism was an improbable subject for a "literary" treatment. Unlike Marx and Engels themselves, most of its adherents had written about it in terms of dry dialectics and pseudoscientific historical "laws." In the work of these sectarian epigones, the intellectual antecedents of Marxism were hazy; the founders' lives were a closed book. Though many had lived and died for these ideas, the moral passion and drama of revolutionary history were strangely absent from this literature. Some intellectuals would sniff at Wilson's mastery of theory, but this was not his goal. Instead, he set out to apply the methods of criticism to both the writing and *acting* of history, imparting a vigorous narrative thrust to what these radicals said as well as what they had done.

More than any other book of Wilson's, *To the Finland Station* called upon the novelistic talent missing from his fiction but vital to his critical essays, with their lucid recapitulations of his wide reading. Wilson needed characters who were given to him, outside of him; he had little gift for introspection but great feeling for social history as it expressed itself in individual lives and idiosyncratic ideas. *To the Finland Station* is essentially a narrative work, a series of lives in their historical settings. The book applies the scenic method of Michelet and Taine to the history of ideas and their actual impact. The earlier historians themselves play cameo roles in Wilson's book, perhaps as his own surrogates. Michelet's discovery of Vico, Taine's shock at the suppression of the Commune, become part of the drama of the book. Taine's belated effort to master politics and economics becomes a parable of Wilson's own conversion.

Through it all Wilson remains the critic—weighing, assimilating, expounding—above all, making his material come alive, as few students of Marxism ever did. To Wilson's detractors this was a form of fabulation: Wilson was the popularizer, the magazine journalist, the "introductory" critic, as he had been in *Axel's Castle*. Yet Wilson's way of drawing connections, of shaping his story line and juxtaposing sources, is always at the service of his strong interpretive bent. It is never simply the middlebrow "story of philosophy" or "story of civilization," or the kind of potted popular biography that elides all the crucial questions. In fact, Wilson was a pioneer in applying new literary techniques to nonliterary texts, including the psychoanalytic approach and the analysis of rhetoric and imagery. Not only did he examine Marx's youthful poetry for clues to his emotional life but in a later chapter, "Karl Marx: Poet of Commodities," he isolated Marx's vivid and violent imagery as a way to "see through to the inner obsessions at the heart of the world-vision of Marx." At about the same time, Kenneth Burke was applying his own critical methods to Hitler's *Mein Kampf* in "The Rhetoric of Hitler's 'Battle' " (1939).

Wilson's conversion to Marxism did not long endure. The purge trials and the Hitler-Stalin pact tore the benign mask off Stalinist Russia for all but the most intransigently committed intellectuals. By 1940, the year his book appeared, Wilson would say that "Marxism is in relative eclipse. An era in its history has ended." What never ended for Wilson was the acute historical awareness, the insistent human concern, that had been amplified by the Depression and his encounter with Marxism. Because of its dogmatic, mechanical character, the Marxism of the thirties produced little criticism of lasting value in the English-speaking world. Even Malcolm Cowley later condemned "the ideological vulgarity of what passed for Marxian criticism in the 1930s." But the encounter with Marxism, the experience of the Depression, was the forge in which the historical criticism of the next generation was tempered. Some writers, disillusioned or deradicalized, lost their bearings, retreated into silence or slipped back toward the kingdom of art for art's sake. But others, deprived of their comfortable Marxist certainties, were immensely invigorated, forced to think for themselves in difficult, intuitive ways. It would be hard to imagine the work of Wilson, Orwell, Cowley, Burke, Trilling, Rahv, or Harold Rosenberg without the Marxist moment early in their lives, the moment from which they never entirely recovered despite their later anti-Communism.

Compared to these writers who would follow him, Wilson's ingrained historicism took him in an unexpected direction. In his *New Republic* years, in *Axel's Castle* and *To the Finland Station,* in his two great collections of longer essays, *The Triple Thinkers* (1938; revised 1948) and the psychoanalytically oriented *The Wound and the Bow* (1941), with its full-scale monographs on Dickens and Kipling, Wilson was very much the cosmopolitan critic. This was an insular period in American culture. The refusal to ratify the Treaty of Versailles or join the League of Nations expressed more than a diplomatic isolationism. Wilson's feeling for European culture had been fostered by Christian Gauss at Princeton. In literature at least, he had something of an expatriate's sensibility, and his criticism did much to introduce the new writers of the twenties and to broaden America's literary taste.

But the Depression, while it turned intellectuals toward Marxism, also turned them inward, toward their own country, where people were suffering through unprecedented calamities. Just when the American Dream appeared more distant than ever, the United States came to seem like a precious enigma. Individual American lives could be scrutinized as keys to a national mystery. Though any excess of subjectivity was sure to be condemned by radical critics, a wave of autobiography followed the success of books like Michael Gold's *Jews Without Money* (1930) and *The Autobiography of Lincoln Steffens* (1931).

Some of these books were immigrant sagas, as if a whole new class of Americans suddenly realized they too had a story to tell. But Edmund Wilson came of old American stock, and as he became more disaffected with America as it was, his turn toward autobiography became an inquiry into the American past, an archaeology of a country that no longer existed, that lay buried under the new "transnational" America that the children of immigrants were helping to create.

The same journalistic impulse, the same restless curiosity, that took him to Harlan County also brought him to Talcottville, in upstate New York, where his mother's family had lived and he had spent some of his childhood and youth. "The Old Stone House" (1933) initiated a vein of autobiography in Wilson that led eventually to his remarkable portrait of his father at the end of *A Piece of My Mind* (1956) and to the best of his late books, *Upstate* (1971), a collection of journals, family memories, and comments on regional culture. This retrospective turn inspired his major postwar work of cultural history, *Patriotic Gore* (1962), a collection of studies of the literature of the Civil War era that had occupied him for nearly two decades. Wilson's criticism after 1940 became, in a sense, the extension of his autobiographical impulse. His excursions into family history spilled over into cultural history and brought out a strength that had been muted in his work on modernism—his subtle, instinctive sense of time and place, of the relationship between individual lives, individual books, and the enveloping flow of the culture around them, something wholly missing in most "textual" criticism. But his work also became a recoil from what America had become.

At the end of *A Piece of My Mind* Wilson had wondered whether he too, like his brilliant but neurotic father, like the old stone house in Talcottville (to which he, like his father, had grown so attached), was now a quaint artifact of an earlier era: "Am I, too, I wonder, stranded? Am I, too, an exceptional case? When, for example, I look through *Life* magazine, I feel that I do not belong to the country depicted there, that I do not even live in that country. Am I, then, in a pocket of the past?" He marvels that his father, despite the tragic foreshortening of his career, had "got through with honor that period from 1880 to 1920," for he himself feels just as alienated from the life of his time.

This hadn't been the case in the twenties and thirties. If Wilson's attraction to the drama of the Finland Station was a form of vicarious revolutionary excitement, it was also a way of living in the present, for Wilson, like all good historical critics, saw the past as the embryo of the present, its intrinsic, revealing prehistory. But in *Patriotic Gore* a reader feels that Wilson simply prefers to dwell among the granite-jawed republican figures of the past, men like Lincoln, Sherman, and Grant—or like Alexander Stephens, the extraordinary vice president of the Confederacy, and Oliver Wendell Holmes, the long-lived Supreme Court justice, who sit for two of the book's most vigorously detailed portraits. Wilson's long introduction, far from bringing this material together or connecting past and present, is a sweeping dismissal of the political history of the twentieth century, above all the two world wars and the cold war. Its tone of patrician aloofness and disdain evokes Henry Adams at his worst, though the canny Adams was never simply dismissive. Part radical, part simply cranky, this astonishingly olympian essay, which sees nations as "sea slugs" who devour each other as if by biological law, is Wilson's grim farewell to the modern world.

For all of Wilson's sense of isolation, his turn inward toward history was characteristic of American critics starting with the thirties. The decade began with an agrarian manifesto against industrial society by many of the same men, including John Crowe Ransom, Allen Tate, and Robert Penn Warren, who would eventually make their mark as New Critics. Their book, *I'll Take My Stand* (1930), was first to be called *Tracts Against Communism,* but the Communists themselves soon began to encourage an interest in the American past. After 1935, during the Popular Front period, they fostered a sentimental cultural nationalism that had wide ramifications in the arts, especially in music and dance, and in government-sponsored arts programs which fed the mural movement, the oral history projects, and commissioned guides to each of the forty-eight states. Studies of the American past flourished as a patriotic prehistory to the New Deal. Common-man versions of Tom Paine, Jefferson, Lincoln, and Whitman, as well as semi-legendary figures like Paul Bunyan and Davy Crockett, became staples of popular biography and populist literary history.

Like the younger *Partisan Review* critics who admired him, Wilson had little sympathy for this middlebrow populism, which was more a form of ersatz folklore and "progressive" mythmaking than criticism. In *Patriotic Gore* he wrote, "there are moments when one is tempted to feel that the cruellest thing that has happened to Lincoln since he was shot by Booth has been to fall into the hands of Carl Sandburg. Yet Carl Sandburg's biography of Lincoln, insufferable though it sometimes is, is by no means the worst of these tributes." Wilson had far more tolerance for the intricate if mannered embroidery of Van Wyck Brooks's literary histories, beginning with *The Flowering of New England* in 1936, for they reminded him of the Taine model that still appealed to him. In a succession of reviews in *The New Yorker* he dissected their weaknesses as criticism but they encouraged his own explorations of American cultural history. Wilson's turn from modernism and Marxism, the twin beacons of his earlier books, was never as sharp as Brooks's recoil from modernism, but it led in the same direction, toward a renewed interest in the American past.

The Rise of American Studies

The same period saw the growth of the American Studies movement, which provided some academic parallels to the later development of Wilson and Brooks. Influenced by the prophetic writings of the early Brooks and his circle, but also, to a degree, by the new work of linguists and cultural anthropologists, this was an effort to overcome the hardening disciplinary boundaries of literature and history and to see American culture as an organic whole. In book after book, starting with V. L. Parrington's *Main Currents of American Thought* (1927–30), Constance Rourke's *American Humor* (1931), and F. O. Matthiessen's *American Renaissance* (1941), critics and historians set out to determine the essential character of American life. Avoiding the diagnostic, polemical vein of Spingarn, Santayana, Mencken, Brooks, and Mumford, they set out to construct a central core of American masterpieces that would differ strikingly from the canon of the genteel critics and their radical successors. Their work was inspired not by the new realists of the prewar years, such as Dreiser, but by the modernists of the postwar period, including Eliot and the New Critics. "In their hands," says Gerald Graff of the new Americanists, "the New Criticism became a historical and cultural method."

Parrington's unfinished work laid out in monumental detail the viewpoint of the progressive Old Guard against which these later Americanists would react. Though Parrington was not a Marxist, his social and economic determinism was congenial to the Marxist decade. (Still, even a Marxist critic, Bernard Smith, found it "crude and vulgar." Smith's 1939 volume, *Forces in American Criticism,* was in fact one of the best-balanced, least programmatic pieces of Marxist literary history, far superior to Granville Hicks's better-known work on American literature, *The Great Tradition.*)

Though Parrington was a professor of English, he chose in this work "to follow the broad path of our political, economic, and social development, rather than the narrower belletristic." In the foreword to his second volume he was even more explicit: "With aesthetic judgments I have not been greatly concerned. I have not wished to evaluate reputations or weigh literary merits, but rather to understand what our fathers thought, and why they wrote as they did." He insisted that he was writing as a historian, not a critic, and he defended the kind of omnivorous antiquarianism that has often brought literary history into disrepute: "The exhuming of buried reputations and the revivifying of dead causes is the familiar business of the historian, in whose eyes forgotten men may assume as great significance as others with whom posterity has dealt more generously. Communing with ghosts is not unprofitable to one who listens to their tales."

Such a ponderous approach, though welcomed by many sociological critics and economic determinists in the thirties, could not survive the decline of radical politics after 1940, and the ascendency of new forms of aesthetic analysis. Parrington is at his best as an intellectual historian, not as a critic of any kind. He insisted that minor works, documents, sermons, and theological polemics were as relevant as works of art. He was the first to carve out a large cultural space for the Puritans, enabling Perry Miller and his successors to correct his own hostile account of them. He explored revolutionary thought in great detail, and paid moving tribute to the progenitors of American liberalism, such as Roger Williams and Theodore Parker, but he was at his worst in his discussions of our greatest writers, from Poe to Henry James. He could deal only with the typical, the representative, never with the singular, the idiosyncratic. His sardonic side enabled him to take the measure of the literary lights of the Gilded Age such as Holmes and Lowell, for they belonged entirely to their cultural moment. But he disposes of Poe in two pages, declaring: "The problem of Poe, fascinating as it is, lies quite outside the main current of American thought, and it may be left with the psychologist and the belletrist with whom it belongs." Poe's psychological problems, he says, "are personal to Poe and do not concern us here. And it is for the belletrist to evaluate his theory and practice of art." But he grudgingly adds that "whatever may be the final verdict it is clear that as an aesthete and a craftsman he made a stir in the world that has not lessened in the years since his death, but has steadily widened."

No student of American culture could fail to learn something from Parrington, but few could be happy with what he gave them. As Alfred Kazin wrote in a balanced epitaph in *On Native Grounds:* "What ailed him, very simply, was indifference to art; an indifference that encouraged him to write brilliantly of General Grant but lamely of Hawthorne; Grant had made 'history'; Hawthorne merely 'reflected' a tradition." Parrington pointed criticism in the direction of social history, only to dissolve social history into the history of ideas, so that even the academic Left, when it revived decades later, found little use for him. His successors were liberal historians like Henry Steele Commager, whose lively biography of Theodore Parker (1936) and broad survey, *The American Mind* (1950), were directly inspired by Parrington.

Constance Rourke offered quite a different alternative to formalist criticism in her study of popular culture, *American Humor*. The difference between Rourke and Parrington, and later between Rourke and Matthiessen, was almost a textbook illustration of the split described by Santayana and Brooks between the upper and lower reaches of the American mind. Instead of attacking the genteel tradition, Rourke looked behind and beneath it. Her sources lay not in novels, sermons, or political pamphlets but in the popular arts.

Though Rourke was no anthropologist, she did her work in the early, pioneering years of that discipline; she has a highly diversified, strongly ethnological sense of American culture.

Whitman in *Democratic Vistas* had attacked a class-bound, European sense of culture, and argued for "a programme of culture drawn out, not for a single class alone, or for the parlors or lecture-rooms, but with an eye to practical life, the west, workingmen, the facts of farms and jack-planes and engineers, and of the broad range of women also of the middle and working strata." Santayana and Brooks had invoked Whitman, but Rourke had a genuinely Whitmanesque sense of American culture, which for her was essentially an oral culture composed of frontier humor, legends and folktales, the performances of strolling players, and ethnic or regional stereotypes. She turns popular jokes about Yankees or black people, tall tales about Mike Fink or Davy Crockett, into the equivalent of a national mythology, and shows how much serious American literature "has had its roots in common soil. . . . an anterior popular lore that must for lack of a better word be called folk-lore." Thus she is able to move on from primitive versions of the Yankee and the backwoodsman to the fictional protagonists of James and Howells, Twain and Bret Harte, right up through the up-to-date satirical figures of Sinclair Lewis. Her emphasis is on the archetype, not the individual work.

Rourke's populism predates the Popular Front and, in its treatment of recurrent myths, formulas, and narrative motifs, foreshadows many later explorations of popular culture. Her aim, like Brooks's, was to define the national character: this was part of Brooks's legacy to American Studies. But unlike Brooks she had "no quarrel with the American character; one might as well dispute with some established feature of the national landscape." Rourke accepts what she finds because she enjoys it; the foibles of popular culture seem rich to her, not crude or ragged. Her book has a lightness of touch that makes Brooks feel dour, that leaves Parrington and Matthiessen looking elephantine.

For almost the same reason, her work was less usable than theirs to the burgeoning academic study of literature. Parrington gave his readers a sweeping overview that helped dislodge the genteel canon; he helped them see American literature as a progress toward the triumph of realism. But his work was deficient in critical judgment and out of touch with both the literature and criticism that developed after the First World War. Rourke's approach, on the other hand, required an unusual kind of learning that was hard to pass on: it was not centered on masterworks that were accessible to criticism. Hence it could scarcely be refined into a method. Yet its cultural emphasis gave an invaluable grounding to American Studies—even after 1945, when the new formalism began to dominate literary study. Here Matthiessen proved to be the greater influence, for he not only set up a pantheon of a few select writers, as Leavis did in England, but offered a method by which they could be closely read—a canon and a method that were remarkably in tune with the literature and criticism of the postwar era.

Matthiessen's work is a tissue of contradictions, but they are rich and interesting contradictions, for his mind never settled into a single groove. His last work on Dreiser is hard to reconcile with his lifelong devotion to James. At the height of the radical thirties, his Christian socialism did not prevent him from writing a pioneering study of T. S. Eliot, as well as withering critiques of Marxist volumes on American literature by V. F. Calverton and Granville Hicks. He was close to the New Criticism, yet he attacked it in his last major essay, "The Responsibilities of the Critic," for bogging down in pedantic exegesis, with its terms used not "as the means to fresh discoveries but as counters in a stale game." He demolished Parrington's method in the preface to *American Renaissance,* arguing that even as a historian "you cannot 'use' a work of art unless you have comprehended its meaning." But by 1949, when Parrington's influence was fading, he described him as "our greatest recent cultural historian," whose "instinct was right, in insisting on the primacy of economic factors in society."

It may simply be, as some scholars have suggested, that Matthiessen's literary method was inconsistent with his politics, just as he himself, as a serious Christian, would never be fully reconciled to his homosexuality. Or it may be that he simply swam against the tide, pursuing a formal approach in the turbulent thirties, partly under the impact of modernism, but turning leftward, disaffected, in the forties, as he saw the New Criticism becoming routinized into pedagogy. Here Matthiessen's own work weighed tellingly, for *American Renaissance* gave a mighty push to the formal and academic study of a handful of American writers who were quite different from the Longfellows, Bryants, and Lowells who once held a key place in American literary history. Matthiessen's canon—Emerson, Thoreau, Melville, Hawthorne, and Whitman—was not original: it was indebted to the previous attacks on the genteel tradition, especially the polemical work of Brooks, Mumford, and Parrington, which cleared the ground that he would build upon. But none of the earlier critics focused on texts in the close analytical way Matthiessen did.

Matthiessen's orientation is not exclusively formal. *American Renaissance* includes cultural history, political analysis, biographical criticism, and even comparisons of writers with painters like Mount and Eakins. But the influential new element is suggested by his close study of the language of Emerson's essays, or his prefatory assertion that all interpretation "demands close analysis, and plentiful instances from the works themselves." He continues: "With few notable exceptions, most of the criticism of our past masters has been perfunctorily tacked onto biographies."

His treatment of Thoreau begins: "Thoreau has not ordinarily been approached primarily as an artist." On Hawthorne, a similar overture: "A total impression of one of Hawthorne's tragedies, in its careful and subtle gradations, demands a closer reading than most critics have apparently been willing to give." The chapter on Whitman is called, somewhat ironically, "Only a Language Experiment," after a remark by the old poet to Traubel about *Leaves of Grass,* to which Matthiessen adds: "It will be interesting, therefore, to begin by seeing how much we can learn about Whitman just by examining his diction."

Matthiessen was uncommonly interesting on all these subjects: on the syntax of Emerson's sentences and paragraphs, on Thoreau's or Melville's imagery, on Whitman's diction, on Hawthorne's fictional structures as well as his tragic vision. To a remarkable degree, Matthiessen created American literature as a subject for academic study. He did this by establishing the formal complexity and tragic seriousness of a few key writers in a way that suited the age of modernism—which was also an era of mass instruction, when the journalistic critic and the "common reader" were giving way to the academic expert and his classroom charges. Unlike some who followed him, Matthiessen had an extraordinary depth of feeling for the writers he discussed. He could hardly have imagined that his way of inhabiting these writers, which was not simply analytical but had an intimate spiritual dimension, would soon be turned into a cottage industry. When he writes of Melville that "he plunged deeper into the blackness than Hawthorne had, and needed more complex images to express his findings," he surely could not have guessed that this would let loose a flood of studies of light and dark imagery in Hawthorne, Melville, and Poe. This was the kind of sterile, mechanical work he criticized in 1949, the year before he took his own life.

Thus, even as Matthiessen helped create American Studies by giving it a critical method, he helped derail it from its cultural mission, which was to focus on a single culture in all its complexity, to overcome the widening gap between literature and history, literature and politics, literature and the other arts. Against his own beliefs and intentions, he helped dehistoricize literature for an age that was already turning away from the historical awareness of the twenties and thirties. Ironically, Matthiessen, like D. H. Lawrence in his *Studies in Classic American Literature,* gave American writers tremendous currency by making them seem more contemporary, more powerfully up-to-date. Boldly examining his writers through the prism of modernism, he rescued them from the stuffy official versions of their work.

"The first awareness of the critic," he later wrote, "should be of the works of art of our own time. This applies even if he is not primarily a critic of modern literature." Matthiessen came to his work fresh from his study of Eliot, and Eliot is only one of the modern writers whose names are sprinkled throughout his text. Just as Perry Miller drew a line from the Puritans through the Transcendentalists to the moderns, Matthiessen compares Thoreau's style to Hemingway's, Hawthorne's allegory to Kafka's, connects Hawthorne through James to Eliot, invokes Lawrence frequently, and compares Whitman not only to Hart Crane and Pound, Carl Sandburg and Archibald MacLeish, but also, at much greater length, to a key modernist icon, Hopkins, as if that improbable linkage could somehow validate Whitman's poetry. (In this sense, the rediscovery of Melville in the twenties made Matthiessen's project possible, for Melville and Emily Dickinson were the Hopkins and Donne of American literature, the "Metaphysical" writers who were too advanced, too difficult for their own contemporaries, only to be redeemed from neglect and incomprehension by a new post-Victorian aesthetic.)

As a result, the American Renaissance writers were reshaped into modern writers, bristling with irony, ambiguity, and the tragic sense of life; other American writers who scarcely fit this pattern, such as the naturalists, were greatly devalued. Here Matthiessen's work dovetailed with the influence of the New York intellectuals who, as anti-Stalinists, disagreed with him politically. Most of the early *Partisan Review* writers began as Marxists in the thirties before breaking with the Communist Party. Schooled in fierce political debate, they retained enough of their Marxist grounding to continue writing historical criticism all through the New Critical era. But their sense of history was quite different from Wilson's or Brooks's. Their sensibilities were formed by the modern masters but they were oriented toward Europe, and only a few had strong interests in earlier American writers. But the impact of those few, especially in the work of Lionel Trilling, as seconded and developed by Richard Chase, ultimately proved decisive.

Trilling as a Cultural Critic

Lionel Trilling's career had begun with an intellectual biography of Matthew Arnold and a brief study of E. M. Forster. But even before and during this English phase, he made his mark on contemporary American writing as a poised and accomplished reviewer for *The Menorah Journal, The Nation, The New Republic,* and after its revival in 1937, *Partisan Review.* While still an undergraduate, Trilling grappled in print with Dreiser's newly published *An American Tragedy,* and later he contributed two distinctly harsh essays, on Eugene O'Neill and Willa Cather, to Malcolm Cowley's *After the Genteel Tradition* (1937), a revaluation of the insurgent writers of the 1910–30 era. With a few exceptions, Trilling disliked the new American realists, whom he compared unfavorably to the great European novelists, above all Balzac and Stendhal, Jane Austen and George Eliot, writers who occupied a key place in his teaching at Columbia.

Trilling's most important and influential book, *The Liberal Imagination* (1950), can be seen as a meeting point between the important historical work he had done on English culture and the journalistic chores he had undertaken in his essays on recent American writers. Trilling's study of Matthew Arnold and his strong identification with Victorian culture are almost never given their due in discussions of his work, except for the customary observation that Trilling later assumed an Arnoldian pose and even, eerily, an Arnoldian prose in his own criticism. (Someone cannily observed that in his anthology *The Portable Matthew Arnold,* it was difficult at times to tell the introductions from the selections.) Trilling called his first book "a biography of Arnold's mind," but it was also saturated with history. It brings to life the mental and political atmosphere of the whole age, centering on the predicament of one critic—as concerned with society as he is with literature—who is caught up in a period of political and cultural upheavals, including the decline of religious sanctions, the shifting positions of poetry, criticism, and fiction, the beginnings of mass education, the sharpening of class antagonisms, and the popular agitation that culminated in the second Reform Bill of 1867, which called forth Arnold's famous polemic *Culture and Anarchy.*

In his notes for an autobiographical lecture toward the end of his life, Trilling reveals that he was first drawn to Arnold's poetry, not his prose:

The Arnold that first engaged my interest was . . . the melancholy poet, the passive sufferer from the stresses and tendencies of his culture. When the book was finished my concern was with the man who had pitted himself against the culture, who had tried to understand the culture for the purpose of shaping it—with the critic, with (perhaps it can be said) the first literary intellectual in the English-speaking world.

Trilling had begun the book, he tells us, as a Marxist but concluded it as an Arnoldian, an engaged cultural critic in the Arnold-Brooks-Bourne mold, impelled to question liberal and progressive views from within the liberal, humanistic consensus. "No sooner was the book out of the way," Trilling adds, "than I found myself confronting a situation that I had inevitably to understand in Arnold's terms." Like Arnold during the battle for Reform or Brooks and Bourne in the waning days of the Progressive era, Trilling saw himself confronting a debased, instrumental liberalism, descended from Stalinism and the Popular Front, whose cultural icons were figures like Dreiser and Parrington, the writers he attacks with unusual polemical vigor in the opening essay of *The Liberal Imagination*.

To labor over a book on Arnold, a dissertation no less, all through the Marxist decade was itself a dissenting gesture. Trilling later expressed warm gratitude to Edmund Wilson for a moment of encouragement; indeed, the book is his closest parallel to Wilson's historical studies. Much later Trilling even attributed a dialectical purpose to his slim 1943 study of Forster, suggesting that it was undertaken as part of his "quarrel with American literature" of that moment, that he had "enlisted Mr. Forster's vivacity, complexity, and irony" against "what seemed to me its dullness and its pious social simplicities." This is precisely the argument that unifies *The Liberal Imagination:* that literature, especially the great tradition of the novel, could enrich the liberal mind with a human and emotional dimension it had lost, could provide it with a model of complexity, variousness, and possibility. Though friendly critics like R. P. Blackmur and Joseph Frank demurred that no actual politics could ever sustain such a nuanced literary vision, that the book was implicitly a blueprint for quietism and aesthetic retreat, Trilling's exquisitely modulated prose itself proposed a model of dialectical tension and reflective inwardness for critics long disenchanted with radicalism.

Trilling's book, composed all through the forties, gives us some essential markers for the passage of criticism from the boisterous Depression decade to the more purely literary world of the fifties. When he began writing it, the cultural nationalism of the Popular Front, with its affinity for harsh realists like Dreiser and protest writers like Steinbeck, still held sway, while the cosmopolitan, modernist outlook of the *Partisan Review* critics seemed at best a marginal force. But after the war, as America assumed its position on the world stage, the old rebels and naturalists, who were still reacting against a bygone Victorian America, gave way to the growing influence of the great modernists, to Hemingway, Faulkner, and Fitzgerald, to Kafka, Joyce, and Proust. Problems of style, along with the brooding concerns of the inner life, became more important to the younger writers than the social documentation of a Farrell or a Dos Passos, or the grandiose, inchoate yearnings of a Thomas Wolfe. American literature was undergoing one of its periodic shifts of sensibility. Thanks in part to Trilling, who forwarded this momentous reconsideration in the closing pages of *The Liberal Imagination,* a large segment of American criticism would soon be following suit.

Yet Trilling's book was not all of a piece. In promoting writers like Kipling, Twain, Henry James, and Fitzgerald over Dreiser and Sherwood Anderson, in giving his primary allegiance to a more Freudian, more introspective literary sensibility, Trilling was in tune with powerful trends in postwar American culture. Though Trilling is usually thought of as a cultural critic far removed from formalism, his emphasis on the complexity and irony of the imagination is quite compatible with the outlook of the New Critics, with whom he remained on graciously respectful terms all through his life. For all their differences, there was a considerable measure of common purpose between the New York intellectuals and the New Critics; both tended to cast the issue in terms of art against politics, modernism against naturalism, the autonomous imagination versus the politics of commitment. Philip Rahv's "political autopsy" on proletarian literature first appeared in the *Southern Review;* Trilling's harsh farewell to Sherwood Anderson, along with other essays of his, came out in John Crowe Ransom's *Kenyon Review.* Both Rahv and Trilling joined the New Critics to help found the Kenyon School of English, an important summer institute.

Yet the New York critics were far more politically explicit, more historically oriented, and more touched by the immediate concerns of contemporary culture. Even in its reasoned recoil from politics, *The Liberal Imagination* was Trilling's most political book, the one he grimly located at "the dark and bloody crossroads where literature and politics meet"—perhaps a deliberate allusion to the crossroads at which Oedipus slays his own father, the place where Trilling enacts his own rebellion against the radical generation, including the radical father in himself. Trilling was above all a reactive critic, finely attuned to the contradictions in his own mind, given, as his published notebooks show, to writing against himself, even against the grain of a consensus he had helped establish. Within a few years of *The Liberal Imagination* he could write that "the American intellectual never so fully expressed his provincialism as in the way he submitted to the influence of Europe. He was provincial in that he thought of culture as an abstraction and as an absolute. So long as Marxism exercised its direct influence on him, he thought of politics as an absolute. So long as French literature exercised its direct influence upon him, he thought of art as an absolute." In the same reactive vein, Trilling would eventually express deep reservations about modernism and, later still, about the uninflected way some neoconservatives had appropriated his own ideas.

Thus in *The Liberal Imagination* it is never possible to tell how much Trilling is reacting against liberalism, or against political criticism in general, and how much he is making the case for a more finely honed political outlook. A certain cordiality toward the New Critics doesn't prevent him, in one essay called "The Sense of the Past," from making a strong case for historical criticism, reminding the formalists "that the literary work is ineluctably a historical fact, and, what is more important, that its historicity is a fact of our aesthetic experience." On the other hand he cautions that "the refinement of our historical sense means chiefly that we keep it properly complicated."

Trilling, with his gift for inclusive and suggestive formulations, even anticipates the skepticism of the deconstructionists by adding that history, like art itself, like all interpretive thinking, is an abstraction from the flux and multitudinousness of experience—in other words, a set of choices: "Try as we may, we cannot, as we write history escape our purposiveness. Nor, indeed, should we escape, for purpose and meaning are the same thing. But in pursuing our purpose, in making our abstractions, we must be aware of what we are doing; we ought to have it fully in mind that our abstraction is not perfectly equivalent to the infinite complication of the events from which we have abstracted."

These cautionary lessons for historical critics were inspired by the excesses of a vulgar Marxism, but Trilling typically framed them in cogently general terms that acquired new resonance decades later, when poststructuralist theorists, retreating to the barricades of a new formalism, lodged similar complaints against all historical criticism. Trilling never considered himself a theorist, but he loved ideas and always pushed from specific cases toward general formulations. In a stern review, he objected to the elder Brooks's version of the American past, because "ideas and the conflict of ideas play little or no part in it." By contrast, Trilling's interior dialogue proceeds by ironies and undulations that set up conflicting viewpoints and general ideas from sentence to sentence. The opening lines of his essay on Wordsworth, a piece unusual for him in concentrating on a single poem, provide a neat instance: "Criticism, we know, must always be concerned with the poem itself. But a poem does not always exist only in itself: sometimes it has a very lively existence in its false or partial appearances." With an elegant bow to the text, he proceeds to open it outward to its many contexts.

Writing about the novel in his influential "Manners, Morals, and the Novel" and its sequel, "Art and Fortune," Trilling drives home the historicity of the literary text strikingly, by emphasizing money, manners, and class as the very substance of great fiction. Discussing the kind of novel that was no longer dominant in an age of modernism, Trilling shows his strong debt to Marxist criticism but also his significant divergence from it. Nothing could be further from the vapid idealization of the "timeless values" of a classic than Trilling's remark that "every situation in Dostoevski, no matter how spiritual, starts with a point of social pride and a certain number of rubles." But Trilling focuses on money not simply as an economic fact but as the fuel of human interaction, expressed in minute details of status, feelings, and social style. "Money is the medium that, for good or bad, makes for a fluent society." His discussion of manners contradicts both the hard Marxist stress on class and the trivial academic stereotype of the novel of manners, which is blind to the deeper links between manners and morals. Manners for him is "a culture's hum and buzz of implication," a subtle aura of intentions and moral assumptions that is more psychological than behavioral. Trilling even deals with class as an element of mind and will, a dimension of character, arguing that "one of the things that makes for substantiality of character in the novel is precisely the notation of manners, that is to say, of class traits modified by personality."

Trilling called this a tradition of "moral realism," perhaps to distinguish it from more strictly economic definitions of realism. His values in fiction bear a close resemblance to those of F. R. Leavis, whose work on George Eliot and Henry James forms part of the ground for Trilling's later essays on Jane Austen. Leavis, like Wilson, had welcomed Trilling's book on Matthew Arnold, and Trilling in turn handsomely reviewed *The Great Tradition* in the pages of *The New Yorker*. Meanwhile some of Trilling's more promising students at Columbia went on to study with Leavis in Cambridge (including Norman Podhoretz, whose first published essay was a review of *The Liberal Imagination* in *Scrutiny*). Both Leavis and Trilling had flirted with Marxism in the early thirties, and both maintained a lifelong interest in connecting literature to social history. Some of Leavis's colleagues, especially Q. D. Leavis in *Fiction and the Reading Public* and L. C. Knights in *Drama and Society in the Age of Jonson,* made valuable contributions to a modest sociology of literature that figures significantly in the early volumes of *Scrutiny*. Long before the mantle of Blakean and Lawrentian prophecy settled on him in his old age, Leavis's studies of seventeenth-century prose and eighteenth-century poetry were strongly bound up with social questions including class. In his teaching at Cambridge he made the social history of English style one of his specialties.

For all his emphasis on practical criticism—the precise configuration of the words on the page—Leavis, like Van Wyck Brooks and Trilling, like T. S. Eliot himself, had deep roots in the Victorian tradition of cultural criticism, as Raymond Williams demonstrated so effectively in *Culture and Society*. Throughout the twentieth century this tradition provided some notable critics with an alternative to both aesthetic formalism and Marxist determinism, offering them both a social strategy and a way of making literature matter in a world in which it seemed to be sinking into insignificance.

Leavis included two essays in *The Common Pursuit* (1952) which defined the relationship between criticism and society in a rough but useful way. In "Literature and Society" he argues that Eliot's notion of Tradition, far from being ahistorical, requires us to read literature in contextual terms, "as essentially something more than an accumulation of separate works." In Eliot's name, Leavis insists on a criticism that stresses "not economic and material determinants, but intellectual and spiritual, so implying a different conception from the Marxist of the relation between the present of society and the past, and a different conception of society. It assumes that, enormously— no one will deny it—as material conditions count, there is a certain measure of spiritual autonomy in human affairs, and that human intelligence, choice and will do really and effectively operate, expressing an inherent human nature." This "measure of autonomy" leaves considerable latitude for the Romantic individualism he felt Eliot's work had undermined.

In the companion essay, "Sociology and Literature," Leavis, saluting the work of Leslie Stephen and G. M. Trevelyan, cautions literary people that practical criticism cannot confine itself to "intensive local analysis ... to the scrutiny of the 'words on the page' in their minute relations, their effects of imagery, and so on: a real literary interest is an interest in man, society and civilization, and its boundaries cannot be drawn." On the other hand, he warns historians and sociologists that "no use of literature is of any use unless it is a real use; literature isn't so much material lying there to be turned over from the outside, and drawn on, for reference and exemplification, by the critically inert." This was the precisely the point Matthiessen had made against Parrington in the introduction to *American Renaissance,* in a passage saluted by Trilling in *The Liberal Imagination.* All three critics were trying not simply to define a select company of great writers—this is a reductive view of their work—but to make cultural history more inward with literature itself, while grounding formal criticism in moral and historical awareness.

But where Leavis remained resolutely insular, almost never leaving Cambridge—where he encountered (and provoked) frequent rejection—and confining his work largely to English literature in relation to English society, Matthiessen and Trilling helped create an American parallel to Leavis's Great Tradition. After defining the novel of manners and moral realism, Trilling writes that

> the novel as I have described it never really established itself in America. ... The fact is that American writers of genius have not turned their minds to society. Poe and Melville were quite apart from it; the reality they sought was only tangential to society. Hawthorne was acute when he insisted that he did not write novels but romances. ... In America in the nineteenth century, Henry James was alone in knowing that to scale the moral and aesthetic heights of the novel one had to use the ladder of social observation.

Trilling's point was coupled with his assault on the social realists America did have, such as Dreiser.

Just as the Marxist critic Georg Lukács had attacked the naturalism of Zola in the name of the "critical realism" of Balzac and Stendhal, Trilling dismissed American realism as a factitious imitation of an essentially European tradition. This was partly a political judgment— many of the American naturalists had been radicals—but ultimately a comment on American society itself, on the lack of social texture which Henry James had observed in his life of Hawthorne. (There James had drawn the lesson that "the flower of art blooms only where the soil is deep, that it takes a great deal of history to produce a little literature, that it needs a complex social machinery to set a writer in motion.") Trilling even argued that American novels "have given us very few substantial or memorable people": mythic figures like Captain Ahab or Natty Bumppo, yes, but few real characters: "American fiction has nothing to show like the huge, swarming, substantial population of the European novel, the substantiality of which is precisely a product of a class existence."

Not all the critics who took up Trilling's point shared his nostalgia for a class-bound culture, the kind in which he himself might never have attended a university or gained a professorship. Richard Chase's 1957 book *The American Novel and Its Tradition*, modeled on Leavis but more indebted to Trilling, traces the American romance from Brockden Brown to Faulkner, and Leslie Fiedler's more Freudian *Love and Death in the American Novel* (1960) emphasizes the popular sterotypes of Gothic melodrama, going back to eighteenth-century works like *La Nouvelle Héloïse* and *The Monk*. Both Chase and Fiedler had contributed to the vogue of myth criticism in the postwar decade, and their books have a close connection to key works of American Studies which, using the same literary canon, tried to identify certain essential myths and symbols of American culture—books like Henry Nash Smith's *Virgin Land* (1950), R. W. B. Lewis's *American Adam* (1955), and Leo Marx's *Machine in the Garden* (1964).

Ultimately all these works, beginning with Matthiessen's *American Renaissance*, would come under attack from younger scholars as examples of "consensus" history or cold-war criticism, as books seeking common ground, a unified vision, yet ignoring fundamental conflicts and tensions in American culture. This had been Trilling's point against Brooks and Parrington, but where Trilling stressed the clash of ideas, the younger critics, returning to the spirit of thirties Marxism, insisted on the conflict of classes and economic forces. With the rise of academic Marxism, feminism, and Third World cultural studies among younger Americanists, this new historicism also put more emphasis on popular authors, women writers, black writers, and nonliterary texts, along with the problems of ideology that such works reflected. Much of the attention that had been focused for decades on the American romance was now directed toward the more politicized tradition of American realism that Trilling, Matthiessen, and their followers had helped to banish. Yet many of the older myth-and-symbol critics, though they had reacted against the doctrinaire historicism of the thirties, had helped keep alive a social and cultural perspective on literature during the period of New Critical hegemony.

Kazin, Rahv, and *Partisan Review*

One major work on American literature that appeared shortly after *American Renaissance* stood apart from these trends. Alfred Kazin was the early exception among the New York intellectuals in the depth and intensity of his interest in the American past. He was only twenty-seven in 1942 when he published his prodigious book *On Native Grounds,* a study of American prose writers since 1890. Trilling saluted his book in *The Nation* as "not only a literary but a moral history," but Kazin's acknowledged models, who became part of the story itself, were Edmund Wilson and Van Wyck Brooks, critics already considered old-fashioned by 1942, when Ransom, Tate, Blackmur, Burke, and Cleanth Brooks had published their first major works. The son of Yiddish-speaking immigrants in the Brownsville section of Brooklyn, Kazin had begun an illustrious career as a reviewer—and a love affair with American literature—while still a student at City College in 1934.

Like so many other cultural critics in this tradition, Kazin was not simply a critic but also a remarkable writer. He brought to criticism an almost preternatural vividness, a breathless aphoristic brilliance that was far more than a reviewer's facility: he could light up a writer's life and work in a single phrase. His aim, always, was to cut through the verbiage of exegesis to find the figure in the carpet, the imaginative core or flaw. On Mencken: "Mencken's technique was simple: he inverted conventional prejudices." On Steinbeck: "Steinbeck's people are always on the verge of becoming human, but never do." On Wilson: "Unlike most critics, he seemed to be taking the part of the reader rather than talking at him; thinking with the reader's mind and even, on occasion, at the reader's pace." On Van Wyck Brooks: "Brooks's conception of the Gilded Age was not false; it was a great literary myth. . . . But as he applied it to Mark Twain it rested on a curious amalgamation of social history and a literary psychoanalysis that was so dazzling and new that it was at once unconvincing and incontestable." And this longer comment on Sinclair Lewis: "What is it about Lewis that strikes one today but how deeply he has always enjoyed people in America? What is it but the proud gusto behind his caricatures that have always made them so funny—and so comfortable? Only a novelist fundamentally uncritical of American life could have brought so much zest to its mechanics; only a novelist anxious not to surmount the visible scene, but to give it back brilliantly, could have presented so vivid an image of what Americans are or believe themselves to be."

This is a young man's work, highly rhetorical criticism of an unusual freshness, energy, and intensity. Proud of its effects, it hurtles along impatiently, certainly not "at the reader's pace." Yet, dispatching author after author in a stunningly definitive way, Kazin's criticism reveals a gift for atmosphere and portraiture that would later make his volumes of memoirs, *A Walker in the City, Starting Out in the Thirties,* and *New York Jew,* so polished and lapidary yet turbulently emotional. Kazin published no fiction but composed his criticism, as Wilson did, in narrative terms. The first chapter of *On Native Grounds,* "The Opening Struggle for Realism," is built around the transformation of William Dean Howells from the young Midwestern acolyte of the genteel tradition to the serious radical and social novelist. Just as Wilson and Brooks built their criticism around narrative moments which were also cultural turning points, Kazin used Howells's move from Boston to New York as the emblem of a shift of cultural power from the old New England Brahmins to the new urban realists.

This is scarcely a new idea, but it sharply contradicts the direction in which Matthiessen and Trilling were leading students of American culture. Their new canon centered on the American Renaissance writers, on James, and on the young modernists of the twenties, and it defined the academic syllabus in American literature for the next three decades. Kazin, on the other hand, though dealing with a period that could be seen as a triumph for modernism, returned to an older critical plot by tracing the progress of realism from Howells's early campaigns to the revival of naturalism during the Depression years. Like James Agee's *Let Us Now Praise Famous Men, On Native Grounds* is a belated work of the thirties, a synthesis of cultural nationalism, modernism, and an idiosyncratic radicalism. Its final chapter, "America! America!," dealing with Depression journalists, biographers, and documentarists like Agee, completes the full arc from alienation to integration that is part of the essential thirties myth—a way of coming home. (In his next book, *A Walker in the City,* Kazin would deal with ethnic New York and his own Jewish background as Trilling's generation, still set on leaving home, could not do.)

Like his mentors Wilson and Brooks, Kazin made his mark not as a close reader but as an omnivorous one. In the period of academic consolidation that followed, Kazin's vast panorama of major and minor talents, including not only novelists but nearly all the critics discussed in this chapter, was largely set aside. A few key writers dominated the courses and the scholarship alike. Kazin's sensibility could not be taught; the writers he discussed were going out of style;

the historical method was losing favor. In Trilling's books even academics eventually found some unifying ideas they could use: the liberal imagination, the adversary culture, the role of biology in Freud, or the ideology of modernism. In Kazin they found only a welter of brilliant impressions and quicksilver insights. Kazin's mind, ignited by passion and enthusiasm, was always on individual writers and their world, not on ideas. Unfashionably, he still practiced criticism as an extension of biography and cultural history, evoking major figures like Wharton and Dreiser through their milieu and their psychological formation, not through the details of individual works. His intuitive, epigrammatic manner was inimitable. Moreover, Kazin remained a staunch defender of Dreiser even as his reputation bottomed out in the fifties, after Trilling's devastating attack—a Dreiser who yielded nothing to a New Critical or modernist approach.

Yet for all his tolerance for Dreiser's stylistic and intellectual flaws, for all his instinctive historicism, Kazin had an unabashed love of art for its own sake that brought him closer to Trilling than to the young academic radicals who returned to Dreiser in the seventies. For him literature was not an expression of ideology and cultural attitudes so much as a drama of momentous inner struggle and verbal achievement. "What was it he had missed?" Kazin says of Howells's limitations at the end of his first chapter. He answers by evoking James, who, for all his own limitations, "had somehow lived the life of a great artist, had held with stubborn passion to the life of art and the dignity of craft." James too was a social realist but, unlike Howells, James had managed to achieve "an inscrutable deceiving intensity, an awareness of all the possible shades and nuances and consequences of art, an ability to wind himself deeper and deeper into the complexities of consciousness."

Kazin wrote this *before* the James revival of the early forties, and it helps define his distance from the thirties social tradition in which he remains fundamentally grounded—the tradition Trilling's work set out to counteract. Perhaps *On Native Grounds* is "explained" by *A Walker in the City* and *Starting Out in the Thirties,* for they show how much Kazin had remained the outsider, the working-class immigrant's boy, compared to Trilling, who honored the values of the middle class, and who reserved for England—really, the idea of England— the kind of ambivalent but all-embracing love that Kazin lavished on American literature, American history, even the American landscape. Thus Kazin and Trilling struck a different balance between art and social consciousness, between modernism and populism, and Kazin— who called the thirties in literature "the age of the plebes"—also felt a peculiarly strong connection to patrician critics like Wilson and Brooks, as well as writers like Howells and Henry Adams, who depended less on sensibility and more on their abiding roots in the culture they so often criticized.

If the strength of Wilson and Brooks was their sense of place, their sense of the past, Trilling's forte was his sense of the present, his remarkable intuition for the mood and temper of the cultural moment. When Kazin wrote about Howells, he made him the archetype of the outsider turned insider who, almost by choice, turns himself into an outsider again: a socialist, an unpopular writer, a patron of unpleasant young artists and radical causes. This is Howells as the thirties might have seen him. When Trilling wrote about Howells ten years later, at the start of the fifties, he praised him as the chronicler of the ordinary world of the middle class, an antidote to the modern sense of extremity and apocalypse. Apart from what this reveals about Trilling's own values, and the burgeoning new sensibility of the fifties, it underlines his propensity for dialectical thinking, his instinctive gift for highlighting the moment by way of something that contradicts it or simply sets it off.

This kind of diagnostic cultural criticism, which had been pioneered by the early Van Wyck Brooks, who had learned it from the Victorians, was a specialty of all the *Partisan Review* critics, especially in their periodic symposia like "The New Failure of Nerve," "Religion and the Intellectuals," and, best known, "Our Country and Our Culture." The mark of these symposia was their emphasis not so much on the country at large as on the changing views of intellectuals, above all the literary and political intellectuals who formed the circle and audience for *Partisan Review*. This was the intellectual class that Trilling embraced, often ironically, in his capacious first-person plural, that he later described as an "adversary culture" at just the time it entered the academic and national mainstream. Other New York critics made their mark as shrewd and biting analysts of intellectual trends, including Harold Rosenberg in the early essays collected in *The Tradition of the New* and *Discovering the Present;* the novelist and critic Mary McCarthy; the exquisite stylist F. W. Dupee, once the literary editor of the *New Masses,* who wrote a superb book on Henry James and many finely sculpted reviews and essays; the young Irving Howe, who in essays like "This Age of Conformity" (1954) preserved a radical stance that put him at odds with other New York intellectuals; and especially Philip Rahv, the longtime coeditor of *Partisan Review,* who, with William Phillips, broke with the Communist Party in the mid-1930s yet continued brilliantly to defend a more eclectic historicism against each new development on the critical scene.

Rahv was perhaps the strongest theorist, the most adept ideologue among the New York critics. Schooled in modern European literature, language, and political controversy, Rahv was a ponderous but adroit polemicist who adapted Marxist methods to anti-Stalinist arguments and to special American problems. He made his debut as a theorist of proletarian writing, but even in the Communist phase of *Partisan Review* from 1934 to 1936, Rahv and Phillips expressed discontent with the narrow limits of proletarian criticism and fiction. Later, in 1939, one of Rahv's first important essays was a devastating attack on proletarian literature as "the literature of a party disguised as the literature of a class." In the same year he published "Paleface and Redskin," a well-focused restatement of Van Wyck Brooks's thesis about the split between highbrow and lowbrow in American culture.

In this essay it was unfortunate that Rahv singled out James and Whitman as his two emblems, and not only because the elder James came to be deeply moved by Whitman's poetry, as Edith Wharton testified; in fact, both writers were too large and comprehensive to suit Rahv's allegorical scheme. (Indeed, Santayana and Brooks had pointed to Whitman as the figure who best transcended the split.) This schematic, even dogmatic quality was one of the drawbacks of Rahv's criticism. Trilling had cloaked his polemical intentions in sinuous dialectics and graceful euphemisms, as for example when he described Stalinism enigmatically as "liberalism." This gave his terms far wider application, so that they proved at once slippery and challenging to other critics. But Rahv, whose range was far narrower, whose work was often complex but never ambiguous, could write as if he were drawing up a position paper for a party meeting, excommunicating writers rather than criticizing them.

Yet when he wrote about Dostoevsky, Kafka, Tolstoy, Gogol, or Chekhov, Rahv, besides proving himself a virtuoso at ideological analysis, revealed a robust, finely tuned sense of literary judgment; above all, he zeroed in decisively on the key critical issues. Like Wilson and Kazin (though far more brusquely), he had the good reviewer's gift for grasping the imaginative core of a writer's work. Chekhov was not someone whose sensibility, measured and delicately ironic, appealed to him as readily as Dostoevsky's. Yet Rahv turns a review of Chekhov's selected letters into a terse, powerful statement. Denying that Chekhov leaves us with with no more than a mood of "delicious depression," but also dismissing the heavier view that takes him "simply as the critic of Russian society at a certain stage of its development," he perfectly grasps the combination of gaiety, pessimism, personal will, and empathy in Chekhov's humane outlook. Thus Rahv seeks out a middle ground in his critical method—between a wholly detached impressionism and a mechanical, deterministic historicism; his writing, though often abstract, attends closely to the concrete world of the author.

Rahv loved art too much to remain a strict Marxist, yet he was too steeped in history and politics to go in for formalism, aestheticism, or art for art's sake, as a few *Partisan Review* writers like Clement Greenberg did. In his final years—he died in 1973—Rahv became even more of a character and curmudgeon than he had always been, issuing marching orders to the New Left, delivering execrations against the counterculture and even against writers whom *Partisan Review* had built up, such as Norman Mailer—in short, behaving like the cultural commissars he had brushed aside in his youth. But in the forties and fifties he was an active opponent of the new formal and technical criticism, including rhetorical criticism, myth criticism, and poetic exegesis as applied to prose fiction. Though never as enthusiastic about Henry James as his most fervent admirers, he not only helped forward the James revival but, in essays like "Notes on the Decline of Naturalism" and "Fiction and the Criticism of Fiction," contributed to James's goal of putting the discussion of fiction on a firmer theoretical basis.

Rahv has often been seen as the quintessential *Partisan Review* critic. His work, situated even more than Trilling's at the "bloody crossroads where literature and politics meet," combines a relatively conservative modernism, which is suspicious of the wilder flights of the avant-garde, with an anti-Communist Marxism, ever alert to signs of his colleagues' backsliding into some form of accommodation with the American scene. Thus Rahv took note acerbically of "the ambiguous, if not wholly conservative, implications" of Trilling's "extreme recoil from radicalism." Yet Rahv's essays on fiction run fundamentally parallel to Trilling's: he appeals to the classical tradition of European realism as a way of attacking naturalism, and he appeals to the great modernists against their contemporary successors, the would-be inheritors of the avant-garde. But where Trilling came to see modernism in increasingly apocalyptic terms, Rahv saw it as a later stage of realism, an attempt to do justice to the disruptions and contradictions of modern life. Modernism was the realism of the twentieth century; postmodernism was its nihilistic caricature. The greatest writers were those who, in a time of general crisis, best explored their own inner conflicts.

Thus Rahv, in true Hegelian fashion, emphasized the concrete universal, the impact of history as felt through the experience of individuals. Where Trilling came to see modernism as a form of spiritual violence, Rahv saw it as the final moment of the great tradition, the inevitable self-realization of a turbulent era. While Trilling located realism essentially in the nineteenth century—to be invoked as an antidote to modernity—to Rahv, as to the novelist Saul Bellow, the principle of realism remained "the most valuable acquisition of the modern mind." And he directed his salvos against critics who, in his view, retreated from this "sixth sense," the sense of history firmly grounded in realism. These opponents included myth critics, who failed to see that symbols and allusions were never the core of a novel but "its overplus of meaning, its suggestiveness over and above its tissue of particulars."

Like Bakhtin and Trilling, indeed like Henry James and D. H. Lawrence before them, Rahv saw the novel as the form of literature most open to experience. Deeply hostile to religion, he considered the vogue of symbolic interpretation as "some kind of schematism of spirit; and since what is wanted is spiritualization at all costs, critics are disposed to purge the novel of its characteristically detailed imagination working through experiential particulars—the particulars of scene, figures, and action: to purge them, that is to say, of their gross immediacy and direct empirical expressiveness." Along with Trilling and other New York intellectuals, Rahv was a reactive critic, arguing in the militant thirties against extreme forms of naturalism, arguing in the depoliticized fifties against "the reactionary idealism that now afflicts our literary life and passes itself off as a strict concern with aesthetic form." As Rahv sums it up, "if the typical critical error of the thirties was the failure to distinguish between literature and life, in the present period that error has been inverted into the failure to perceive their close and necessary relationship."

Similarly, Rahv attacks stylistic and formal criticism of fiction as "the superstition of the word," the result of an "infection of the prose sense by poetics." Some formal critics are "inclined to overreact to the undeniable fact that fiction is made up of words, just like poetry." But, he argues, the language of fiction "only intermittently lends itself to that verbal play characteristic of poetic speech, a play which uncovers the phonic texture of the word while releasing its semantic potential." If indifferent stylists like Tolstoy and Dostoevsky can be greater novelists than Turgenev or Jane Austen, he says, this shows that other formal elements predominate over local effects of language: "character creation, for instance, or the depth of life out of which a novelist's moral feeling springs, or the capacity in constructing a plot (plot, that is, in the Aristotelian sense as the soul of an action) to invest the contingencies of experience with the power of the inevitable."

Style is simply the narrative rhythm that best suits the writer's imagination of reality. "A Dostoevsky story cannot be appropriately told in the style, say, of Dreiser, as that style is too cumbersome and the pace too slow." And Dreiser, whom Rahv had once attacked, he now sees as unquestionably a better novelist than Dos Passos, who is the better writer. As for Dostoevsky, "Dostoevsky's style has a kind of headlong, run-on quality which suits perfectly the speed of narration and the dramatic impetuosity of the action. . . . The principle of Dostoevsky's language is velocity; once it has yielded him that it has yielded nearly everything that his dramatic structure requires of it."

Formulated more theoretically than Trilling's essays on fiction, Rahv's views add up to a powerful statement that could speak for many of the socially oriented critics of the first half of this century, including many Marxists like Georg Lukács and the Frankfurt school, who also combine a conservative epistemology, a traditional sense of form, with left-wing politics. Whatever their degree of sympathy for the avant-garde, their work is firmly rooted in the ethics and aesthetics—and above all in the historical outlook—of the nineteenth century. They see literature essentially as a reflection of reality, a reconstitution of immediate experience that has the power to criticize that experience. They focus on realism as a weapon of social criticism, an instrument of self-examination.

While the Marxist critics usually insist on a close correspondence between life and literature, between history and literary history, the Anglo-American culture critics, estranged from Marxism, insist on the relative autonomy of the individual and the crucial mediations of literary form—which, in Rahv's words, can "invest the contingencies of experience with the power of the inevitable." They show the influence of Freud and Anglo-American empiricism and individualism. As the phrase suggests, their "sixth sense," the historical sense, is more often a matter of intuition and sensibility than hard theory; they rarely pursue such exact parallels between literature and history as we find in Lukács's *Goethe and His Age, The Historical Novel,* or his essays on Balzac and Stendhal, though their understanding of fiction has been formed around many of the same writers. Thus when Edmund Wilson connected the "inexorable doom" of Edith Wharton's protagonists with "the mechanical and financial processes which during her lifetime were transforming New York," he was making a suggestive analogy—invoking a social fact that gives individual fates their resonance—not describing a direct cause and effect.

By and large, the Marxist critics were antimodernist, profoundly suspicious of what they saw as a literature of decomposition and disintegration. On the other hand the culture critics, especially those born in the twentieth century, saw modernism as a further development of realism, an acute reflection of contemporary life, marked by what Rahv calls "the crisis of this dissolution of the familiar world," the decay of the old rational order of nineteenth-century science and stability. Yet their modernism was essentially conservative: the same accusations their elders leveled against modernism—charges of incoherence, irresponsibility, frivolous pessimism—they directed against late modernism and postmodernism. If Lukács and Wilson would attack Kafka, Rahv, as early as 1942, could direct his fire at Kafka's imitators: "To know how to take apart the recognizable world is not enough, is in fact merely a way of letting oneself go and of striving for originality at all costs. But originality of this sort is nothing more than a professional mannerism of the avant-garde." Of the "genuine innovator" he insists, almost classically, that "*at the very same time that he takes the world apart he puts it together again.*" This is perfectly consistent with his attacks on formal criticism, his emphasis on art as experience.

The socially oriented critics generally showed far more affinity for the political novel than for the experimental work of the avant-garde. Wilson and Rahv, both fluent in Russian, were entranced by the spiritual intensity with which the Russian writers grappled with social, moral, and political issues but, resolute secularists themselves, paid much less attention to their religious concerns. Rahv's first essay on Dostoevsky dealt with *The Possessed,* Dostoevsky's feverish assault on the radical generation of the 1860s. Wilson brilliantly illuminated Flaubert's *Sentimental Education* in his essay on "The Politics of Flaubert." Both essays projected the political viewpoint of the thirties back into the nineteenth century. Trilling was drawn to the anti-radical politics of James's most atypical novel, *The Princess Cassamassima;* other critics including Leavis focused on similar themes in Conrad's *Secret Agent.* Trilling himself wrote a novel of ideas and ideologies, *The Middle of the Journey;* its most interesting character was modeled on the Dostoevskian figure of Whittaker Chambers. The first major critical work by Rahv's colleague at Brandeis University, Irving Howe, was an influential collection of essays, *Politics and the Novel.* This book identified a whole tradition of political fiction extending from

Stendhal to Orwell, from bourgeois realism to anti-utopian fable. In some chapters Howe was trying to reclaim for the independent Left what Trilling had mobilized for his critique of ideology. Always a socialist, never a communist, equally at home in politics and literature, Howe eventually became both the inheritor and the historian of the New York intellectual tradition.

Orwell: Politics, Criticism, and Popular Culture

This new interest in political fiction, like many of the novels themselves, was the fruit of the encounter with Marxism; indeed, it was a consequence of all the political traumas of the twentieth century, especially the rise of totalitarian dictatorships. This minor but engrossing literary tradition embraced writers like Arthur Koestler and Victor Serge, who had themselves been revolutionaries and whose books, like the famous essays in *The God That Failed,* explored the grandiose hopes and bitter betrayals that inevitably beset intellectuals in politics. One of these novelists, George Orwell, who had fought with the anarchists in Spain, was also an avid student of this political writing. Almost alone among English critics, who showed little interest in intellectuals and ideology, he was repeatedly drawn to the work of ex-Communists like Koestler and to anti-utopian novels like Jack London's *Iron Heel* and Zamyatin's *We,* which became the model for his own *Nineteen Eighty-Four.*

After his disillusionment with Communism in Spain, Orwell became far more of a political writer than any critic we have discussed here. He would later say that "every line of serious work that I have written since 1936 has been written, directly or indirectly, *against* totalitarianism and *for* democratic Socialism, as I understand it." As a result, Orwell, much discussed as a novelist, praised and damned as a prophet, widely imitated as a stark, transparent stylist and essayist, revered as a man of exceptional probity and decency, has been comparatively neglected as a critic. His name figures in none of the standard histories of criticism. Yet Orwell's combination of quasi-novelistic journalism, political controversy, and what he called "semi-sociological literary criticism" is strikingly characteristic of the American critics we have already considered and of the Continental intellectuals they most admired, as Orwell did.

Orwell corresponded with Rahv and contributed a regular London Letter to *Partisan Review* from 1941 to 1946. Rahv, Trilling, and Diana Trilling were among those who acclaimed *Nineteen Eighty-Four* on its first appearance. Trilling helped shape American perceptions of Orwell as a truthful, decent man, a man of conscience and virtue, with his 1952 introduction to *Homage to Catalonia,* Orwell's book on the Spanish war. Irving Howe wrote frequently about Orwell over several decades and described him as one of his models: "For a whole generation—mine—Orwell was an intellectual hero."

Much of this identification with Orwell was political. The Trillings, Rahv, and Howe had long been embattled against Stalinism and its intellectual sympathizers. Orwell's book on Spain offered the kind of first-hand evidence of Communist perfidy that fellow travelers made it their business to ignore. Many later Orwell essays attacked the willful blindness of the left-wing intelligentsia, their preference for ideological abstractions over concrete realities and simple moral imperatives. Orwell's conversion in Spain had given him a cause bordering on a passion. By 1946 he could write that, "looking back through my work, I see that it is invariably where I lacked a *political* purpose that I wrote lifeless books."

Since Orwell's literary criticism has received little attention, its close relationship to his political writing has rarely been noted. Even Trilling, in passing, expresses only a reserved approbation: "His critical essays are almost always very fine, but sometimes they do not fully meet the demands of their subject—as, for example, the essay on Dickens." With considerable point, through not without a touch of condescension, Trilling adds: "And even when they are at their best, they seem to have become what they are chiefly by reason of the very plainness of Orwell's mind, his simple ability to look at things in a downright, undeceived way."

While Trilling doesn't pause over the political implications of this last statement, his point is clear enough: Orwell is no "genius"; his common sense, though not a sufficient basis for literary criticism, enabled him to avoid the traps of more brilliant, more theoretical minds, the occupational pitfalls of intellectuals. But apart from Dickens, who was one of Trilling's special authors, few of Orwell's critical subjects truly interested Trilling. Nor was he genuinely drawn to the kind of allegorical fable Orwell wrote in *Nineteen Eighty-Four* and *Animal Farm,* which belonged neither to nineteenth-century realism nor to twentieth-century modernism. Trilling's own criticism showed little interest in this kind of message novel, which ran counter to his view of fiction as an open, unencumbered form.

The most striking and, ultimately, influential feature of Orwell's literary criticism is his fascination with popular culture. By the end of the fifties Orwell's work in this field, combined with the continuing impact of *Scrutiny* and of working-class English Marxism, would help bring forth a new kind of sociocultural criticism from Raymond Williams, Richard Hoggart, and the Birmingham school of cultural studies. Yet when Orwell was alive, nothing could have appealed less to New York intellectuals, modernist intellectuals, than a serious critical approach to popular culture.

There were a few American echoes of Orwell's work. It would be hard to imagine Robert Warshow's essays on gangster films and Westerns as fundamental American myths, or his pieces on comic books and on Chaplin, without Orwell's example. But by and large the New York viewpoint on popular culture was more influenced by the haughty attitude of emigré intellectuals who recoiled from the American scene. It was best articulated by Clement Greenberg in 1939 in "Avant-Garde and Kitsch" and by the early work of Dwight Macdonald: a sweeping denigration of mass art and thirties populism in the name of modernist intransigence, abstraction, and aesthetic complexity. On the other hand, Orwell's complicated involvement with popular culture wasn't confined to his famous essays on boys' weeklies, penny postcards, and hard-boiled crime thrillers. If we adjust our lens slightly, nearly all his other critical writings can be seen as "Studies in Popular Culture," the subtitle of one of his collections.

Orwell's first book of criticism, *Inside the Whale* (1940), which was favorably noticed by Q. D. Leavis in *Scrutiny,* contained three long essays—on Dickens, on boys' weeklies, and (the title essay) more or less on Henry Miller. Orwell's Dickens, to Trilling's evident dismay, was not the modern Dickens discovered by Wilson but the popular Dickens long beloved by ordinary English readers, above all, the preternaturally vivid Dickens characters that all English children had grown up with. Acutely attuned to class differences, Orwell draws up a social and moral inventory of the Dickens world, extracting a tendency or "message" from each of the writer's works. This emphasis on argument, not form—on social, not verbal texture—is guaranteed to curl the hair of any New Critic—or, for that matter, any New York critic, since Orwell's rationale is that "every writer, especially every novelist, *has* a 'message' " and, anyway, "all art is propaganda."

Though radicals since Ruskin and Shaw had made free use of Dickens's attacks on English society, Orwell shows that Dickens's social criticism is "exclusively moral," not Marxist. Yet he argues that it is no less subversive: "A good tempered antinomianism rather of Dickens's type is one of the marks of Western popular culture." Thus Orwell turns Dickens—and popular culture generally—into the epitome of the common man outlook, as opposed to the inhumane absolutism of the typical intellectual. "The common man is still living in the mental world of Dickens," a world of instinctive human generosity and indignation, of simple pleasures and dastardly abuses, "but nearly every modern intellectual has gone over to some or other form of totalitarianism."

Thus, just as Trilling appealed to the novel for its anti-ideological character, its openness to experience, Orwell's essays invoke popular culture as a rebuke to the abstract thinking of intellectuals, especially their worship of power, whether Marxist or Fascist. Popular culture was simply one facet of Orwell's affinity for the "lower depths." V. S. Pritchett described him as a man who had "gone native in his own country." Of the mildly pornographic penny postcards, Orwell writes: "Their whole meaning and virtue is in their unredeemed lowness. . . . The slightest hint of 'higher' influences would ruin them utterly. They stand for the worm's-eye view of life." Robert Warshow later made a similar point about the tramp figure in Chaplin.

Orwell exalts writers who create a sense of limitless human abundance, like Shakespeare and Dickens, but also others like Swift, Gissing, Smollett, Joyce, and Henry Miller who specialize in the unpleasant truths most writers leave out. We cherish Dickens, he says, because of his "fertility of invention"; the Dickens world is like life itself. "The outstanding, unmistakable mark of Dickens's writing is the *unnecessary detail*." Shakespeare he defends against the puritan moralism of the aged Tolstoy who, no longer content with a writer's "interest in the actual process of life," now demands a literature of "parables, stripped of detail and almost independent of language." Like a modern ideologue, Tolstoy now wants "to narrow the range of human consciousness."

Yet Orwell is even more attracted to writers who, though strikingly limited themselves, descend obsessively into the lower depths that polite literature shuns. Swift was "a diseased writer," a permanently depressed figure whose worldview "only just passes the test of sanity." Yet he possessed "a terrible intensity of vision, capable of picking out a single hidden truth and then magnifying it and distorting it." This is in line with Orwell's oft-stated belief that "for a creative writer possession of the 'truth' is less important than emotional sincerity." Orwell's criticism itself is less interesting for its explicit arguments, where he himself can sound like a Tolstoyan ideologue, than for the way he fleshes them out; his best work as a novelist can be found in the descriptive vividness of his essays. Thus he likens Tolstoy's scorn for Shakespeare's profligate abundance to the reaction "of an irritable old man being pestered by a noisy child. 'Why do you keep jumping up and down like that? Why can't you sit still like I do?' In a way the old man is in the right, but the trouble is that the child has a feeling in his limbs that the old man has lost." Hostile to all forms of spirituality, skeptical of empty idealisms, Orwell grounds ideas in the physical basis of life. "Saints should always be judged guilty until they are proved innocent," he wrote of Gandhi in *Partisan Review* in 1949, shortly after his assassination. "The essence of being human is that one does not seek perfection."

The same insistence on the physical helps explain his affinity for Swift, including the Swiftian disgust that surfaces often in his own work. Again, Orwell's version of this is intensely concrete and deliberately shocking: "Who can fail to feel a sort of pleasure in seeing that fraud, feminine delicacy, exploded for once? Swift falsifies his picture of the world by refusing to see anything in human life except dirt, folly and wickedness, but the part which he abstracts from the whole does exist, and it is something which we all know about while shrinking from mentioning it." Thus, in a single sentence, Swift epitomizes both the (bad) abstracting intellectual and the (good) concrete imagination, reminding us of unpleasant facts as Orwell prided himself in doing. Orwell on Swift is also Orwell on Orwell, exposing himself as he drives his point home: "In the queerest way, pleasure and disgust are linked together. The human body is beautiful: it is also repulsive and ridiculous, a fact which can be verified at any swimming pool. The sexual organs are objects of desire and also of loathing, so much so that in many languages, if not in all languages, their names are used as words of abuse."

Orwell has it both ways: he is the student of language yet also the spokesman for the common wisdom; the Freudian intellectual, anticipating Norman O. Brown on Swift, but also the critic of intellectuals; the common man but ever the iconoclast. For Orwell, the unregenerate popular mind—filled with irregular bits of ordinary patriotism, decency, common sense, lust, and even a touch of heroism—*is* a species of iconoclasm. His long essay "Inside the Whale" is the most naked example of a dialectic that underlies Orwell's criticism. Beginning and ending with Henry Miller, this is an acidulous history of the relation between writers and politics between the wars. Miller becomes the standard of ordinary experience by which the political follies of intellectuals, such as the Auden-Spender group, can be judged.

Orwell had reviewed *Tropic of Cancer* and *Black Spring,* corresponded with Miller, and even visited him on his way to fight in Spain, when Miller supposedly called him an idiot for risking his own skin. In his essay Orwell compares him to Joyce, Céline, and especially

Whitman for his passivity toward experience, his rejection of "higher" goals. Just as Joyce's "real achievement had been to get the familiar on to paper," so "what Miller has in common with Joyce is a willingness to mention the inane squalid facts of everyday life." Thanks to his passive acceptance of life, "Miller is able to get nearer to the ordinary man than is possible to more purposive writers." Writers like Auden, on the other hand, grew increasingly politicized, which brought them into casual complicity with tyranny and violence. In Auden's hard-boiled poem on Spain, the phrase "necessary murder," says Orwell, "could only be written by someone to whom murder is at most a *word*. . . . Mr Auden's brand of amoralism is only possible if you are the kind of person who is always somewhere else when the trigger is pulled." A master polemicist as well as master of the plain style, Orwell can devastate a writer with one or two well-chosen phrases. Like Howe and Rahv, he brings the habits of political controversy into literary criticism—but also the subtleties of a literary sensibility into political writing.

"Inside the Whale" is something of a mess; it's really two essays, one on Miller, the other on the left-wing English intelligentsia. The parts come together only by an act of will. Yet it is precisely the *kind* of piece that socially oriented critics often produce: diagnostic, polemical, using writers as emblems of larger cultural attitudes. Orwell touches on a dozen writers from Housman and Eliot to Auden and Miller, connecting each with his social moment, his class, and the historical burden of his message. He identifies the pastoral writing of Housman and Rupert Brooke with the disillusionment that followed the war, and links the radicalism of Auden and Spender with their soft, middle-class, public school education, their inverted snobbery, their "sense of personal immunity." The narcissistic, bohemian spirit of Henry Miller becomes one of Orwell's masks, enabling him to strike the pose of the common man, the enemy of intellectual cant.

As a critic Orwell is better when he explores the common man more directly, not as an adjunct to social prophecy. As direct observation *The Road to Wigan Pier* (1937) is a masterpiece; as analysis it's often cranky and absurd. But Orwell grew rapidly as an essayist. His classic pieces on boys' weeklies and penny postcards ("The Art of Donald McGill") are both evocative and shrewdly observant. They affectionately explore these subcultural materials as reflections of the popular mind but also as specimens of ideology, little doses of safe, conformist thinking with which the masses are always being inoculated. Thus Orwell anticipates both the sociologists of mass culture, who take best-sellers and hit songs as an index of public attitudes, and the ideological critics of the Frankfurt school and, later, the Birmingham school, who see modern mass culture as part a process of "hegemonic" indoctrination.

Orwell's essays combine a remarkable tenderness toward popular art (especially in its older, Edwardian forms, which take him back to his own childhood) with a shrewd, detached insight into its social and political outlook. By the end of 1941, as he himself turns less radical, he sees its "antinomianism" less as a form of radical criticism than as a safety valve within an essentially conservative society. The McGill postcards give us something like "the music-hall world where marriage is a dirty joke or a comic disaster, where the rent is always behind and the clothes are always up the spout, where the lawyer is always a crook and the Scotsman always a miser, where the newlyweds make fools of themselves on the hideous beds of seaside lodging houses," and so on. "Like the music halls, they are a sort of saturnalia, a harmless rebellion against virtue."

Conclusion: England and America

Orwell is an unlikely but useful figure to round off this survey of the largely American cultural criticism of the first half of the twentieth century. Though his disillusionment with communism enabled him to forge strong links with American intellectuals and to win a large cold-war audience, he was the kind of writer only England could have produced. He was also something of a loner, certainly a less typical English critic than his school friend Cyril Connolly, who edited *Horizon*. Despite his aesthete's pose as an indolent sybarite and professed failure, the boorish but well-connected Connolly was a prolific reviewer and baroque man of letters. Connolly's mandarin style was remote from Orwell, who believed that "good prose is like a window pane." But both men came of age under conditions that never existed in America and gradually passed even in England as the century wore on.

England had a number of traditions that made the careers of writers like Orwell or Connolly or V. S. Pritchett possible. Since the founding of the great reviews like the *Edinburgh* or the *Quarterly* at the beginning of the nineteenth century, England had a long, rich, and uneven history of literary journalism, which expanded dramatically at the turn of the century with the effects of compulsory education. But despite the growth of a mass audience, England remained to a significant degree a class-bound society, as well as one in which literature still mattered. Though Orwell, in a grim moment, likened the professional book reviewer to someone "pouring his immortal spirit down the drain, half a pint at a time," it was far easier for a literary journalist to survive in England than in America, where book reviewing was a more marginal, more mechanical pursuit and where, except for a brief period in the thirties, government support for culture or communications was nonexistent. (Orwell worked unhappily for the BBC during the war years.)

More than in England, book reviewers in America tended to be functionaries of the marketplace rather than guardians of literary values, a role which fell more and more to the growing professoriat. A surprising number of important English writers were also supple, assiduous reviewers, at once supporting themselves and enhancing the literary culture. Though their pieces were impressionistic and unsystematic, Arnold Bennett, Virginia Woolf, E. M. Forster, and D. H. Lawrence all did significant work as critics; the same could be said about few American novelists after James and Howells. (The criticism of Mary McCarthy was a rare exception.) This cross-hatching with the world of the novel not only enlivened the prose and the creative empathy of English criticism but also sharpened its social perspective. The kind of attention to class and manners we find in Orwell was a staple of English criticism left and right. In America, a more open society, the novel of manners was an extremely minor enterprise. As literary criticism became more formal, analytical, and academic, social criticism was left to the old-style historians and pop sociologists. For critics it was a minority pursuit bordering on the unpatriotic.

The growth of higher education, with its need for a new mass pedagogy, proceeded far more slowly in England than in America. Only after World War II did a university education become more widely available. The New Criticism as machinery for the production of close readings was never institutionalized in England; it lacked the necessary industrial base. In England, aestheticism was long hobbled by its associations with upper-class decadence, symbolized by the fate of Wilde, Beardsley, and the *Yellow Book*. It took a brilliant generation in the twenties to gain approval for the formal study of English literature in Cambridge, a more modern university than Oxford. The interwar figures who stood for criticism as against historical scholarship—critics like Eliot, Leavis, Richards, and Empson—were anything but pure formalists. Their close approach to language and style was saturated with historical considerations. The same could be said of the first American New Critics, before their work was routinized.

By 1950—the year Orwell and Matthiessen died, the year Trilling published *The Liberal Imagination,* the year Edmund Wilson, at the low ebb of his reputation, collected his *New Yorker* pieces under the deliberately casual title of *Classics and Commercials*—historical criticism was far more beleaguered in America than it would ever be in England, a nation with a longer moral tradition and a more ingrained, more conservative sense of the past. Victorian cultural criticism remained a living body of work, especially for the English Left. Always suspicious of modernism, the English, bereft of empire, began turning inward. The welfare state, the Movement (in poetry), and the Angry Young Men became cultural features of Little England. For many young postwar writers, Thomas Hardy became the man of the moment, not Proust, Kafka, or Joyce.

Historical criticism in America was by then primarily a counter tradition, a minority enterprise, but it was also far less insular and more cosmopolitan than its English counterpart. Trilling's subjects in 1950 ranged from Tacitus to the Kinsey Report, from Kipling and Scott Fitzgerald to Freud. Wilson's book, though not as various as his earlier work, included a delicious evisceration of *Brideshead Revisited,* an iconoclastic assault on detective stories, and a book-length study of the new California hard-boiled writers.

Both books avoided the kind of technical criticism already fashionable in the academic world. Like most traditional criticism from Johnson to Arnold, they were the product of close reading, not the minute record of it. They were the work of public critics: essayistic, conversational, accessible to any intelligent reader. Their concerns were contemporary, not antiquarian, but their methodology, if they had one, was rooted in the familiar essay of the nineteenth century. As if to highlight his somewhat old-fashioned allegiance to social history, Wilson included no less than three reviews of his friend Van Wyck Brooks's Makers and Finders volumes, pieces more sympathetic to Brooks than his earlier dissection of *The Pilgrimage of Henry James.* Though Wilson again emphasized Brooks's shortcomings as a practical critic, he was most impressed by the quality of the writing, by the intricately patterned mosaic of major and minor figures, and by the keen sense of time and place that enabled Brooks to locate American literature so firmly in the American landscape. Brooks's own goal, as he tells us in his 1953 envoi, *The Writer in America,* was "to show the interaction of American letters and life." This was a goal Wilson admired without sharing Brooks's nationalism and antimodernism. Like every other critic we have considered here, Brooks and Wilson would have agreed with Leavis that "one cannot seriously be interested in literature and remain purely literary in interests."

7

The Return to History?
A Dialogue on Criticism Today

The following conversation takes place over drinks after a particularly heated session of the English Institute in Cambridge, Massachusetts. One speaker, here called A., is about fifty years old, a Left Arnoldian who teaches English at a large state university not far from New York City. His views bear some resemblance to those expressed in the foregoing pages, though he's more partisan and intemperate. It's been quite a long time since he's seen his friend B., almost forty, who is currently an associate professor of English at Yale and seems more respectful of recent developments in academic criticism. What follows is the gist of the conversation, not its exact wording. A few quotations have been silently corrected by the editor.

B. You used to be an avid reader of literary criticism. Do you still follow the critical scene closely?

A. I don't read as much criticism as I used to. It's gotten far too professionalized. I can remember when the New Critics were attacked for being narrow formalists and technicians. They were called the plumbers and pedagogues of criticism. But the recent stuff makes the essays of Allen Tate, Cleanth Brooks, and John Crowe Ransom look like belles lettres. They wrote like writers who could still imagine they had some nonprofessional readers. Remember Blackmur's wonderful phrase for criticism: "the formal discourse of an amateur." That sounds like a thousand years ago, doesn't it?

B. But things have gotten much better since deconstruction began to fade. Don't you see the shift away from technical analysis and language games, toward a more personal, more autobiographical criticism? Look at Skip Gates's recent essays in places like *Dissent* and the *Times*.

He started out by mastering the current jargon, synthesizing theory and Black Studies. Now he's taken aim at the larger audience that reads personal essays and literary journalism. The same is true for feminist critics. Aren't these straws in the wind? Isn't readable prose coming back, even among theorists? Why, Gilbert and Gubar are even writing in dialogue!

A. I like the change in style and I find some of these essays quite touching. Especially for blacks and women, these issues are personal or they're nothing at all. But the shift isn't as innocent as you imply. There's been a war on over the canon and "political correctness." After taking over quite a bit of territory in academe, then losing ground with a broader public, blacks and feminists are legitimately making their pitch to a wider audience through the mass media, just like the conservatives. The academic radicals haven't done this till now. It's such a mandarin Left anyway. They showed contempt for ordinary readers and ordinary language, which helps explain why they're on the defensive now. They had no public language in which to respond to the charges made against them. I still find most of today's academic criticism hopelessly recondite and cut off from the way people live and think. Nowadays, I find myself looking back to earlier critics at least as often as reading new ones. They deliver the goods.

B. Then you're depriving yourself of some good work, even if it can be rarefied and special. Your favorite critics' notions of culture excluded whole groups of people who deeply interest us today, or included them only when they played the high culture game. Black critics have gone beyond the occasional, impassioned essay on Baldwin, Ellison, or Wright; they're developing whole new ways of thinking about African-American culture. Feminist and gay critics have not only rediscovered lost works but are recasting our view of familiar writers. And the New Historicists are doing for us today exactly what you admire in Wilson, Lukács, and Trilling, seeing literature in its historical context without losing a sense of its literariness.

A. But doesn't the programmatic, politically committed side of their work make you uneasy? Wilson, Trilling, Rahv—indeed, all the New York intellectuals—were closely involved with Marxism. But they did their best work when they broke with Marxist orthodoxy yet remained in an uneasy tension with it. They had to work out their own viewpoint: an independent, nondogmatic historicism which left room for individual genius, for the mysterious and unexplainable. The same can't be said for the sixties generation. Much as I agree with their political ideas about community, equality, and social justice, I don't find them particularly useful when they're applied, with all the academic trappings, to culture and the arts.

B. I see you're hard to please. I thought you'd be delighted at the return to history in the latest criticism. Apparently you find this work both too academic and too political. That seems like a contradiction to me.

A. But that's just the contradiction we find in the present scene, isn't it? I don't share the neocon hostility toward "tenured radicals," which implies that academics with safe jobs should be bland and neutral and should have no politics, as conservatives supposedly have no politics. On the contrary, I find many tenured radicals politically unserious— arcane and conformist at the same time; they're the proverbial "herd of independent minds." They've taken the utopian dream of social justice and equality that people have spilled blood over, and turned it into a professional method, squeezing the sap of life out of it. And they preach to the converted: their articles always assume what needs to be proved. They're so sure that the West is polluted with colonialism, racism, and sexism that they find them wherever they look. But who's listening?

B. There may be some automatic radicalism out there, but you're wrong to see it as simple careerism or conformity. Ever since the sixties, since Vietnam and Watergate, there's been an endemic skepticism about the Official Story, whatever it is. Now it's spread from a well-deserved suspicion of our political leaders to a suspicion of the whole Western cultural project. The West has a great deal to answer for what it did to blacks, Jews, women, gays, and the colonial peoples who inhabited those dark places on the map. We've hardly come to terms with the legacy of slavery, for example.

A. I agree with you politically, but that doesn't mean that the influence on literary criticism has been a good one. A wholly politicized criticism is as bad as a wholly unpolitical criticism. It leaves no room for the freedom and contingency of the writer within any given social system. Or for the Byzantine complexity of art's relationship to power. You didn't mention the impact of French theory, which promoted not only the antibourgeois, antihumanist impulse but the tendency to be paradoxical and abstract. Under this influence, criticism, instead of keeping its eye on the object—the writer, the work, the immediate social and personal milieu—has vaporized the object into an assortment of influences, determinants, contexts.

B. Surely you can't blame the French for all you dislike in American criticism. The French intellectuals have veered sharply away from their own obsessions with '68. They've become more centrist than we are; they've even discovered Anglo American liberalism. I hear there's a new fashion in Paris for our Founding Fathers.

A. The French can afford these fashions because they don't take them seriously. Soon they're onto something else. But we still seem caught in the French influences of twenty-five years ago. For all their concern with problems of interpretation, none of the leading French theorists of that era—Lévi-Strauss, Foucault, Derrida, Lacan, Althusser— were genuine literary critics, people for whom art really mattered. (Lacan hung around with the surrealists when he was young, but I suppose Lévi-Strauss came the closest. He wrote at least one book that will live, *Tristes Tropiques*.) After Sartre and Blanchot, Roland Barthes was the only one of the lot who had a genuine literary sensibility. You'll agree that he wrote astonishing prose. He also shifted amazingly from book to book.

B. But you've always been a believer in the critic as an intellectual, a generalist. It's disturbing to hear you fall back on the idea of the purely literary. The fact that Marx and Freud weren't primarily literary doesn't mean that critics had nothing to learn from them. In "Freud and Literature" Trilling insisted that you had to learn from psychoanalysis itself, not from Freud's own narrow ideas about art. This is doubtless true of leading figures in structural linguistics, anthropology, cultural theory, and philosophy as well. Recent criticism has helped turn English from an isolated "field" into a confluence of strong intellectual currents. This has been a heady time, even a golden age for critical thinking. I'm sorry it hasn't moved you more.

A. For me, I suppose, the golden age came between the twenties and the sixties, a period of great, classically trained European scholars like Spitzer and Auerbach, idiosyncratic writers like Blackmur, Benjamin, and Leavis, and major public critics like Wilson and Trilling. The more recent ferment in criticism has engaged me more as spectacle than for its insight or theoretical progress. Those intellectual crosscurrents aren't automatically valuable unless they teach us more about actual literary works. Most of the influences you describe, far from promoting a better understanding of the relationships between literature and society, have helped rupture the cognitive connection between the text and the world. Instead of bracketing and isolating the text, as some New Critics did, they bracket the whole notion of reality: they textualize the world. Now they're turning the study of history into the academic game that literature has become.

B. But the new, more self-conscious way of looking at history in terms of competing discourses and interpretive paradigms has had genuine value. For example, it's had a radical effect on our understanding of the French Revolution.

A. "Radical" is not quite the word for it. I remember seeing a show in Paris in 1989 on the fall of the Bastille. The visual images of the Bastille were exceptionally powerful—its image spread quickly thoroughout Europe as a trigger, a talisman. But the accompanying texts insisted that there was no Bastille, only infinite layers of symbolism, myth, and misunderstanding—the eighteenth-century equivalent of a media image. To read the new French historiography, you'd never guess that the French Revolution had acutally happened: it was only a set of interpretive discourses. I suppose this is where the old and new historicism part company.

B. You can't repeal the recent work in problems of historical or literary interpretation. The old quest to recapture history "wie es eigentlich gewesen" is a chimera. It's hard today to imagine returning to a naive view of the critic or historian as objective observer. Once the serpent of skepticism has crept into the garden of reading, there's no way to keep your innocence intact.

A. Actually, I don't find much skepticism in cultural studies today, especially those that focus on race, class, and gender. For all their debunking tone, they're full of political certainty. They talk about difference and diversity but can be remarkably intolerant. They criticize the West but, unlike the French, ignore the traditions of pluralism that made their rebellion possible. I find the same narrow-mindedness in conservatives whose ossified ideas of the canon discredit the traditions they defend. Both sides need each other to confirm their stereotypes.

B. I didn't think we wanted to get into a discussion of political correctness, which has become a club used indiscriminately to bash every liberal idea of the past thirty years. I'll concede that the best Marxist criticism—Adorno, Benjamin, and the Frankfurt school, for example—had to break with Stalinism to do justice to art. There's plenty of work on race, class, and gender that avoids the orthodoxies that trouble you. There will be much more. Even a cursory reading of, say, Elaine Showalter's anthology of feminist criticism or Harold Veeser's on the New Historicism shows how much these critics differ among themselves.

A. They differ, as professionals do, on a few acceptable issues, within fairly limited parameters. They differ tactically, but not politically. After all, the aim of such anthologies is to carve out space within the field, to focus attention on their views. They collect scattered writings buried in academic journals and pitch them for classroom adoption. Don't get me wrong: such books may have commercial and professional designs on us, but they're very useful for keeping abreast of the field. The two you mentioned were especially comprehensive and well edited. They included some really thoughtful, challenging essays; but the contributors differ only within a broader consensus.

B. Certainly there are no antifeminists or antihistoricists among them. They're all leftists to some degree, and the only challenges they take seriously are from critics more orthodox than themselves—Marxists and radical feminists, for example. They share a theoretical terminology and don't disagree on the validity of theory. But some of the issues that divide them can be quite important, like the question of whether there's a solid world out there, a world of ascertainable facts on which the historical critic can rely.

A. A naive question like that shows me how much they're out of touch with the assumptions on which we all live. This is where theory has left us: with fascinating metacritical issues that have almost nothing to do with how people read. I hope they find a way back from theory to the individual writer and the individual work. Perhaps that makes me sound like more of a New Critic than I think I am. Still, criticism should be primarily about writing, not about the critical process. I go to criticism to make sense of work that intrigues me, as I go to reviews to shed light on new art and performance. I don't get much of that from recent academic criticism, though there's still plenty of good literary journalism out there. Perhaps my problem with academic criticism is generational: critics who've grown up on theory are highlighting issues that don't mean that much to me. They intrigue me notionally but don't often touch my experience as a reader. Their game isn't my game. Perhaps that's true whenever there's been a major paradigm shift.

B. You may be right. Every generation uses different categories to reshape the canon and rewrite the books that have endured. But commenting on writers and texts is not what most recent criticism is about. It's more concerned with exploring the conditions under which any writing occurs, and what happens to it once it enters the world. At a meeting of a theory group not long ago, a colleague of mine commented, "I'm tired of talking about what literature *means*. I'm more interested in how it's been *used*." Literature as an institution, as an instrument of social power or an expression of powerlessness— that's what's preoccupied recent criticism. This is hard to swallow for those who are used to criticism as interpretation, as a discursive (re)transcription of a book's form and meaning. But certainly it's something that any social view of literature should want to consider.

A. That's pretty presumptuous, isn't it? It used to be seen as presumptuous and pedantic to analyze closely what a poem meant. But that kind of respectful commentary now seems modest, when many critics have learned to put writers in their place. For a long time I complained that critics doing academic explication had given up on value judgments. They were playing with ideas, but weren't responding fully to what they were reading. But now many critics have become arrogantly judgmental, even hostile toward literature, eager to show they're not to be taken in by it. They simplify literature into ideology, and teach their students to distrust what they've read. Sometimes they have grounds; at other times they're simply tone-deaf aesthetically. Often they have programmatic reasons for withholding themselves, like the feminist film critic Laura Mulvey, who wrote an essay called "Visual Pleasure and Narrative Cinema," arguing that women had to resist the blandishments of film so as not to identify with the demeaning roles men were projecting on them. Judith Fetterley later applied the same idea to American novels in a book called *The Resisting Reader*. Resistance, withholding, suspicion—these were devices women would use to deconstruct the roles in which men had cast them. But they also became watchwords for criticism in general, the famous "hermeneutics of suspicion," with authors guilty until proven innocent.

B. Despite your own doubts, you're giving a pretty fair account of what these critics are doing. What offends you about it? Does the critic or even the ordinary reader have to become the worshipful acolyte of the artist? Wasn't that one of the flaws of both the old impressionistic criticism, with its vague raptures, and of the New Criticism, trying to weave every accidental detail into a perfect pattern?

A. Instead of hiding behind a blanket suspicion of art, the critic might take more interest in the messy lives of actual artists. Think about the choices, contingencies, and compromises that go into any piece of writing or painting or music. These "works," these "texts," are also chunks of someone's flesh and blood. They're personal performances, at times desperate ones.

B. You can hardly criticize poststructuralist critics on that score. They certainly don't idealize the finished work as the New Critics often did. Like today's nostalgic Great Books promoters, the New Critics tended to think of a poem or novel as a finished product, a perfectly sculpted monument set off from history, biography, and the reading process. Poststructuralists will go after any scrap of evidence: a fragment of an unpublished draft, some parallel text, an odd biographical detail. It's true they resist seeing texts as little unmediated bits of human experience. They insist on the trickiness of language. But they've shown far more speculative daring than the New Critics.

A. You seem to be forgetting the original shock of the New Criticism, which scandalized people by focusing on minute, ambiguous details, or on unconscious patterns of rhetoric and imagery. But the poststructuralists were as grimly predictable in exposing internal contradictions—in showing how texts were undermined by their own language—as the New Critics had been in finding organic unities. Dressed up as theory, deconstruction was the Second Coming of the New Criticism.

B. That's why you should find the return to history and biography exciting after these text-based approaches. The New Historicism was the hot critical movement of the eighties, but it was simply one version of a more widespread reaction against New Criticism and deconstruction: a general shift from text to context that includes feminist criticism, the resurgence of a non-Stalinist Marxism, a powerful current from cultural anthropology that's affected both critics and historians, a serious new interest in popular culture, and so on.

A. You're right. I'm much more delighted by the broad move toward a new historicism, lower case, than by the semiofficial movement, which (despite differences among its participants) yields far too much to deconstruction and poststructuralism. I'm pleased by the wealth of historical information that now gets into many critical essays. Look how Hawthorne has been transformed: from an author of romances, quite detached from society, to a remarkable student of earlier American culture. Not so long ago, this stuff was considered critically irrelevant, an "extrinsic" approach, as Wellek and Warren called it in their *Theory of Literature*. I doubt that so much social and political detail about Elizabethan England has ever previously been brought to bear on Shakespeare's plays.

B. There's been a remarkable shift within a few short years. It's spread from Renaissance studies to work done on the Romantic period, on American writers, in film studies. It's completely overturned the histories of nineteenth-century art. I'm struck by the great interest in Courbet and French realism, and the important new critical work on the French impressionists, who were discussed entirely in formal terms until the day before yesterday. No one can write a literary history nowadays as a selection of discrete, canonical masterpieces. I was sampling a history of the French cinema the other day, looking for material on Jean Renoir. It wasn't published that long ago, but it was still in the New Critical, or auteurist, style—all peaks and highlights, no surrounding terrain. Today you couldn't ignore Renoir's deep involvement with the Popular Front shortly before he made films like *Grand Illusion*, *La Marseillaise*, *La Bête Humaine*, and *The Rules of the Game*. You can't understand why the audience reacted as it did to *Grand Illusion* or *The Rules of the Game* without understanding the politics of the late thirties. But for that kind of critic, politics is too mundane to have much to do with a certified masterpiece. It was a history with the history left out.

A. But surely films as great as *Grand Illusion* or *The Rules of the Game* survive because, to a great extent, they leave their circumstances behind. I won't say they're universal, but surely they've transcended their cultural moment.

B. Frankly, I don't think the survival of a novel or film depends on any trans-historical quality. The more richly embedded it is in its cultural moment, the more deeply it may affect us. *Grand Illusion*, for example, is all about crossing borders, borders of class, language, gender, even nationality. It begins with a piece of Popular Front sentimentality: the captured French officers sitting down to eat with their German counterparts and paying tribute together to a fallen French pilot. But by the end of the film, with the aristocratic Fresnay sacrificing himself to enable Gabin and Dalio to escape, with Gabin's bilingual affair with Dita Parlo and the men's actual flight across the border, the pieties of the Popular Front and left-wing antinationalism have been triumphantly validated. This is a political film through and through, with a dense set of cultural references.

A. The links you draw between the film and its cultural context are more suggestive than exact. They remind me of the intuitive approach of the older critics I admire, like Blackmur, Trilling, and Arnold, rather than of more recent historicists. You wouldn't call the earlier critics "historicists"; the word seems more suitable for their academic contemporaries. You'd say they were critics with a finely tuned sense of history, the "sixth sense," as Rahv called it, a sense of the moment. That's also true of the favorite ancestor of recent theorists, Kenneth Burke. You couldn't find a more idiosyncratic book than his *Attitudes Toward History*.

B. You've hit upon one of the differences between academics and intellectuals. Because they have graduate apprentices and a well-delineated "field," academics have always felt obliged to have a "method." In *Professing Literature* Gerald Graff showed that "theory" is what each new wave of English professors have been doing since the 1880s. Academics and professionals need something systematic, a piece of machinery that can be kept well oiled and passed on to the next generation, which of course will want to devise its own machinery. This is their way of perpetuating themselves, but it's quite alien to how intellectuals operate. They tend to be generalists: haphazard, unsystematic, and (as the dry-as-dust scholars used to say) "unsound."

A. I thought it was *my* role to be sarcastic about professionalism and to praise the inspired critical amateur. This is finally what I object to most about much of the work done recently on race, class, and gender. Here were subjects that were unfairly neglected, except by the occasional maverick like Leslie Fiedler. Here were outsider groups and new materials that the politics of the sixties put on the cultural agenda. But they've been caught up in the iron law of academic routinization and conformity. This was just what happened to the New Criticism twenty or thirty years after its ideas were fresh: they were turned into pedagogic methods. By 1990, race, class, and gender were what irony, paradox, and ambiguity had become by 1960: catchwords, predictable gambits, the academic tombstones of critical originality.

B. As usual, you're exaggerating. There's plenty of interesting work being done under the head of race, class, and gender. Historians have been especially creative in writing a new social history, "history from below," focusing on groups long hidden from view: workers, peasants, women, gays, black slaves, immigrants, Native Americans. Think back to the work done by E. P. Thompson and Richard Hoggart on English working-class culture. Think of the studies by Eugene Genovese and Herb Gutman of religion and family life during the slavery era. There's been path-breaking work on labor history, women's history, gay history. And except for a few implacable traditionalists like Gertrude Himmelfarb—whose own brand of intellectual history was a breakthrough two generations ago, when diplomatic and political history were dominant—the historical profession has accommodated itself to this shift.

A. You're talking about the "new" work of the sixties; that's history, as they say. It's also revealing that you cite historians rather than literary critics when you look for good work in race, class, and gender. Most of the young social historians are probably on the left politically, but as far as method goes they play by the rules of evidence they learned in graduate school. They labor in the archives. Their findings are exhaustively documented. Their approach remains empirical, whatever the political impact they hope to make. You can't say the same about the radical literary scholars, who too often insist that the whole game is rigged, that Western culture is corrupt, brutal, and exploitative, and that clear writing and empirical canons of evidence are themselves implicated in "hegemonic" forms of authority.

B. That's nonsense. Impressionistic standards of argument and evidence have always been allowable in lit crit. That's why social scientists and philosophers usually looked down on us. Critics have borrowed some of their creative freedom from literature itself. They relied on sensibility, on association, on apodictic aphorism. You can't tell me that when Van Wyck Brooks writes about the highbrow and lowbrow, or when Trilling talks about the nineteenth-century figure of the Young Man from the Provinces, they're formulating arguments that would satisfy any positivist.

A. Well, they weren't historians, they weren't even "historicists" in the academic sense. As I was saying before, Brooks and Trilling, like Wilson and Kazin, simply had in their bones what James called a "sense of the past," a sense of historical continuity or rupture. It was a habit of thinking, a way of making connections, rather than a strict historical method. It's striking how much of the "history" they wrote was really about their own times, or about how the recent past—the last decade, the last generation, even the last century—had somehow produced the present world. There was always an instinctive Hegelianism at work in critics influenced by nineteenth-century historicism. (I'm reminded of Lukács's notion that the authentic historical novel is about a period still within living memory—Scott's *Waverley* rather than his *Ivanhoe*. Lukács was another Hegelian, like most good Marxist critics.)

B. But you're saying that the historical critics you admire aren't really doing much history.

A. In a strange way that's true. For most of the New York intellectuals, as I've said about Trilling, the sense of the past was really a sense of the present. Influenced by modernism, by the pressures of political debate, by their own drama of acculturation, they saw everything in relation to the contemporary. This was why Arnold and the Victorians were meaningful for them; it was why they identified with the great Russians: they lived with a similar sense of crisis, of a society in anguish and transition. Trilling's essay on Howells is a good example of this tendency to see the past in contemporary terms. Had Philip Rahv really read any writer before Hawthorne and Dostoevsky—in other words, the proto-modernists?

B. You're describing a special kind of critic and intellectual. What you say is certainly not true of the New Historicists, who have worked up an intricate knowledge of distant periods.

A. Well, the New Historicism, like other work in race, class, and gender, does have a political program. It's against racism, colonialism, sexism, and so on; its adherents make this explicit time and again. They feel it justifies their whole enterprise. But unlike the cultural critics from Brooks to Kazin, they're scholars—learned specialists in periods like the Renaissance—who've gone back to the contextual approaches of the scholars who preceded the New Criticism. I don't want to bear down too hard on the academic nature of their work.

But can you imagine anything in *Representations* appearing in the old *Partisan Review*? Can you conceive of anything in *Critical Inquiry,* which is after all a fairly ecumenical journal, coming out in the old *Kenyon* or *Sewanee?*

B. You can't expect the intellectual style of one generation to be reproduced in another, especially after criticism has gotten more centered in the university. The difference between critics and scholars has lost much of its meaning. Academic departments are no longer in the hands of philistines, narrow positivists, and dry textual scholars. The leading lights of *Representations,* writers like Stephen Greenblatt and Philip Fisher, may be learned but they're also wide-ranging, thoughtful, lucid; they're critics in every sense of the word. Like most historicists, they don't throw up the same barriers of style the deconstructionists did.

A. Greenblatt and Fisher are very attractive writers. So are a number of other lower-case historicists like Edward Said, Jerome McGann, and Sacvan Bercovitch. They're eclectic writers who've tried to put historical criticism on a new basis, and they've had enormous influence on younger scholars. But as far as the much-discussed New Historicism itself, I can't see that it's really made a clear break with deconstruction. It's deconstruction with a human face.

B. What's wrong with that? The human face is what you were looking for, isn't it? The return to history should satisfy everything you demand out of criticism. It shows that works of art and literature, far from being isolated artifacts, belong to the world around them in innumerable, intricate ways. What's your problem then?

A. First, we risk replacing the narrow concern with the text with a too sweeping emphasis on context, imagining that historical information, some of it merely analogous, selective, or anecdotal, can account for everything of significance in a literary work. Some New Historicists worry about this, as do some feminists, but essentially they leave no room for aesthetic autonomy. In their turn to history, they don't leave room for texts to escape *from* history, since all such "escapes" are forms of ideology produced by their age.

B. Continue. You're obviously on a roll. I'll save my rebuttal for later.

A. The New Historicism developed partly as a response to the deconstructionists' skepticism that any text could represent the world. Indeed, they had insisted that the world was simply another text. We all know Derrida's famous dictum that "there is no outside-the-text," no Archimedean vantage point from which we can know anything with certainty. The deconstructionists argued, often brilliantly, that language was so slippery that it could never fully express either the intended meaning of its speaker or the configurations of an "objective" reality. In a few succinct pages in his book *Does Deconstruction Make Any Difference?* Michael Fischer shows how all of Derrida's terms—supplement, difference, presence, *différance,* trace—even his puns, stylistic involutions, and seeming citations, simply erode our sense that language, including his own, could correspond to any wider, experiential world. My sense is that most New Historicists would be perfectly comfortable with Derrida's dictum, since they too see the world as a larger social text, or at least as an entity we can know only through textual traces. They seem to take us outside the text, but what they take us to is simply another text.

B. Well, they're right, aren't they? Do you think there's any way to achieve a direct, unmediated knowledge of the past?

A. They're right in the trivial sense, that all that we know is fragmentary, mediated by selection and interpretation; we turn hints and traces into larger narratives. But that doesn't mean that the world is unknowable or subjectively constructed. That's where theory would take us. The debate over "referentiality" in the eighties was exactly like the debate over "indeterminacy" in the seventies, which shows how the New Historicism labors in the epistemological shadow of deconstruction. In the earlier case, just because texts couldn't be tied to a single stable meaning—who ever thought they could?—it was argued that no sign truly corresponded to anything outside itself. This was the view most New Historicists applied to the text's relation to history: because it couldn't correspond perfectly, the correspondence was simply a constructed one, a matter of interpretation. Again true, but only in a trivial way. It leaves no room for strong probability, the loose fit, the broad consensus that might differ only in detail.

B. But we never actually *have* the events of the past, we only have the words. Remember the conclusion of Paul de Man's 1969 essay "Literary History and Literary Modernity," where he says that "the bases for historical knowledge are not empirical facts but written texts, even if those texts masquerade in the guise of wars or revolutions."

A. That's a theoretical viewpoint that undermines any historicism whatever. Yet the New Historicists have tried to accommodate it, indeed, have based their work on its assumptions. That's what Louis Montrose calls "the textuality of history," which he explains by saying that "we can have no access to a full and authentic past, a lived material existence, unmediated by the surviving textual traces of the society in question." This is an admirably precise passage, but isn't it a formula for *anti*-historicism? Don't words like "full," "authentic," "lived," and "unmediated" set up a straw man? Who now thinks that we can know the past in a direct, immediate, existential way? Literature probably brings us closest to that kind of elusive, inward knowledge. That's why historians and sociologists should pay more attention to it.

B. If not for Derrida's critique of "presence" and immediacy, you probably would never have acknowledged the grain of truth in Montrose's definition. Now you say it's obvious but exaggerated. Yet, as Gordon Wood complained in the *New York Review,* even historians like Simon Schama have begun questioning the old empirical faith. Like the anthropologists, they've become more conscious of the pitfalls of the interpretive process. You know the work of Hayden White since his book *Metahistory.* In a recent English Institute paper another historian, Lynn Hunt, says that "no particular fact or anecdote that comes from the past can be presumed to have any particular truth status just because it comes from the past," since "history is not an unproblematic ground of truth." On the other hand, she acknowledges that the *goal* of objective truth is crucial for the historian, though it's elusive and unattainable. This strikes me as a good middle ground.

A. Would it surprise you to learn that de Man himself made the same point about literary interpretation in a late essay? It's certainly not a passage the acolytes of indeterminacy are fond of quoting. He says this: "What makes a reading more or less true is simply the predictability, the necessity of its occurrence, regardless of the reader or of the author's wishes. . . . It depends, in other words, on the rigor of the reading as argument. . . . This does not mean that there can be a true reading, but no reading is conceivable in which the question of its truth or falsehood is not involved."

B. Well that should dispel the notion that, thanks to poststructuralism, anyone can say anything, since it's all error or misreading. At least in this passage de Man achieves the right balance: you seek the "truth" yet know it can never be definitive. You're in quest of something always just out of reach. It's a version of the New Critical "trust the tale, not the teller."

A. Either de Man was no de Manian, as Marx said he was no Marxist, or else he was responding to strong attacks on deconstruction as a nihilistic, "anything goes" theory. So he takes cover where a philosopher would, behind an appeal to coherence of argument.

B. Still, de Man was pretty strongly set against any form of historical interpretation. In one of his best-known essays, "The Resistance to Theory," he said blatantly that "literary theory can be said to come into being when the approach to literary texts is no longer based on nonlinguistic, that is to say, historical and aesthetic, considerations." Once, during the question period after a lecture at the English Institute, he advised a student of literature rather brutally to go into another field, like sociology, if he insisted on pursuing such extraneous matters. Certainly such remarks take on a different meaning, once we've heard about his early collaborationist articles.

A. But it's hard to know whether to take them as an unspoken apology, a cover-up, or the coded expressions of a guilty conscience. In other words, was de Man's resistance to historicism primarily anti-Marxist or belatedly anti-Fascist? In either case, history was the nightmare from which he was trying to awaken.

B. Surely there's no way you can say the New Historicists share this animus. After all, the other part of Montrose's formula, besides the textuality of history, was "the historicity of texts," which he defined as "the cultural specificity, the social embedment, of all modes of writing." It's true that the New Historicists refuse to see literary works as straightforward reflections of some objective reality. But the questions you raised about the world, the text, and the critic are precisely the ones endlessly debated by the New Historicists themselves.

A. We shouldn't be conflating the problems of historians and those of literary critics, just because both involve the interpretation of "texts." Frankly, I'm sorry I've gone along with that trendy word. It's convenient, but the point of using it is to level all differences, to textualize everything. Lynn Hunt and de Man aren't playing on the same field. Documents about the French Revolution or the American Civil War still require interpretation, but not in the same way as a novel about those subjects. De Man will merely concede that a novel is more honest in its fictionality. For him, wars and revolutions were fictions too, rhetorical constructions. Deconstructionists feel that the moment they've opened even a slight wedge between the words on the page and the world they describe, they've opened up an abyss— between language and its referents, between signs and what they signify. Much of this is sheer hyperbole.

B. But the New Historicists clearly do establish significant correspondences between literary texts and the actual world.

A. Not quite. Like the more skeptical historians who've been influenced by cultural anthropology, they see every account simply as one person's "narrative," with little claim to truth value. And they accept the whole poststructuralist attack on the self as a coherent, originating agency. Under the influence of Foucault, they came to see every text as part of a socially constructed "discourse," and they resist analyzing texts in relation to the "real" world. The late Joel Fineman, a brilliant purist of New Historicism, once attacked Greenblatt for not being sufficiently rigorous in excluding all reference to objective reality. Surely this is the main dividing line between old and new historicists. The older types still believe that events like the French Revolution and the Civil War actually happened. As David Simpson remarked, it was ironic to watch de Man's defenders boning up minutely on World War II, as if history suddenly mattered. Unlike him, they hadn't previously given history much thought. In a sense, he'd taught them not to. They also couldn't resist testifying to what they knew of his character, falling back on that other fossil of the old criticism—the sense of an integral, continuous self.

B. I don't see why you should object to some healthy skepticism about historical knowledge, causation, and even "referentiality." What virtue is there in remaining naive about it? We all know how hard it is to reconstruct even the recent past. Besides, all modern movements in the arts, from impressionism to modernism to postmodernism, were keenly self-conscious about the relation of the observer to what is observed. This is as true for anthropologists and documentary filmmakers as for symbolist poets. It needn't lead to solipsism or nihilism.

Why shouldn't we apply some of the same skepticism to historical writing and to literary interpretation?

A. No, I agree with Jerome McGann and Herbert Lindenberger that there's no way to restore a lost innocence. If historical criticism is effectively revived, it will be on a different basis. That's why some of the most history-minded critics have either proceeded by analogy and intuition rather than hard-and-fast evidence, or else have remained modestly informational, filling in some background and allowing you to draw your own conclusions.

B. Ah, but that's just where the newer historicisms have made a significant advance. Where the old literary historians thought of the text as the foreground and of history as mere "background," the younger students of Romantic poetry or American literature really understand how historical forces constitute significant elements in the text itself.

A. That's just what I worry about: turning culture or history into a single all-determining "author" of the text. This was what vulgar Marxist criticism once did, until it was discredited for its impoverished conception of art. Some New Historicists are simply Marxists in post-modern dress. But where Marxists used Class as their master term, the New Historicists, influenced by Foucault, use Power, which can be just as rigid and monolithic. New Historicists share too much of the antihumanism of Foucault and the deconstructionists. As Tzvetan Todorov has remarked, you can't be for human rights at the same time you deconstruct the human subject.

B. Not so fast. Greenblatt himself expresses the same qualm about a monolithic emphasis on power in his recent book on Shakespeare. Just as there were good and bad Marxist critics, there are marked differences among the New Historicists. You yourself greatly admire humanistic Marxists like Raymond Williams and Walter Benjamin, who eschew any rigid economic determinism. There are New Historicists who avoid the Iron Cage, the Foucauldian vision of the pervasiveness of power, and leave room for what E. P. Thompson calls "human agency," our ability to shape our own history, despite forces that manipulate us. In an article in *PMLA* not long ago, Theodore B. Leinwand developed the term "negotiation," already used by Greenblatt, to refer to the complicated relationships between power and individual autonomy. He pointed to "compromise, negotiation, exchange, accommodation, give and take"—not something that would appeal to a doctrinaire Marxist or Foucauldian, but surely closer to how societies actually operate.

A. Well, with the help of Leinwand, Lynn Hunt, and others, you've finally outlined a version of New Historicism I can accept. I only wish it existed—I mean, as a fully developed view of the relationship between literature and history. But I'm afraid many New Historicists, like some Marxists, are as insensitive to art as they are blind to the possibilities of human autonomy. This isn't true of Stephen Greenblatt, of course. He's an appealing example because he writes well and he's refreshingly self-critical, ambivalent. It's hard to forget the closing words of his book *Renaissance Self-Fashioning:* "I want to bear witness at the close to my overwhelming need to sustain the illusion that I am the principal maker of my own identity." Of course the book has tried to show that it *is* an illusion, so this is something of a rhetorical ploy, albeit an honest one. Increasingly, he has tried to accommodate the sense of wonder, the sense of human autonomy. But many New Historicists are quite free of such mixed feelings. Like many Marxists, they simply see art as they see the idea of man, as part of the superstructure, as ideology.

B. No, though the critique of ideology is an important part of their program, they also see art institutionally, materially, as part of a process of production, transmission, and consumption. I would have expected this to appeal to you more than an ahistorical conception of art as a set of timeless universals. You know very well that art and literature are themselves modern concepts that we've projected back onto the cultural productions of the past, when what *we* call literature had a quite different social function.

A. Frankly, I hate this language of "cultural production" and "social function" even more than I dislike talking about "texts." You yourself have conceded something to the autonomy of art. No real critic could operate without it. This materialist language of "cultural production," like so much academic critical jargon, belongs to the domain of technology, the worship of system, the cult of the professional. It's fundamentally suspicious of art.

B. No, it's only suspicious of the extreme Kantian/Romantic conception of the autonomy of art. It's based on the idea that art isn't produced by some mystical (and mystified) process of inspiration and individual "genius," but under concrete material conditions that can be closely examined without spoiling our sense of art as art.

A. I'm all for this kind of social analysis of art, provided it's not oblivious to aesthetic and human issues. Much as I've admired historical criticism, it was often insensitive to art. This remains as true today as it was before the New Criticism, when the "facts" had priority. Or else individual writers were subsumed within larger Hegelian schemes of periods and movements. When I was a student, beginning to read criticism, I often couldn't see the artist for the isms: classicism, romanticism, aestheticism, impressionism, expressionism, and so on. Artists and writers don't think that way, and neither do good critics. But something even worse has happened today. Many historical critics have begun writing *against* their subjects, whose work they portray as carriers of ideology, as if it were a contagious disease. This too follows from deconstruction, which usually saw texts as divided against themselves, full of subtexts and countertendencies. In a sense, the New Historicists have simply put deconstruction in the service of a political viewpoint, a critique of "hegemony" and "domination."

B. Because you grew up in the New Critical era, dominated by a Romantic idealization of art, you still think the appropriate posture of critics toward writers is on their knees. Why shouldn't a more critical approach to art be just as illuminating?

A. I don't rule it out. I said before that criticism had to be evaluative as well as interpretive. To say what we like and dislike is an instinctive part of our nature. It's the way critics put their whole sensibility on the line. It's *how* it's done that can be impoverishing. Earlier Marxist and Freudian critics were among the first to write against their authors, to know much more than they did. They put them in the political dock, or on the couch. The critics of ideology, though no doubt drawn to writers by a love of literature, as we all are, seem afraid of being taken in, of letting a writer's vision dominate their own. They dread being the passive agents of art's sinister designs upon us. They're the proverbial latecomers who stand on the shoulders of giants and see so much farther.

B. There are some superb works of ideological critique like Richard Slotkin's book *The Fatal Environment,* on the Custer myth and its far-reaching influence. It's infused with a density of research and historical detail and a fine political anger. Do you find tendentiousness only in works you disagree with?

A. I liked the Slotkin book and learned a great deal from it. Since I've always loved Westerns, I can't avoid having mixed feelings at witnessing the dismantling of the mythology of the West, though I see its political and historical point. But I'm truly disturbed by some of the work of younger Americanists and Romanticists who strike me as fatally out of sympathy with what they're writing about. In most cases, even when they tell us something new, they're grinding a political ax. Historicism itself is a Romantic invention. Because of the upheavals that followed the French Revolution, there has always been some good historical work on Romanticism. Specialists on Shelley were often political radicals themselves, as well as good historical scholars. There were good books on the Romantics by David Erdman and Carl Woodring, right down to more recent books by Marilyn Butler and Jerome McGann. But younger scholars, raised on Foucault, Derrida, and Althusser, have been much more mistrustful of the fatal attraction of Romantic writing, like feminists on film. Perhaps the most notorious example was Marjorie Levinson, who attacked Wordsworth for leaving out the beggars around Tintern Abbey— actually, except for the title, the poem has nothing to do with Tintern Abbey—making him the epitome of those Romantics who suppressed social reality and withdrew unconscionably into a private realm. This is pretty close to Stalinist criticism—you remember those Zhdanovite attacks on bourgeois subjectivism that made life hell for writers in Russia. So Wordsworth becomes a selfish creature who averted his eyes from the beggars and the homeless, though no writer then or since drew more profound attention to the pathos and dignity of old age, beggary, and solitary poverty.

B. But Wordsworth turned blind beggars into timeless emblems of the human condition. Wasn't he against helping them by social and political means? Take "The Old Cumberland Beggar" or "Animal Tranquillity and Decay." He clings to the traditional style of almsgiving. He sees those who suffer as sources of strength for *others,* as in "Resolution and Independence" or "The Ruined Cottage"—emblems of fortitude in dealing with the human condition. Is it illegitimate to criticize this attitude?

A. It's a rare case when the best way to criticize a poem is to disagree with it. Literary works aren't simply expressions of *opinion* that we can take or leave as we see fit. If you're not moved by Wordsworth because you find him politically objectionable—or, worse still, if you *are* moved but distrust him for it—you're in a pretty bad way. Why not make all writers more hygienically acceptable?

B. I think we've gone far afield. We started out describing the New Historicism as a reaction against New Criticism and deconstruction, with their insistence on excluding what is "outside-the-text." Then you suggested that the New Historicism was fatally compromised by seeing events themselves as texts and discourses. Now you're trying to show that the New Historicism is simply deconstructing literary works in a different fashion—debunking them, undermining them, showing their internal contradictions. Don't you see anything of value in the current return to history?

A. What I like of the new historicism, what's valuable about the recent work on race, class, and gender, is not the politically tendentious part of the program, designed to unmask Western values. It's the recovery of neglected writers, the restoration of a historical viewpoint, the renewed sense of the cultural matrix of art. Art belongs to a human world. This is what good journalistic critics, with a minimum of fancy footwork, explore intuitively every day. So do good academic critics like Harold Bloom. They look for how books bear upon our common life. They write with feeling, write in a personal voice. They renew the connections "advanced" critics have been busy severing.

B. Is this where we've been leading, to a defense of the public critic— the reviewer, the amateur, the generalist—against the theorist and the professional? Haven't you read *The Rise and Fall of the Man of Letters* and *The Last Intellectuals?* Are you trying to turn back the clock?

A. Criticism as direct human discourse about art and letters, politics and society, will never be outdated. It answers to our basic need for explanation, for consolation—for conversation about culture. Books, paintings, films, plays are part of our experience, besides being *about* our experience. They're not just part of the baggage of learning we drag around with us from college. But such criticism as experience will never be popular in the university: it can't be systematized, it can't be "theorized."

B. Aren't race, class, and gender part of our experience as well? Where do they fit into your humanistic discourse, your "conversation"? They certainly were neglected by some of your earlier humanists, who universalized the experience of their own class.

A. Of course they belong to our experience, just as they belong to our literature. Recent criticism has helped us to see that. But when such categories are "theorized," when history itself is theorized into a magic bullet, they seem to lose touch with reality. I used to loathe empiricism for its limited horizons; I loved utopian and totalizing systems. But I've come to feel that only a genuinely modest and personal approach to race, class, and gender, anchored in facts and individual feelings, will really work. Otherwise we risk reducing criticism to a technical jargon, a political program, or a meaningless game. Theory can be thrilling as an intellectual challenge; it raises enormous questions, sometimes even answers them too; but it can also be narcissistic, self-perpetuating, sterile, and hermetic—an ego trip rather than an authentic journey.

B. So it all comes down to your problems with theory, even with political and literary ideas you happen to agree with. You're still fundamentally an Arnoldian. You share the English no-nonsense empiricism, the suspicion of theory and method. You share their Protestant faith in sincerity and inwardness, the mark of the Wordsworthian. But the world has changed since the Arnoldians ruled the roost. Revolutions have come and gone. Women have asserted themselves. Both England and America have become multi-ethnic societies in a way that would have been inconceivable a hundred years ago. There's no way the homogeneous, Arnoldian idea of culture, with its cozy consensus about "the best that is known and thought in the world," could ever reestablish its authority. The approach to cultural studies today is precisely an attempt to deal with difference, marginality, multiplicity rather than consensus. It's decentered, or rather it presumes many centers.

A. The goals are noble, the methods often flawed. Don't confuse literary criticism or historical writing with self-validation. I'm surprised at your caricature of Arnold, though it's a common one. He was already aware of the changes you describe. You see it in *Culture and Anarchy,* or in his essays on democracy, equality, and the function of criticism. For all their wry urbanity, his formulas for culture and criticism are really acts of desperation. He looked for a radically humanizing role for culture as a *response* to growing social differences. Besides, it's not Arnold's specific ideas I appeal to; it's his model, the role he played: by day a mild-mannered school inspector, on weekends the scourge of barbarians and philistines—the engaged critic as double agent trying to balance art and social concern.

B. How backward of you to round off this conversation by praising Matthew Arnold, who's been dead for over a century. You know he's not exactly the hot ticket in criticism today.

A. It's not Arnold I praise, but the public critic rather than the technical critic; the novelist and poet as critic; the personal critic rather than the systematizer; the critic as intellectual and generalist rather than the ideological critic Arnold loved to attack. Edmund Wilson called this creature "The Critic Who Does Not Exist," though *he* did, and there are quite a few others today, even if they don't practice what academics recognize as criticism. As long as we still have public discourse, not just faculty symposia, as long as we can imagine a community, such a criticism will continue to exist, because we need it.

B. I suppose we can agree to disagree.

Notes

Chapter 2

1. Matthew Arnold, "Democracy" (1861), in *The Portable Matthew Arnold,* ed. Lionel Trilling (New York: Viking, 1949), p. 436.

2. Jonathan Swift, "An Argument Against Abolishing Christianity," in *Gulliver's Travels and Other Writings,* ed. Louis A. Landa (Boston: Houghton Mifflin, 1960), p. 412.

3. Matthew Arnold, "Last Words on Translating Homer," in *Matthew Arnold's Essays: Literary and Critical* (London: Everyman's Library, 1906), p. 366. (Hereafter cited as *Essays.*)

4. Matthew Arnold, "Emerson," in *Philistinism in England and America,* ed. R. H. Super (Ann Arbor: University of Michigan Press, 1974), p. 168.

5. Ibid., p. 177.

6. Ibid., "George Sand," p. 189.

7. Park Honan, *Matthew Arnold: A Life* (New York: McGraw-Hill, 1981), p. 334.

8. Matthew Arnold, "Joubert; or a French Coleridge," in *Essays,* p. 172.

9. Matthew Arnold, *On the Classical Tradition,* ed. R. H. Super (Ann Arbor: University of Michigan Press, 1960), p. 19.

10. "On Translating Homer," in *Essays,* p. 249.

11. Matthew Arnold, "Marcus Aurelius," in *Essays,* pp. 189, 192.

12. Matthew Arnold, *Culture and Anarchy,* ed. J. Dover Wilson (Cambridge: Cambridge University Press, 1969), p. 150.

13. Matthew Arnold, "The Function of Criticism at the Present Time," in *Essays,* p. 23.

14. *Culture and Anarchy,* p. 132.

15. *The Selected Writings of Walter Pater,* ed. Harold Bloom (New York: New American Library, 1974), p. 139.

16. Ibid., p. 137.

17. *Culture and Anarchy,* p. 39.

18. Ibid., pp. 45, 46.

19. "The Function of Criticism," in *Essays,* p. 8.

20. Ibid., pp. 19, 23.

21. Ibid., p. 14.

22. Ibid., pp. 15–16.

23. Matthew Arnold, "Memorial Verses: April, 1850," ll. 43–44.

24. Peter Brooks, review of *Camus*, by Patrick McCarthy, *New York Times Book Review*, September 12, 1982, p. 26.

25. "Last Words," in *Essays*, pp. 342–43.

26. Ibid., pp. 1, 249.

27. Quoted by Honan, *Matthew Arnold*, p. 391. Original in "A French Critic on Goethe" in Matthew Arnold, *Essays Religious and Mixed*, ed. R. H. Super (Ann Arbor: University of Michigan Press, 1972), p. 254.

28. David Bromwich, "The Genealogy of Disinterestedness," *Raritan*, Spring 1982, p. 69.

29. Leavis, "Literary Criticism and Philosophy," in *The Common Pursuit* (London: Chatto & Windus, 1952).

30. Matthew Arnold, "A French Critic on Milton," in *Essays Religious and Mixed*, p. 186.

31. Matthew Arnold, "The Literary Influence of Academies," in *Essays*, p. 36.

32. Ibid., p. 42.

33. Quoted in "A French Critic on Milton," in *Essays Religious and Mixed*, p. 187.

34. "Last Words," in *Essays*, p. 342.

35. Edmund White, review of Roland Barthes, *The Empire of Signs*, *New York Times Book Review*, September 12, 1982, p. 34.

36. "The Function of Criticism," in *Essays*, p. 24.

37. Ibid., p. 16.

38. *Culture and Anarchy*, p. 111.

39. Matthew Arnold, *Essays in Criticism: Second Series*, ed. S. R. Littlewood (New York: St. Martin's Press, 1960), p. 62.

40. Pater, *Selected Writings*, p. 26.

41. Ibid., p. 173.

42. *The Letters of Matthew Arnold to Arthur Hugh Clough*, ed. Howard Foster Lowry (London: Oxford University Press, 1932), p. 97.

43. Matthew Arnold, "George Sand" in *Philistinism*, p. 188.

44. Honan, *Matthew Arnold*, p. 282.

45. J. Hillis Miller, *the Disappearance of God* (Cambridge, Mass.: Harvard University Press, 1963), p. 27.

46. Pater, *Selected Writings*, pp. 174, 177.

47. Matthew Arnold, "The Function of Criticism," in *Essays*, pp. 4, 5.

48. Arnold, *Essays in Criticism: Second Series*, pp. 95–96.

Chapter 4

1. Virginia Woolf, *Reviewing*, with a Note by Leonard Woolf (London: Hogarth, 1939), p. 29.

2. George Orwell, "Confessions of a Book Reviewer," in *The Collected Essays, Journalism, and Letters of George Orwell*, ed. Sonia Orwell and Ian Angus (Harmondsworth, England: Penguin, 1970), vol. 4, p. 217. Cyril Con-

nolly, "The Blue Bugloss," in *Enemies of Promise* (1938; London: André Deutsch, 1973), pp. 103–7.

3. Alfred Kazin, *Contemporaries* (Boston: Atlantic-Little, Brown, 1962), p. 504.

4. Ibid., p. 472.

5. Jeffrey's reviews are reprinted in *The Romantics Reviewed,* ed. Donald Reiman (New York: Garland, 1972), vol. 2, p. 217. See also John O. Hayden, *The Romantic Reviewers, 1802–1824* (Chicago: University of Chicago Press, 1969).

6. John Clive, *Scotch Reviewers: "The Edinburgh Review," 1802–1815* (London: Faber & Faber, 1957), p. 157n.

7. Reiman, ed., *The Romantics Reviewed,* vol. 2, p. 429.

8. See Hayden, *Romantic Reviewers,* p. 11.

9. Clive, *Scotch Reviewers,* p. 32.

10. For many provocative insights into the history of British journalism, see *Newspaper History: From the Seventeenth Century to the Present Day,* ed. George Boyce, James Curran, and Pauline Wingate (London: Constable, 1978).

11. See John Gross, *The Rise and Fall of the Man of Letters* (London: Weidenfeld & Nicolson, 1969), a lively book which suffers from its own journalistic limitations. It devolves into a series of individual profiles, but it's the closest thing we have to a critical history of reviewing in England.

12. Henry James, *Literary Reviews and Essays,* ed. Albert Mordell (1957; reprint, New York: Grove Press, 1979), p. 133.

13. C. A. Sainte-Beuve, "To Love Molière," in *Sainte-Beuve: Selected Essays,* ed. and trans. Francis Steegmuller and Norbert Guterman (Garden City, N.Y.: Doubleday-Anchor Books, 1964), pp. 126–27.

14. Gerald Graff, unpublished essay. See also his *Professing Literature* (Chicago: University of Chicago Press, 1987), pp. 226–43.

15. Sainte-Beuve, "To Love Molière," p. 126.

16. Walter Bagehot, "The First Edinburgh Reviewers," in *Literary Studies* (London: S. M. Dent & Sons, 1911), vol. 1, pp. 1–35.

17. Edgar Allan Poe, *Essays and Reviews,* ed. G. R. Thompson (New York: Library of America, 1984), p. 1025. This superb volume makes Poe's critical journalism widely available for the first time.

18. Ibid., p. 1029.

19. Quoted by John Paul Pritchard, *Criticism in America* (Norman: University of Oklahoma Press, 1956), p. 85.

20. Poe, *Essays and Reviews,* p. 1025.

21. Henry James, "The Science of Criticism" (1891), in *Literary Criticism: Essays on Literature, American Writers, English Writers,* ed. Leon Edel, with Mark Wilson (New York: Library of America, 1984), pp. 95, 98.

22. Edmund Wilson, "The Critic Who Does Not Exist," in *The Shores of Light* (1952; reprint, New York: Farrar, Straus & Giroux, 1961), p. 369.

23. Herman Melville, "Hawthorne and His Mosses," reprinted in *The Shock of Recognition,* ed. Edmund Wilson (1943; reprint, New York: Farrar,

Straus and Cudahy, 1955), p. 197. Though confined largely to what our best writers wrote about each other, this volume is probably the best single anthology of American literary journalism. Its idiosyncratic choices are full of exciting rediscoveries, including Poe, early Lowell, and D. H. Lawrence's then-neglected writings on American literature.

24. Wilson, *The Shores of Light,* pp. 367–68.

25. Ibid., p. 372.

26. Quoted by René Wellek in *A History of Modern Criticism, 1750–1950, vol. 4: The Later Nineteenth Century* (New Haven, Conn.: Yale University Press, 1965), p. 217. Wellek's commodious *History* is the only one which gives any substantial attention to the mass of critical journalism, though he too concentrates on major figures. What is needed is a sociological and critical study of the growth of literature as an institution and the many-sided role that reviewing has played in that development.

Sources and Suggestions
for Further Reading

Most of the books on modern criticism written in the last three decades are grounded in recent academic trends and reflect one or another strain of literary theory. They do scant justice to the alternative traditions of criticism discussed in this book, including historical criticism, cultural criticism, and literary journalism. The same is true of earlier books reflecting the viewpoint of the New Criticism, such as William K. Wimsatt, Jr., and Cleanth Brooks, *Literary Criticism: A Short History* (New York: Knopf, 1957), which never even mentions some major critics included here, such as Van Wyck Brooks. A far more comprehensive work is René Wellek, *A History of Modern Criticism: 1750–1950*, 7 vols. (New Haven, Conn.: 1955–91). Especially relevant to the present book is volume 6, *American Criticism, 1900–1950* (1986). An unusually inclusive work from the academic viewpoint is Vincent B. Leitch, *American Literary Criticism from the Thirties to the Eighties* (New York: Columbia University Press, 1988), though it leaves out important critics who did not belong to distinct schools or "ally themselves with theoretical shifts." The same disability limits the usefulness of Patrick Brantlinger's thorough but politically correct survey of recent cultural studies in Britain and America, *Crusoe's Footprints* (New York and London: Routledge, 1990).

From a Marxist viewpoint, Terry Eagleton makes interesting use of Jürgen Habermas's notion of the "public sphere" in the early chapters of *The Function of Criticism* (London: Verso, 1984), a far better book than its widely read but tendentious predecessor, *Literary Theory* (Minneapolis: University of Minnesota Press, 1983). Gerald Graff has provided a guide to theory from sharply differing viewpoints in *Literature Against Itself* (Chicago: University of Chicago Press, 1979); *Criticism in the University*, coedited with Reginald Gibbons (Evanston: Northwestern University Press, 1985); and *Professing Literature* (Chicago: University of Chicago Press, 1987). *Professing Literature* contains enormously valuable historical material on the growth of English and American studies, but *Criticism in the University* is closest to my own defense of nonacademic criticism.

Other general books well worth consulting include Frank Lentricchia, *After the New Criticism* (Chicago: University of Chicago Press, 1980); Michael Fischer, *Does Deconstruction Make Any Difference?* (Bloomington: Indiana University Press, 1985); and Tzvetan Todorov's highly critical *Literature and*

Its Theorists, trans. Catherine Porter (1984; Ithaca, N.Y.: Cornell University Press, 1987), with its resounding appendix, "Traveling Through American Criticism," a damning backward glance at the theory years. Another powerful humanistic critique of literary theory is Eugene Goodheart, *The Skeptic Disposition,* rev. ed. (Princeton, N.J.: Princeton University Press, 1991), which begins with Arnold and concludes with recent ideological critics.

Not to be neglected are the books on criticism by writers who are themselves theorists of notable stature, including Geoffrey Hartman, *Criticism in the Wilderness* (New Haven, Conn.: Yale University Press, 1980); Edward W. Said, *The World, the Text, and the Critic* (Cambridge, Mass.: Harvard University Press, 1983); and Paul de Man, *Blindness and Insight,* rev. ed. (Minneapolis: University of Minnesota Press, 1983). As Lindsay Waters has pointed out, de Man did not share his supporters' antipathy toward newspaper criticism and literary journalism. Besides his notorious articles written during the Nazi occupation of Belgium between 1940 and 1942, his occasional essays and reviews were collected with a valuable introduction in *Critical Writings, 1953–1978,* ed. Lindsay Waters (Minneapolis: University of Minnesota Press, 1989). His defenses of theory can be found in a companion volume, *The Resistance to Theory* (1986). Valuable essays on criticism are scattered through Geoffrey Hartman's collections, which include *Beyond Formalism* (New Haven, Conn.: Yale University Press, 1970); *The Fate of Reading and Other Essays* (Chicago: University of Chicago Press, 1975); and *Easy Pieces* (New York: Columbia University Press, 1985).

The major study of cultural criticism remains Raymond Williams, *Culture and Society* (New York: Columbia University Press, 1959). The only significant study of the history of literary journalism is John Gross, *The Rise and Fall of the Man of Letters* (New York: Macmillan, 1969). But both books deal exclusively with English critics. Some American parallels can be found in Edmund Wilson's anthology *The Shock of Recognition* (1943; New York: Farrar, Straus and Cudahy, 1955), and in two studies of American intellectuals: Daniel Aaron, *Writers on the Left* (New York: Harcourt, Brace and World, 1961), and Christopher Lasch, *The New Radicalism in America, 1889–1963* (New York: Knopf, 1965). A more recent study of our cultural critics in relation to later theorists is Giles Gunn, *The Culture of Criticism and the Criticism of Culture* (New York: Oxford University Press, 1987). On cultural criticism see also Eugene Goodheart, *Culture and the Radical Conscience* (Cambridge, Mass.: Harvard University Press, 1973), and *The Failure of Criticism* (Cambridge, Mass.: Harvard University Press, 1978).

Arnold and His Successors

The major works by and about Matthew Arnold can be found in the endnotes to chapter 2. Here I need only single out the famous intellectual biography by Lionel Trilling, *Matthew Arnold* (1939; New York: Meridian Books, 1955); Park Honan, *Matthew Arnold: A Life* (New York: McGraw-Hill, 1981); and

F. R. Leavis, "Arnold as Critic," in *The Critic as Anti-Philosopher,* ed. G. Singh (Athens: University of Georgia Press, 1983). Other important essays on critics by Leavis and the *Scrutiny* group can be found in Leavis's collections: *The Common Pursuit* (London: Chatto and Windus, 1952), which includes his credo, "Literary Criticism and Philosophy"; *Anna Karenina and Other Essays* (London: Chatto & Windus, 1967), which includes essays on T. S. Eliot and Dr. Johnson as critics; and *A Selection from Scrutiny,* 2 vols. (Cambridge: Cambridge University Press, 1968). Eliot's view of Arnold is expressed in "Arnold and Pater," *Selected Essays* (New York: Harcourt, Brace, 1932), and *The Use of Poetry and the Use of Criticism* (Cambridge: Harvard University Press, 1933). John Henry Raleigh studied Arnold's influence on American critics from Henry James to Eliot and Trilling in *Matthew Arnold and American Culture* (Berkeley: University of California Press, 1957).

Useful anthologies of Arnold's writings include Lionel Trilling's *Portable Matthew Arnold* (New York: Viking, 1949); A. Dwight Culler, *Poetry and Criticism of Matthew Arnold* (Boston: Houghton Mifflin, 1961); and Christopher Ricks, *Selected Criticism of Matthew Arnold* (New York: New American Library, 1972). All students of Arnold are indebted to R. H. Super's edition of *The Complete Prose Works of Matthew Arnold,* 11 vols. (Ann Arbor: University of Michigan Press, 1960–77). Walter Pater's critical writings can be sampled in Harold Bloom, *Selected Writings of Walter Pater* (New York: New American Library, 1974).

Practical Criticism

The three works of practical criticism I deal with in detail in chapter 3, representing idiosyncratic versions of New Criticism, structuralism, and deconstruction, are I. A. Richards, *Practical Criticism* (1929; New York: Harcourt, Brace and World, 1956); Roland Barthes, *S/Z,* trans. Richard Miller (1970; English trans., New York: Hill and Wang, 1974); and a bilingual edition of Jacques Derrida, *Spurs: Nietzsche's Styles,* trans. Barbara Harlow (Chicago: University of Chicago Press, 1979). I won't try to enumerate their other books here, since they are well known, but the works of Barthes I mention, representing different phases of his career, include *Mythologies* (1957; English trans., 1972), *The Pleasure of the Text* (1973; English trans., 1975), *Roland Barthes* (1975; English trans., 1977), and *Camera Lucida* (1980; English trans., 1981), all published by Hill and Wang. His journalistic essays on modern writers like Brecht and Robbe-Grillet, first published in French in 1964, can be found in *Critical Essays* (Evanston: Northwestern University Press, 1972). For a critique of Barthes from a poststructuralist viewpoint, see the recently discovered 1972 essay by Paul de Man, "Roland Barthes and the Limits of Structuralism," *Yale French Studies* 77 (1990).

Almost as little has been written on the history of practical criticism as on the development of literary journalism. Evidently, the response to actual writers and their works lies a little outside the purview of most historians of criticism, who prefer the more abstract issues raised by aesthetics and critical theory. But nearly all the recent books on contemporary criticism begin with a chapter on the New Criticism, if only to provide the formalist ground from which later theorists can be said to depart. Frank Lentricchia broke with this pattern in *After the New Criticism*, when he argued that Paul de Man's deconstruction was actually a *return* to the ahistorical formalism of Cleanth Brooks (though de Man had devoted an essay in 1956 to the "The Dead-End of Formalist Criticism," first translated into English for the 1983 edition of *Blindness and Insight*). A recent piece that sheds additional light on the growth of close reading in the fifties is Richard Poirier, "Hum 6, or Reading Before Theory," in *Raritan* (Spring 1990). For a far-reaching discussion of "indeterminacy" in interpretation, see David J. Gordon, "The Story of a Critical Idea," *Partisan Review* 47:1 (1980).

Journalism as Criticism

My major sources for chapter 4 can be found in the endnotes. A sharp early attack on journalistic and cultural criticism in the name of theory was Stanley Edgar Hyman's *The Armed Vision* (New York: Knopf, 1948). Hyman suppressed his violent diatribe against Edmund Wilson, his colleague at *The New Yorker,* in the paperback edition (New York: Vintage, 1955). Ironically, Hyman himself later became one of the last of the authoritative critical journalists. His biweekly review essays for *The New Leader* from 1961 to 1965, collected in volumes like *Standards* (New York: Horizon Press, 1966), make up an engrossing literary chronicle of the age, comparable to earlier collections by Wilson and Malcolm Cowley.

Criticism Among the Intellectuals

The major book of Trilling's discussed in chapter 5 is *The Liberal Imagination* (New York: Viking, 1950), but I also use material from other key works including *The Opposing Self* (New York: Viking, 1955) and *Beyond Culture* (New York: Viking, 1965, 1968), as well as posthumous publications such as "Art, Will, and Necessity" (1973), in *The Last Decade,* ed. Diana Trilling (New York: Harcourt Brace Jovanovich, 1979), and excerpts from his journals printed in *Partisan Review* 51:4 (1984), ed. Christopher Zinn. The best of several books on Trilling is Mark Krupnick, *Lionel Trilling and the Fate of Cultural Criticism* (Evanston: Northwestern University Press, 1986). The most revealing piece of biography, apart from his own fiction, is Diana Trilling, "Lionel Trilling: A Jew at Columbia," appended to her selection of his uncollected reviews and essays, *Speaking of Literature and Society* (New York: Harcourt Brace Jovanovich, 1980), which also includes his review of Norman O. Brown. Diana Trilling's full-length biographical work is said to be forthcoming.

The main work of R. P. Blackmur discussed here is the posthumous *A Primer of Ignorance,* ed. Joseph Frank (New York: Harcourt, Brace, 1967). Blackmur's classic essays on modern poets were collected in *Language as Gesture* (New York: Harcourt, Brace, 1952) and in paperback in *Form and Value in Modern Poetry* (Garden City, N.Y.: Doubleday Anchor, n.d.). His essays on prose, including Trilling's *Liberal Imagination,* were collected in *The Lion and the Honeycomb* (New York: Harcourt, Brace, 1955). His essays on European fiction, including studies of all of Dostoevsky's major novels, can be found in *Eleven Essays in the European Novel* (New York: Harcourt, Brace, 1964). Much of his uncompleted book on Henry Adams finally appeared in *Henry Adams,* ed. Veronica A. Makowsky (New York: Harcourt Brace Jovanovich, 1980). The volume includes a foreword by Denis Donoghue, who also edited Blackmur's *Selected Essays* (New York: Ecco, 1986).

Russell Fraser wrote *A Mingled Yarn: The Life of R. P. Blackmur* (New York: Harcourt, Brace, 1979). Eileen Simpson's luminous memoir *Poets in Their Youth* (New York: Random House, 1982) deals with John Berryman, Delmore Schwartz, and Robert Lowell, as well as Richard and Helen Blackmur. On Blackmur and Berryman see also a good critical study by James D. Bloom, *The Stock of Available Reality* (Lewisburg: Bucknell University Press, 1984). Blackmur also figures in the recollections of Lincoln Kirstein, who gave him his start at the legendary little magazine *Hound and Horn.* See *The Hound & Horn Letters,* ed. Mitzi Berger Hamovitch (Athens: University of Georgia Press, 1982).

The main work of Northrop Frye discussed here is *The Modern Century* (Toronto: Oxford University Press, 1967). His best book was his first, a magisterial study of Blake, *Fearful Symmetry* (1947; Boston: Beacon Press, 1962). Other major works are *Anatomy of Criticism* (Princeton, N.J.: Princeton University Press, 1957) and his synoptic study of the Bible, *The Great Code* (New York: Harcourt Brace Jovanovich, 1982). Other books included *A Study of English Romanticism* (New York: Random House, 1968) and *The Critical Path* (Bloomington: Indiana University Press, 1971). Some of his best work, because it was the most concrete, can be found in collections of essays like *Fables of Identity* (New York: Harcourt, Brace and World, 1963) and *The Stubborn Structure* (Ithaca, N.Y.: Cornell University Press, 1970).

Frye's work is discussed by M. H. Abrams in *Doing Things with Texts,* ed. Michael Fischer (New York: Norton, 1989); by Geoffrey Hartman, Angus Fletcher, Murray Krieger, and W. K. Wimsatt, Jr., in *Northrop Frye in Modern Criticism,* ed. Murray Krieger (New York: Columbia University Press, 1966); by Tzvetan Todorov, from a structuralist viewpoint, in *The Fantastic* (1970; Ithaca: Cornell University Press, 1975) and, from a broader perspective, in *Literature and Its Theorists;* and by Frank Lentricchia in *After the New Criticism.* A fine short study of his career is Ian Balfour, *Northrop Frye* (Boston: Twayne, 1988).

Memoirs of the New York intellectuals, all published within a short time of one another, include William Barrett, *The Truants* (Garden City, N.Y.:

Anchor Doubleday, 1982); Irving Howe, *A Margin of Hope* (New York: Harcourt Brace Jovanovich, 1982); William Phillips, *A Partisan View* (New York: Stein and Day, 1983); Lionel Abel, *The Intellectual Follies* (New York: Norton, 1984); and Sidney Hook, *Out of Step* (New York: Harper & Row, 1987). But there has also been a rising tide of historical studies, among them James B. Gilbert, *Writers and Partisans* (New York: Wiley, 1968); Alexander Bloom, *Prodigal Sons* (New York: Oxford University Press, 1986); Terry A. Cooney, *The Rise of the New York Intellectuals* (Madison: University of Wisconsin Press, 1986); Alan M. Wald, *The New York Intellectuals* (Chapel Hill: University of North Carolina Press, 1987); and Neal Jumonville, *Critical Crossings* (Berkeley: University of California Press, 1991). An outstanding early overview was Irving Howe, "The New York Intellectuals," in *Decline of the New* (New York: Horizon Press, 1970).

The King of the Cats (New York: Farrar, Straus and Giroux, 1965) was a sparkling collection of F. W. Dupee's reviews and essays. A second, much enlarged edition, with an introduction by Mary McCarthy, was brought out by the University of Chicago Press in 1984. Dupee also wrote *Henry James,* rev. ed. (Garden City, N.Y.: Doubleday Anchor, 1956). His lively account of the student uprising at Columbia first appeared in *The New York Review of Books,* September 26, 1968, and was reprinted in *The Oxford Reader,* ed. Frank Kermode and Richard Poirier (New York: Oxford University Press, 1971).

The major work of Alfred Kazin discussed here is *An American Procession* (New York: Knopf, 1984), the last of a trilogy that includes his best book, *On Native Grounds* (1942; Garden City, N.Y.: Doubleday Anchor, 1956), and a study of postwar fiction, *Bright Book of Life* (Boston: Atlantic-Little, Brown, 1973). His collections of essays include *The Inmost Leaf* (1955; New York: Noonday, 1959) and *Contemporaries* (Boston: Atlantic–Little, Brown, 1962). His superb volumes of memoirs include *A Walker in the City* (New York: Harcourt, Brace, 1951); *Starting Out in the Thirties* (Boston: Atlantic–Little, Brown, 1965); and *New York Jew* (New York: Knopf, 1978).

The Critic and Society, 1900–1950

The sources for chapter 6 are too numerous to be listed here. Apart from the voluminous Edmund Wilson, I single out a few key works for each critic not already mentioned earlier. What follows is an alphabetical listing by author:

Bourne, Randolph. *History of a Literary Radical.* Ed. Van Wyck Brooks. New York: B. W. Huebsch, 1920.
———. *The Radical Will: Selected Writings, 1911–1918.* Ed. Olaf Hansen. New York: Urizen Books, 1977.

Brooks, Van Wyck. *Van Wyck Brooks: The Early Years.* Ed. Claire Sprague. New York: Harper & Row, 1968.

———. *Three Essays on America.* 1934; reprint, New York: E. P. Dutton, 1970. Includes *America's Coming-of-Age* (1915), *Letters and Leadership* (1918), and "The Literary Life in America" (1921).

Chapman, John Jay. *Selected Writings.* Ed. Jacques Barzun. New York: Farrar, Straus and Cudahy, 1957.

Chase, Richard. *The American Novel and Its Tradition.* Garden City, N.Y.: Doubleday Anchor, 1957.

———. *The Democratic Vista.* Garden City, N.Y.: Doubleday, 1958.

Cowley, Malcolm. *Exile's Return.* 1934; rev. ed., 1951. New York: Viking, 1956.

———, ed. *After the Genteel Tradition.* 1937; rev. ed., Carbondale: Southern Illinois University Press, 1965.

———. *—And I Worked at the Writer's Trade: Chapters of Literary History, 1918–1978.* New York: Viking, 1978.

[Cowley, Malcolm, and Kenneth Burke.] *The Selected Correspondence of Kenneth Burke and Malcolm Cowley, 1915–1981.* Ed. Paul Jay. New York: Viking, 1988.

Fiedler, Leslie A. *Love and Death in the American Novel.* 1960; rev. ed., New York: Stein and Day, 1966.

———. *The Collected Essays of Leslie Fiedler.* 2 vols. New York: Stein and Day, 1971.

Hicks, Granville. *The Great Tradition.* New York: Macmillan, 1933.

Howe, Irving. *Politics and the Novel.* New York: Meridian, 1957.

———. *A World More Attractive.* New York: Horizon Press, 1963. Includes "This Age of Conformity" (1954).

———. *Decline of the New.* New York: Horizon Press, 1970.

James, Henry. *The Art of the Novel.* Ed. R. P. Blackmur. New York: Scribner's, 1934.

———. *Literary Criticism.* 2 vols. Ed. Leon Edel, with Mark Wilson. New York: Library of America, 1984.

Leavis, F. R. *The Great Tradition: George Eliot, Henry James, Joseph Conrad.* London: Chatto and Windus, 1948.

———. *The Common Pursuit.* London: Chatto and Windus, 1952.

Lewis, R. W. B. *The American Adam.* Chicago: University of Chicago Press, 1955.

Marx, Leo. *The Machine in the Garden.* New York: Oxford University Press, 1964.

Matthiessen, F. O. *American Renaissance: Art and Expression in the Age of Emerson and Whitman.* New York: Oxford University Press, 1941.

———. *The Responsibilities of the Critic: Essays and Reviews.* Ed. John Rackliffe. New York: Oxford University Press, 1952.

Mencken, H. L. *A Book of Prefaces.* New York: Knopf, 1917.

———. *Prejudices*. 6 vols. New York: Knopf, 1919–27.

———. *The Vintage Mencken*. Ed. Alistair Cooke. New York: Vintage, 1955.

———. *Prejudices: A Selection*. Ed. James T. Farrell. New York: Vintage, 1958.

Mumford, Lewis. *The Golden Day*. New York: Boni & Liveright, 1926.

———. *The Brown Decades*. 1931; New York: Dover, 1971.

Orwell, George. *The Road to Wigan Pier*. 1937; New York: Harcourt, Brace, 1956.

———. *The Collected Essays, Journalism and Letters of George Orwell*. Ed. Sonia Orwell and Ian Angus. London: Secker & Warburg, 1968.

Parrington, V.L. *Main Currents in American Thought*. 3 vols. New York: Harcourt, Brace, 1927–30.

Rahv, Philip. *Literature and the Sixth Sense*. Boston: Houghton Mifflin, 1969.

———. *Essays on Literature and Politics, 1932–1972*. Ed. Arabel J. Porter and Andrew J. Dvosin. Boston: Houghton Mifflin, 1978.

Rosenberg, Harold. *The Tradition of the New*. New York: Horizon, 1959.

———. *Discovering the Present*. Chicago: University of Chicago Press, 1973.

Rourke, Constance. *American Humor*. New York: Harcourt, Brace, 1931.

———. *The Roots of American Culture and Other Essays*. Ed. Van Wyck Brooks. New York: Harcourt, Brace & World, 1942.

Santayana, George. *Selected Critical Writings of George Santayana*. 2 vols. Ed. Norman Henfrey. Cambridge: Cambridge University Press, 1968.

Schorer, Mark. *The World We Imagine*. New York: Farrar, Straus and Giroux, 1968. Includes "Technique as Discovery" and "Fiction and the 'Analogical Matrix.' "

Smith, Henry Nash. *Virgin Land: The American West as Symbol and Myth*. Cambridge, Mass.: Harvard University Press, 1950.

Spingarn, Joel. *Creative Criticism and Other Essays*. 1917; New York: Harcourt, Brace, 1931. Includes "The New Criticism."

Warshow, Robert. *The Immediate Experience*. Garden City, N.Y.: Doubleday, 1962.

Wilson, Edmund. *Axel's Castle*. New York: Scribner's, 1931.

———. *To the Finland Station*. New York: Harcourt, Brace, 1940.

———. *The Wound and the Bow*. Boston: Houghton Mifflin, 1941.

———. *The Triple Thinkers*. 1938; rev. ed., New York: Oxford University Press, 1948.

———. *Classics and Commercials*. New York: Farrar, Straus, 1950.

———. *The Shores of Light*. New York: Farrar, Straus and Young, 1952.

———. *Patriotic Gore*. New York: Oxford University Press, 1962.

———. *The Bit Between My Teeth*. New York: Farrar, Straus and Giroux, 1965.

———. *Upstate*. New York: Farrar, Straus and Giroux, 1971.

————. *Letters on Literature and Politics, 1912–1972.* Ed. Elena Wilson. New York: Farrar, Straus and Giroux, 1977.

Many of the above critics have discussed one another in important essays. These include Edmund Wilson on Brooks (in *The Shores of Light* and *Classics and Commercials*); Lionel Trilling on Parrington (in *The Liberal Imagination*), on Orwell (in *The Opposing Self*), and on Wilson and Leavis (in *A Gathering of Fugitives*, 1956); and Alfred Kazin on Brooks, Mencken, Parrington, and Wilson (in *On Native Grounds*), and again on Wilson (in *The Inmost Leaf, Contemporaries,* and *New York Jew*).

Randolph Bourne and his era are discussed by Christopher Lasch in *The New Radicalism in America* (New York: Knopf, 1965). Bourne's friend Brooks is the subject of a succinct study by James R. Vitelli, *Van Wyck Brooks* (New York: Twayne, 1969), a revealing biography by James Hoopes, *Van Wyck Brooks* (Amherst: University of Massachusetts Press, 1977), and a fine essay by F. W. Dupee, "The Americanism of Van Wyck Brooks," *Partisan Review* (Summer 1939). Bourne, Brooks, and Malcolm Cowley all figure in Daniel Aaron's *Writers on the Left* (1961).

The best of several books on the criticism of F. R. Leavis are Francis Mulhern, *The Moment of 'Scrutiny'* (London: New Left Books, 1979), and R. P. Bilan, *The Literary Criticism of F. R. Leavis* (Cambridge: Cambridge University Press, 1979). There is an older biography of Orwell by Bernard Crick, *George Orwell: A Life* (1980; New York: Penguin, 1982), and a recent "authorized" one by Michael Shelden, *Orwell* (New York: HarperCollins, 1991). A major study of Orwell's changing image and influence is John Rodden, *The Politics of Literary Reputation* (New York: Oxford University Press, 1989).

Among the numerous studies of Edmund Wilson, there are books written during his lifetime by Sherman Paul, *Edmund Wilson* (Urbana: University of Illinois Press, 1965), and by Leonard Kriegel, *Edmund Wilson* (Carbondale: Southern Illinois University Press, 1971), as well as a fine recent study by George H. Douglas, *Edmund Wilson's America* (Lexington: University Press of Kentucky, 1983). See also *The Portable Edmund Wilson*, ed. Lewis M. Dabney (New York: Penguin, 1983), and the composite portraits of Wilson, Leavis, and Trilling in Philip French, *Three Honest Men* (Manchester, Eng.: Carcanet New Press, 1980).

The growth and transformation of American Studies can be traced in Richard Ruland, *The Rediscovery of American Literature* (Cambridge, Mass.: Harvard University Press, 1967); in Gerald Graff, "The Promise of American Literature Studies," in *Professing Literature* (Chicago: University of Chicago Press, 1987); in Walter Benn Michaels and Donald E. Pease, eds., *The American Renaissance Reconsidered* (Baltimore: The Johns Hopkins University Press, 1985); and in Sacvan Bercovitch and Myra Jehlen, eds., *Ide-*

ology and Classic American Literature (Cambridge: Cambridge University Press, 1986).

The Return to History?

The sources and references for this highly opinionated dialogue seem hard to pin down, apart from all the works already mentioned in this bibliography. The two anthologies mentioned are Elaine Showalter, ed., *The New Feminist Criticism* (New York: Pantheon, 1985), and H. Aram Veeser, ed., *The New Historicism* (New York and London: Routledge, 1989). The latter includes the essays by Louis Montrose and Joel Fineman cited in this dialogue. More concrete examples of feminist reading can be found in another anthology by Elaine Showalter, *Speaking of Gender* (New York and London: Routledge, 1989). For some radically different views, see *French Feminist Thought,* ed. Toril Moi (Oxford: Basil Blackwell, 1987). Laura Mulvey's widely debated essay "Visual Pleasure and Narrative Cinema" first appeared in *Screen* in 1975. Judith Fetterley wrote *The Resisting Reader* (Bloomington: Indiana University Press, 1978).

The essays by Paul de Man cited here are: "Literary History and Literary Modernity" (1969), in *Blindness and Insight;* his foreword to Carol Jacobs, *The Dissimulating Harmony* (1978), reprinted in de Man's *Critical Writings, 1953–1978;* and "The Resistance to Theory" (1982), in *The Resistance to Theory.* All three de Man volumes are published by the University of Minnesota Press (1983, 1989, 1986). David Simpson's essay on the historical ironies of the de Man case can be found in *The Yale Journal of Criticism* (Fall 1989). Among the many other valuable articles devoted to the affair, an essential point of departure is Geoffrey Hartman, "Looking Back on Paul de Man," in *Reading de Man Reading,* ed. Lindsay Waters and Wlad Godzich (Minneapolis: University of Minnesota Press, 1989).

Stephen Greenblatt's books include *Renaissance Self-Fashioning* (Chicago: University of Chicago Press, 1980); *Shakespearean Negotiations* (Berkeley: University of California Press, 1988); an anthology, *Representing the English Renaissance* (Berkeley: University of California Press, 1988); and most recently, *Marvelous Possessions* (Chicago: University of Chicago Press, 1991). A recent contribution to discussions of the New Historicism mentioned here is Theodore B. Leinwand, "Negotiation and New Historicism," *PMLA* (May 1990), part of an issue devoted to "The Politics of Critical Language," with an introduction by Herbert Lindenberger. Richard Slotkin's *The Fatal Environment* (New York: Atheneum, 1985) is a good example of the new approach to myth and ideology in American Studies. See also the Michaels-Pease and Bercovitch-Jehlen volumes cited in the previous section.

Jerome McGann's case for a New Historicist and ideological critique of Romanticism, with many literary examples, can be found in a series of books: *The Romantic Ideology* (Chicago: University of Chicago Press, 1983); *The Beauty of Inflections* (Oxford: The Clarendon Press, 1985); and *Social Values and Poetic Acts* (Cambridge, Mass.: Harvard University Press, 1988). His former student Marjorie Levinson's controversial essay on Wordsworth's "Tintern Abbey" can be found in *Wordsworth's Great Period Poems* (New York: Cambridge University Press, 1986). M. H. Abrams criticizes both McGann and Levinson in an essay "On Political Readings of *Lyrical Ballads,*" in *Doing Things with Texts,* ed. Michael Fischer (New York: Norton, 1989).

A challenging argument against historicist criticism, written from a deconstructionist viewpoint, can be found in J. Hillis Miller, *The Ethics of Reading* (New York: Columbia University Press, 1987). Using de Man's work as evidence, Miller tries to refute the notion that deconstructive reading is a form of extreme skepticism or nihilism. This might be compared to another study of the reading process that criticizes both historicism and deconstruction, Robert Alter's *The Pleasures of Reading in an Ideological Age* (New York: Simon and Schuster, 1989), and Geoffrey Hartman's thoughtful and balanced new book, *Minor Prophecies* (Cambridge, Mass.: Harvard University Press, 1991), which reflects an evolution from theory toward public and historical concerns.

Historian Lynn Hunt's skeptical review of the recent debates about history is "History as Gesture; or The Scandal of History," in *Consequences of Theory,* ed. Jonathan Arac and Barbara Johnson (Baltimore: The John Hopkins University Press, 1991). John Higham has written a superb study of the growth of historical writing in America, *History,* with Leonard Krieger and Felix Gilbert (Englewood Cliffs, N.J.: Prentice-Hall, 1965).

Index

PS
78
D554
1992

WITHDRAWN
From Library Collection

DATE DUE

JUL 15 1999		
SEP 3 0 1999		

Demco, Inc. 38-293

WITHDRAWN
From Library Collection

REINSCH LIBRARY
MARYMOUNT UNIVERSITY
2807 NORTH GLEBE ROAD
ARLINGTON, VIRGINIA 22207